T0301842

The Economics of Sport and the Media

NEW HORIZONS IN THE ECONOMICS OF SPORT

Series Editors: Wladimir Andreff, *Department of Economics, University of Paris 1 Panthéon Sorbonne, France* and Marc Lavoie, *Department of Economics, University of Ottawa, Canada*

For decades, the economics of sport was regarded as a hobby for a handful of professional economists who were primarily involved in other areas of research. In recent years, however, the significance of the sports economy as a percentage of GDP has expanded dramatically. This has coincided with an equivalent rise in the volume of economic literature devoted to the study of sport.

This series provides a vehicle for deeper analyses of the demand for sport, cost–benefit analysis of sport, sporting governance, the economics of professional sports and leagues, individual sports, trade in the sporting goods industry, media coverage, sponsoring and numerous related issues. It contributes to the further development of sports economics by welcoming new approaches and highlighting original research in both established and newly emerging sporting activities. The series publishes the best theoretical and empirical work from well-established researchers and academics, as well as from talented newcomers in the field.

The Economics of Sport and the Media

Edited by

Claude Jeanrenaud

Professor of Public Economics, University of Neuchâtel, Switzerland

Stefan Késenne

Professor of Economics, University of Antwerp and Catholic University of Leuven, Belgium

NEW HORIZONS IN THE ECONOMICS OF SPORT

Edward Elgar
Cheltenham, UK • Northampton, MA, USA

Published by
Edward Elgar Publishing Limited
The Lypiatts
15 Lansdown Road
Cheltenham
Glos GL50 2JA
UK

Edward Elgar Publishing, Inc.
William Pratt House
9 Dewey Court
Northampton
Massachusetts 01060
USA

Reprinted 2009, 2015

A catalogue record for this book
is available from the British Library

Library of Congress Cataloguing in Publication Data

The economics of sport and the media / edited by Claude Jeanrenaud, Stefan
Késenne.
    p. cm. — (New horizons in the economics of sport)
  Includes bibliographical references and index.
1. Television broadcasting of sports–Economic aspects–United States. 2.
Television broadcasting of sports–Economic aspects–Europe. 3. Radio
broadcasting of sports–Economic aspects–United States. I. Jeanrenaud,
Claude. II. Késenne, Stefan. III. Series
  GV742.3.E36 2006
  070.4'497960973–dc22
                            2006040648

FSC
www.fsc.org
MIX
Paper from
responsible sources
FSC® C013604

ISBN 978 1 84542 743 6

Printed and bound in Great Britain by the CPI Group (UK) Ltd

Contents

List of Contributors   vi
Acknowledgements   vii

1.   Sport and the Media: An Overview   1
     Claude Jeanrenaud and Stefan Késenne

2.   Competitive Balance and the Sports Media Rights Market:
     What are the Real Issues?   26
     Bill Gerrard

3.   Broadcasting Rights and Competition in European Football   37
     Wladimir Andreff and Jean-François Bourg

4.   Joint Purchasing of Sports Rights: A Legal Viewpoint   71
     Adrian Fikentscher

5.   Broadcaster and Audience Demand for Premier League Football   93
     David Forrest, Robert Simmons and Babatunde Buraimo

6.   International Television Sports Rights: Risky Investments   106
     Harry Arne Solberg

7.   The Relationship between Sport and Television: The Case of TF1
     and the 2002 Football World Cup   126
     Michel Desbordes

8.   Why have Premium Sports Rights Migrated to Pay-TV in Europe
     but not in the US?   148
     Stefan Szymanski

9.   Economic Perspectives on Market Power in the Telecasting of
     US Team Sports   160
     Andrew Zimbalist

10. Baseball and the Broadcast Media   179
     Paul D. Staudohar

Index   199

Contributors

Wladimir Andreff, Université de Paris 1, Centre d'Economie de la Sorbonne, France.

Jean-François Bourg, Centre de Droit et d'Economie du Sport, University of Limoges, France.

Babatunde Buraimo, Lancashire Business School, University of Central Lancashire, UK.

Michel Desbordes, University Marc Bloch University, Strasbourg, France.

Adrian Fikentscher, Juristische Direktion, Bayerische Rundfunk.

David Forrest, School of Accounting, University of Salford, UK.

Bill Gerrard, Leeds University Business School, UK.

Claude Jeanrenaud, Institute for Research in Economics, University of Neuchâtel, Switzerland.

Stefan Késenne, Economics Department, University of Antwerp and Department of Human Kinesiology, Catholic University of Leuven, Belgium.

Robert Simmons, The Management School, Lancaster University, UK.

Harry Arne Solberg, Trondheim Business School, Sør-Trøndelag University College, Norway.

Paul D. **Staudohar**, School of Business and Economics, California State University, USA.

Stefan Szymanski, Tanaka Business School, Imperial College London, UK.

Andrew Zimbalist, Department of Economics, Smith College, USA.

Acknowledgements

This volume contains a set of original essays, written by eminent European and North American sports economists. The aim of the volume is to present recent research results on the sports–media relationship and to analyse developments, prospects and key policy concerns related to this issue. The draft version of the chapters was originally presented at the Fifth Conference of the International Association of Sports Economists (IASE) held in Neuchâtel (Switzerland) in May 2003. The Conference was jointly organised by IASE and the Neuchâtel International Center for Sports Studies (CIES), an academic research and education institution founded in 1995 by FIFA and the University of Neuchâtel.

We would like to express our special gratitude to the CIES Director, Mr Denis Oswald, International Olympic Committee (IOC) Executive Board member and sports law professor at the University of Neuchâtel, for his key financial and technical support of the IASE Conference. The organisation and conduct of the Conference, as well as the subsequent edition of this volume were greatly facilitated by the help we received from the staff of both the CIES and the Institute for Economic Research (IRENE) at the University of Neuchâtel. Special thanks also to Mrs Martine Chavaz for her assistance in editing the various versions of the chapters.

1. Sport and the Media: An Overview

Claude Jeanrenaud and Stefan Késenne

Before radio and television, the only way of watching a sports contest was to go to the stadium. Today, the majority of spectators watch their games on television. Sports events were first broadcast on radio and the medium had a major impact on both the profile of the events and their audiences. The first radio broadcast of a sports event was the Jack Dempsey–Georges Carpentier heavyweight title fight in July 1920. The following year, a radio station in Newark, New Jersey, broadcast baseball's World Series. The television era – and with it sport on television – dawned around ten years later with the 1936 Olympic Games in Berlin. Three television cameras filmed the events and closed-circuit images were shown in public halls near the games venues. In June 1937, the 20,000 British households who owned a television set were able to watch the Wimbledon tennis championships and, in April the following year, the FA Cup Final. These were the first sports television broadcasts made by the BBC. The start of television sports broadcasting in the USA was a baseball game between Columbia and Princeton Universities at Baker Field in May 1939, but low television penetration rates meant that only some 400 households were able to watch the game. Production and transmission techniques were fairly basic. Only one camera filmed the game and there was no question of live images being sent across the country. By the 1960 Winter Olympics at Squaw Valley, it was still a question of the events first having to be filmed and then for the films to be flown to Europe to be shown two days later (Reimer, 2002). It was not until the 1964 Tokyo Olympics that the games were first transmitted live to countries around the world.

Initially, television needed sport more than sport needed television. Sport was perfect content for the networks, firstly as a means of selling more television sets – NBC and CBS were both involved in the business of making and selling them – and then as a way of increasing audiences (Baran, 2004). Sports broadcasting was both a means for networks to gain big audiences and an ideal way of raising the profile of events and building team recognition. By attracting new fans, who, previously, would not have gone to a game, it attracted increased attention from sponsors. Until the end of the 1970s, the number of broadcasters remained small, which enabled them to keep television rights fees down. With liberalisation and the arrival of digital television in the 1980s, competition for audiences intensified as new broadcasters entered the market. The outcome was a sharp rise in rights fees. Rights holders benefited from the absence of close substitutes along with a seemingly endless demand from broadcasters for premium sports events.

The amount broadcasters were willing to pay for premium sporting rights cannot be solely explained by what they were able to earn from advertising revenues and subscription fees. By showing the most popular sports, broadcasters expected to benefit in terms of a better image and identity, a stronger market position and a sustained increase in viewers. A trend towards globalisation can also be observed. Today, fans of the big clubs – who, by extension, are the people that sponsors are targeting – are spread across the globe. One of the consequences of this is the increased number of signings of Japanese, Chinese and Korean players by European football clubs. This is not because clubs are getting better value for money in terms of players' performance on the field, but because these players raise the clubs' profile in new markets that sponsors are keen to enter. Similarly, sponsor expectations also explain the strategy behind the choice of host countries for mega-events; choices which are sometimes detrimental to audiences in traditional markets because of the drawbacks created by time zone differences.

The arrival of new broadcasters on the scene has not only led to an explosion in the value of sports rights but also in the amount of sport that is shown (for example a 300 per cent increase in the UK between 1995 and 2000). In the USA today, more than 60,000 hours of televised sports are programmed every year by four major networks, cable television, and the various digital channels and local sports cable networks, against about 1,000 hours three decades before. A final comment on the way the relation between sport and television has developed is that television has led sport into becoming a spectacle, and that professional sport and the entertainment industry have become increasingly entwined. Jacques Blociszewski (1999), a French sports journalist, believes that 'television is increasingly transforming sport into pure spectacle … televised sport loses the magic of a collectively-experienced event … leading to a kind of genetically modified sport'. This has led him to wonder if 'television is not in danger of destroying the very thing that enables it to make big profits'. In his view, televised events have become a sort of video game with advertising, suitably adapted for the market the broadcaster is serving.

While sport and the media both need each other, it is a relationship which raises many issues and problems. Given this, the overview and the nine chapters in this volume address the following questions:

- Is financial dependence on media revenue a threat to sport's independence and integrity? Are sports federations running the risk of changing the nature of sport by giving the media – and, indirectly, sponsors – what they want, thus ultimately reducing fan interest?
- To what extent is sport a private good (one which can be optimally allocated through market mechanisms)? Or does sport possess characteristics of a public good which mean that sports rights negotiations require some form of regulation (rather than relying on the market to determine the allocation of rights)?
- What are the consequences – both for consumers and sport itself – of sports broadcasts moving to pay–TV? If large parts of the population cannot watch live sport, is there a risk of eroding the future fan base?
- What are the outcomes for consumers, along with the competitive effects in downstream markets, of the current business model (exclusivity, joint selling and, in some cases, joint purchasing)? Do antitrust policies meet the needs of consumers and the public interest?
- Are demand determinants for televised sport (from broadcasters and viewers alike) the same as those for live attendance?
- Commercial broadcasters are not interested in sports that are less suited to television or which are not so popular. Given that these sports play just as important a social role as mainstream sports, are there public interest arguments for broadcasting them on a regular basis?
- What path will sports broadcasting rights follow in the future? Have they reached a ceiling in the USA and Europe or will their value continue to rise?

A CHANGED MEDIA SCENE

In Europe, from the 1950s until the middle of the 1980s, each country had a public broadcaster and a sports federation. At the pan-European level, national federations belonged to a European federation, while national television broadcasters were members of the European Broadcasting Union (EBU), which acted on behalf of its members as the sole television rights buyer (European Commission, 1998). This model – a bilateral monopoly with a single buyer and a single seller – explains the modest increase in rights values which lasted until these monopolies disappeared.

Until the end of the 1970s, the sports programming scene in the USA was dominated by the three major national networks. It was only at the end of the decade that competition restrictions for cable television were lifted. This move, along with the development of satellite television, sharply increased the competition for television rights and enabled rights owners to extract a greater part of the economic rent.

Several technological innovations resulted in a transformation of European and US broadcasting rights markets. Until the beginning of the 1980s, free-to-air television was the dominant platform. Since then, new technologies have radically changed the market environment. Today, rights owners can use a number of different platforms and delivery mechanisms to market their products. The arrival of digital television in the early 1990s – offering the possibility of encoded signals and a huge increase in transmission capacity – boosted the development of pay-TV and pay-per-view.

In Europe, new technologies and liberalisation transformed the audiovisual sector by allowing private broadcasters to enter the television market. The middle of the 1980s saw the end of public monopolies and greater competition for sporting rights as the number of private broadcasters significantly increased. This resulted, for example, in the value of television rights for the top league in English football (formerly the First Division and now the Premier League) increasing in real terms from £5.4m in 1985 to £476m in 2001 (Szymanski, 2000).

The rapid growth in the demand for television rights affected both Europe and North America, although the structure of the market meant that it was in America where increases were first felt. The BBC paid only £1500 to the organising committee to show the 1948 Olympics; the first games to be broadcast live (*The Economist*, 1996). For the 1960 Squaw Valley Winter Olympics, CBS paid $50,000 for the broadcasting rights and spent another $450,000 on production costs. While television revenue from the 1980 Summer Olympics in Moscow came to $88m, it had reached $1493m for the 2004 Athens games. The extra competition resulting from the development of pay-TV – premium pay-TV and pay-per-view – contributed to the rapid rise in the price of sports rights but this was also fuelled by the fact that pay-TV broadcasters, unlike their free-to-air counterparts, found it easier to appropriate a larger part of viewers' consumer surplus (see Szymanski's contribution to this volume).

There are fears that as sports broadcasts move to paid channels, the public's interest will ultimately be reduced. These fears are partly justified, but it has to be noted that rights owners are not always short-term profit maximisers. The federations know – or ought to know – that it is in their interests to maintain a wide audience in order to guarantee the future popularity of the sports that they represent. For this reason, rights do not always go to the highest bidder. This is illustrated by the IOC's policy statement on this issue:

> The fundamental IOC television policy as set forth in the Olympic Charter is to ensure maximum presentation of the Olympic Games to the world. To ensure the widest possible television audience for the Olympic Games, Olympic broadcast rights are sold to broadcast networks that can guarantee the broadest free-to-air coverage... (IOC, 2005).

Experience shows, however, that those in charge of the leagues and federations often express a strong preference for the present and use a tender procedure designed to maximise short-term revenue. Such a position provides a rationale for market regulation aimed at preserving sporting traditions and the public interest.

SPORT AND TELEVISION: A SYMBIOTIC RELATIONSHIP

Sport and the media are closely tied in with each other, with television rights being the main source of income for many sports and sport being a key factor in attracting television audiences. In Europe, broadcasting rights often make up 30 per cent or more of a sport's total revenue. Television income is particularly important for football: on average, it accounts for 44 per cent of income for an English Premier League club and 37 per cent for a club in Italy's Serie A. The share can be as high as 70 per cent, outstripping revenue from sponsorship and gate receipts (Ungerer, 2003). In smaller leagues, which offer fewer opportunities for broadcasters and advertisers, clubs have to make do with more modest television revenues; around 10 per cent or less of total revenue. For example, revenue from television rights accounts for less than 10 per cent of Celtic Football Club's total revenue, and revenues from television represent on average only 5 per cent of total revenue for Swiss Top League football clubs (Champions League revenue not included). In the USA, 'approximately 60 per cent of the revenues of the average NFL club come from the joint presentation of NFL games on national television networks' (Tagliabue, in Senate Judiciary Committee, 1999), while about a third of revenue for professional basketball and baseball comes from broadcasting (Cave and Crandall, 2001). For ice hockey, 8 per cent of its 2002–2003 revenue ($449m) came from broadcasting and new media contracts (Levitt, 2004).

Media coverage is not only a major revenue source; it also raises a sport's profile, generating interest among the public and sponsors alike. The relationship between rights owners, broadcasters and advertisers is now so symbiotic that some federations have changed the rules or introduced new ones: such as the possibility of scoring in each exchange in volleyball, the tie-break in tennis and television timeouts in basketball and American football (European Commission, 1998, Baran, 2004). Equally, organisers have agreed to change the competition schedule to accommodate the needs of broadcasters and sponsors. Thus, the US Tennis Open is the only major tournament where the semi-finals and finals are played on consecutive days, so that matches are played on Saturdays and Sundays, when audiences are higher. While there is something in it for the American Tennis Federation (the tournament is its main source of income) and the event's sponsors, it is unlikely that the players appreciate this arrangement (Lambert, 2001).[1] In North America, sport is seen as a commodity which has to be redesigned as viewers' preferences or sponsors' requirements change. In Europe, by contrast, sport is considered as part of the cultural heritage. The dominant opinion in Europe is that sport cannot be reduced to being merely an audience-generating mechanism and that there is a need to preserve both its identity and independence (European Commission, 1999).

Not all sports are equally appealing for television, and commercial broadcasters are only interested in games that suit television and are popular – football in Europe and American football, basketball, baseball and, to a lesser degree, hockey in the USA. Other sports get less airtime and, where they do, it is usually on public channels. In France, football accounts for 25 per cent of programming and, of the other sports, only tennis has a significant market share (slightly above 10 per cent). This is reflected in broadcasters' acquisition budgets, with football accounting for 42 per cent of television rights expenditure in Germany, 51.6 per cent in the UK and 65.2 per cent in Italy. Putting these figures in perspective, Zimbalist (1992) noted that in 1946 only 3 per cent of revenue for Major League Baseball came from radio and television rights. The choices made by broadcasters vary from country to country. While football is widely popular across Europe, cycling is popular in France and Spain, tennis in the UK and Spain, and rugby in the UK and France (CSA, 2000).

Sports broadcasting also has a major impact on the downstream market. Sports rights are now a key issue through sport being an essential component of media companies' business strategies. In the early days of television, the attractiveness of sport to US television networks 'was not advertising dollars. Instead, broadcasters were looking toward the future of the medium, and aired sports as a means of boosting demand for television' (Baran, 2004). Today, sport accounts for more than 20 per cent of television companies' acquisitions budgets, and can even go as high as 40 per cent. Along with first-run major box-office films, sport forms the major 'premium' content that channels use as a means of standing out from their competitors and to increase both audience size and subscriber numbers. Sport has a clear advantage over films for the advertisers as it attracts a more homogenous audience. The viewers are most likely to be young, male and affluent (Tonazzi, 2003). This underlines the importance of exclusivity clauses, found in many contracts. In Europe, football rights have been the driving force in the development of pay-TV, and in Britain the acquisition of exclusive rights for live Premier League matches was a key element in Sky's strategy to dominate the satellite television industry (Forrest *et al.* in this volume). In the USA, at the start of the 1960s, ABC's gamble of increasing the amount of sport it broadcast paid off in terms of audience growth and the widening of its network of affiliates. The fact that sport is relatively cheap to produce is a further advantage, which was a decisive factor in the early days of television when advertising revenue was still modest.

THE RELEVANT BUSINESS MODEL

The first issue concerns the ownership of broadcasting rights: should the home club be regarded as the sole broadcasting rights owner or do rights belong to both the home and the visiting clubs or to the league? Co-ownership of rights between the clubs and the federation is also a possible arrangement (see European Commission, 2003, Section 6.5.1. 'League rights and individual football clubs' rights'). This leads to the issue of who produces the service – the clubs, the league or both? According to some, the league (as organiser of the competition), and not the clubs, should be regarded as the relevant business unit. The value of the service does not stem from the independent activities of each club but from the existence of a recognisable brand in the form of an organised competition. As Veljanovski (2000) rightly points out, going for the championship is an essential element of the service that the teams jointly produce. Sloane (2000) makes the same point when he argues that it is more appropriate to see leagues as multi-plant firms rather than as cartels. The argument of leagues being a single economic unit is not generally accepted. Tonazzi, for example, questions its validity, notably for European football, considering that clubs are separately owned and benefit from a large commercial and organisational autonomy. Furthermore, the fact that leagues in Europe are open makes it difficult to consider them as a single economic entity. The 'single entity theory' is certainly convenient for leagues or federations in search of an antitrust exemption, but does not reflect reality (Tonazzi, 2003, p. 22–23). Looking at cases that have gone to court in

Europe, it emerges that clubs are, in principle, the rights owners, but criteria and practices vary from country to country (European Commission, 2003).

INDIVIDUAL OR JOINT SELLING AND EXCLUSIVITY

Two central issues concerning the marketing of sports rights are joint selling and exclusivity. Central marketing of media rights generates several benefits. First, it reduces transaction costs and represents a more efficient way of selling broadcasting rights ('single point of sale argument'). For the media operator, central marketing makes it easier to acquire a complete rights package covering the whole season. It also needs to be borne in mind that team sports have characteristics which make them different from other economic activities. Clubs are not simply competitors who seek to maximise economic and/or sporting success by eliminating weaker competitors. All need each other in order to create an appealing product, the value of which will be higher when there is greater uncertainty of outcome. A system where clubs own individual rights and have the chance of selling them to the highest bidder (as is the case for the First and Second Division Italian Football League games[2]) favours the big-market clubs as the value of local broadcasting rights is related to the size of the broadcasting market, while the smaller clubs find it difficult to get the resources needed to remain competitive on the field. Thus individual selling increases the spread in club revenues (Scully, 2004). Of course, individual rights sales do not preclude revenue sharing among clubs, but it does make it more difficult in practice. When rights are sold collectively, the league can redistribute funds from richer to poorer clubs, as a way of achieving competitive balance.

Exclusive deals are a widespread practice in the sports rights market. Obviously, the aim is to guarantee the value of a program and, from the property owner's point of view, to derive maximum value from broadcasters. Exclusivity has a particular importance in the case of sport because rights lose most of their value once there is no longer any uncertainty over the result. Indeed, if several broadcasters were able to show the same live event in the same region, acquiring the rights would no longer enable a broadcaster to differentiate itself from its competitors. There is a second reason why broadcasters accept to pay an 'exclusivity' premium: when rights are sold exclusively, owners are able to extract a larger share of economic surplus compared with non-exclusive rights deals. This is a basic principle that is well understood by sports federations.

COLLECTIVE SELLING AND COMPETITION POLICY

On both sides of the Atlantic, the competition authorities have closely monitored the way the television rights market has developed and the practices which restrict competition. In the United States, attention has focused on the major professional leagues and on the college leagues, while in Europe the focus has been on football rights sales (Cave and Crandall, 2001). It needs to be remembered that the US Sport Broadcasting Act of 1961 gave the leagues limited antitrust exemption. The Act permits joint selling agreements and for broadcasting rights to be sold as a single package to the network or networks. The law also includes the 'blackout rule', which is aimed at protecting a home team from locally-broadcast competing games on a day when it is playing at home. The antitrust exemption applied to the major professional leagues for American football, basketball, baseball and ice hockey. Vertical integration of teams and regional sports networks, along with bundling by cable companies, restrict competition and harm consumers' interests and, as Zimbalist stresses in his contribution to this volume, these practices ought to receive greater attention from the competition authorities. In recent years, however, it has been Europe that has fuelled discussions over this issue. The impact of collective selling on both the way the market works and on consumer welfare is probably more serious in Europe because the interests of audiences and broadcasters are focused on a single sport (football) whereas in the USA a variety of popular team sports compete for viewers' interests (see Szymanski, 2000 for a discussion of this issue).

From a competition policy perspective, it is a matter of whether joint selling is a barrier to competition and, if so, whether the costs incurred by restricting competition are offset by expected benefits for consumers (Sloane, 2000). Contracts generally contain an exclusivity clause conferring broadcasting rights on a single broadcaster in the same area. The impact of joint selling and exclusivity is felt in both upstream and downstream markets. Selling rights collectively produces the same outcome as that of a cartel, namely a higher price and a restricted output. Often, some of the rights remain unused rather than being sold on, the aim being to avoid potential cannibalisation by television or non-TV products (notably those delivered by new media). In principle, such practices are a violation of competition rules (Art. 81(1) of the EC Treaty, EU, 2002). However, an exemption can be granted by the European Commission if the arrangement represents an improvement in economic terms and consumers receive a fair share of the benefit (Art. 81(3) of the Treaty). When rights are sold collectively, transaction costs are reduced and the league is able to sell a league-branded quality product that is more attractive than one that would emerge if rights were sold individually by clubs. Another argument – though probably not a key one – is linked to the specificity of sport. Clubs are not simply competitors, as there is a need to cooperate in order to make a tournament possible. Leagues argue that joint marketing makes it possible to reduce revenue disparities between clubs ('solidarity argument') and thus to improve the balance within the league. Such an argument is not wholly convincing, however. As Tonazzi (2003) points out, the Italian Football League experience, following the prohibition of collective selling, shows that individual selling does not necessarily have a negative impact on competitive balance if a suitable system for redistributing television revenue from big-market clubs to small-market clubs is set up. The more fundamental question is whether such an equalising arrangement actually improves competitive balance. If the distribution of revenue between the different teams in the league becomes more equal, it seems obvious that the outcome of the championship will be more uncertain. But theory suggests that it is not necessarily the case. Depending on the assumption regarding the stock of playing talents and the teams' utility function (profit maximisers or win maximisers), revenue sharing can improve the competitive balance, leave it unchanged, or make it worse (see Késenne, 2000, Szymanski and Késenne, 2004, Goddard and Sloane, 2005).

The problem is not one of exclusivity and joint selling as such, but rather with the special conditions within the contracts: excessive length, block sales of large packages, the absence of a transparent bidding process, and automatic renewal. Exclusivity is a condition of the product's value, a fact acknowledged by all parties. In the downstream market, exclusivity combined with an inelastic demand results in higher prices and a lower output (Sandy *et al.*, 2004). Indeed, what interest would a broadcaster have in holding the rights to show a sporting event if all its competitors enjoyed the same right? In order to avoid anticompetitive practices and market foreclosure, the European Commission requires rights owners to offer several packages in an open bidding process. The question of whether rights being bundled in multiple packages will indeed lead to a reduction in price, and thus improved consumer welfare, remains open. Harbord and Ottaviani (2001) argue that this may simply create multiple downstream monopolies with no benefit to the consumer. If one is really after a solution that benefits consumers, then rights should be sold non-exclusively to multiple broadcasters (Harbord and Szymanski, 2004). At first sight, this argument seems convincing, but then one wonders why the leagues – notably the Football Association Premier League (FAPL) – are frightened off from dividing rights into several balanced packages if there is no effect on their total value. It is hard to imagine a broadcaster willing to pay a huge fee for the right to broadcast league games if its competitors will be able to show games at the same time which are broadly just as attractive. Holding back some of the rights is another risk associated with exclusivity, as the example of the Premier League shows, where only 100 of the 400 official matches played were broadcast (see Toft, 2003 and Szymanski in this volume).

The inclusion of rights for new media – the internet and 3G/UMTS mobile rights – within a large bundle, along with the fact that the rights are often not used, is a cause for concern, since it risks hampering innovation and the development of new media. Leagues and teams fear that non-TV products – notably those associated with new media – will have a cannibalising effect on viewing and thus reduce broadcasters' core revenues. In this regard, the position favoured by the European Commission is one known as 'fall-back', where clubs regain the rights not sold by the league (Menshing, 2003). When deciding upon a possible exemption from the rules, the Commission looks carefully at upstream and downstream market structures and the degree of market power of the parties involved. An important issue is the degree to which broadcasting rights for different events are close substitutes. In other words, whether each event constitutes a separate (and distinct) market as opposed to a single market defined in terms of events that are held at the same time. This is an important issue because the narrower the market, the greater is the risk that a dominant position (such as a league owning the broadcasting rights for all league games) will be considered as an infringement of competition rules (Scheuer and Strothmann, 2004; Fikentscher, in this volume). Wachtmeister (1998) notes 'that there is little substitutability between sports for fans. For football supporters, television coverage of athletics or golf is not a good substitute'. However, it is true that there may be some substitutability between sports for sponsors. In its decision regarding Eurovision, the Commission expressed the opinion that the behaviour of those watching a major sports event (such as Winter and Summer Olympic Games, the FIFA World Cup, and the Wimbledon Finals) is not influenced by other major events that are being shown at the same time, which indicates that products are not substitutes and that each event constitutes a distinct market. Broadcasters are willing to pay extremely high prices to win the exclusive rights to events regarded as 'irreplaceable'. If all European football league games constitute a single market, a French broadcaster could, for example, buy the broadcasting rights to Spanish Premier League games (undoubtedly for a reasonable fee) and thus compete with Canal+ (a private broadcaster) which had paid dearly for the rights for French First Division games. French fans will undoubtedly consider the *La Liga* games to be a poor substitute for those of their own national championship.[3] There is no doubt that the French and the Spanish football leagues constitute two separate markets.

A good illustration of the European Union's position is the joint selling arrangement used by UEFA for the Champions League broadcasting rights. In

1999, the Commission decided that UEFA's selling arrangement could not be granted an exemption from competition rules. Article 81(3) of the EU Treaty allows the Commission to exempt restrictive agreements if they 'contribute to improving the production or distribution of the goods or to promoting technical or economic progress, while allowing consumers a fair share of the resulting benefit'. UEFA's initial arrangement did not meet these conditions: exclusive rights were offered in a single package to a single broadcaster for a long period (4 years). Two of the consequences of this arrangement were that some games were not broadcast and that new media were excluded from the market. UEFA then came up with a new arrangement to meet the Commission's objections. The principle of central marketing of media rights is maintained, but rights are divided into 14 packages and sold through a transparent bidding procedure. The duration of the contract was also reduced to three years. The two main packages (Gold and Silver) were to be sold to a free-to-air and a pay-TV broadcaster, meaning that in each country at least two broadcasters would hold the rights. Up to a certain date, clubs could sell some rights (either live or recorded) that UEFA had not been able to sell. UEFA and individual clubs could sell images of the Champions League games to internet and UTMS operators (European Commission, 2003, Toft, 2003). All the same, the Commission's stance in relation to UEFA's new offer seemed somewhat naive. In terms of creating a competitive environment and preventing prices from increasing above their competitive level, the composition of the packages is as much, if not more, important than the number of packages sold. Packages which vary substantially in quality present the same drawbacks as single packages: high prices, reduced output, and limited competition in downstream markets. The Commission should only consent to an exemption from the prohibition on agreements which restrict competition in cases where a number of identical packages (at least two) are put on the market in each country. This is effectively the only means of seriously limiting a single seller's market power.

FREE-TO-AIR OR PAY-TV AND THE PUBLIC INTEREST

In Europe, the liberalisation of the television market and the arrival of digital television have led to sports programs moving away from free-to-air television and towards pay-TV. This has had major consequences for consumers. Indeed, when pay-TV channels acquire exclusive rights to show sporting events, viewers who do not have a subscription, or who are unwilling or unable to pay to watch a specific event, are deprived of access to the event. Are there grounds for government intervention in order to protect the right to information or to correct some kind of market failure? If so, what is the nature of this market failure and what makes the broadcasting of sports events different from other marketable goods? The answer to these questions amounts to deciding whether the broadcasting of sporting events is just like any other marketable good or whether it is a special case (Sloane, 2000). Governments have different opinions on this issue.

The first issue deals with the specific nature of the good: is broadcast sport a public or a private good? Broadcasting has several elements of a public good. A viewer watching a game does not prevent other viewers from watching the same game. There is thus non-rivalry in consumption, which also means that the social value of the product is the sum of its value to viewers and advertisers. Non-rivalness represents market failure: restricting access to fee-payers and depriving fans of the opportunity of watching the games clearly represent a welfare loss because the additional service could have been provided at zero cost (Department for Culture, Media and Sport, 1999). Looked at in this way, arguments based on the theory of public goods may provide some justification for a government intervention in this area. Broadcast sport is certainly not a pure public good: a cable broadcaster has the characteristics of a club (its members being its subscribers). The service provided by a cable operator can thus be regarded as a club good, not a pure public good (Buchanan, 1965).

By distinguishing between free-to-air and pay television (subscription or pay-per-view), we can say that the first possesses the characteristics of non-rivalness in consumption and non-excludability (the latter being a *de facto* situation as exclusion is easily achievable). Subscription and pay-per-view television send an encrypted signal and exclude those who would be interested in the program but whose willingness-to-pay is below the subscription fee or the price charged to watch the event. There is thus a case of market failure, because a group of fans cannot watch their favourite team despite the fact that the service could have been provided at no additional cost. Thus, at first sight, free television appears to maximise welfare, as pay-TV would make the price of television higher than the programs' marginal cost. However, account needs to be taken of another form of market failure linked to the absence of a pricing mechanism. Free-to-air broadcasters, which rely on advertising or taxpayers' money to cover their costs, have less knowledge of viewers' preferences than broadcasters that charge for the service and can use price discrimination and bundling strategies. This brings us back to the Samuelson-Minasian debate (Minasian, 1964, Collins, 2002, Cave, 2004). One could also argue that viewers always have to reveal their willingness-to-pay whatever the platform – pay-per-view, pay-TV, or free-to-air television – in terms of a price for a specific game, a subscription fee or through the time spent watching commercials. In any case, consumers can 'exit' if they think the value of the program doesn't match the price charged.

Given the present state of knowledge, it is not possible to say which of the two forms of market failure leads to the greater welfare loss.

There is no doubt that amateur sport generates positive externalities such as improved health, education, character building, and creating a sense of team spirit. For reasons such as these, sport is encouraged by governments through incentive programmes or tax breaks and by providing sports facilities. Do professional sport and sports broadcasting also generate positive externalities? Viviane Reding, the European Commissioner for Information Society and Media, regards sport as an important means of building social cohesion and believes that audiovisual media have a

> 'fundamental role in the development and transmission of social values ... [television] has a major influence on what citizens know, believe and feel and plays a crucial role in the transmission, development and even construction of cultural identities'.

The Commissioner goes on to say that the audiovisual industry is not like other industries, it is above all a cultural industry. Both sport and television are means of passing on essential values like tolerance, respect, solidarity and team spirit (Reding, 2002 and 2003). This explains why the amended version of the European Union Directive 'Television without Frontiers' embodies the principle and objective of protecting major events, particularly sporting ones.

The revised EU Directive allows each Member State to take steps to ensure that events considered to have a national or cultural significance (hence the term 'crown jewels' as a way of describing them) are accessible on free-to-air television (i.e. advertising-supported). Each country can draw up a list of national and international events that it believes should be accessible to a large part of the population. Italy's list contained eight events, including the Olympic Games, the football World Cup final, the Tour of Italy cycling race and the Italian leg of motor racing Formula 1 Grand Prix. In its response to the consultation process, UEFA said that it supported the goal set out in the article in the Directive concerning the broadcasting of major events. However, it considered that it should be left to sporting bodies to find the right balance between free-to-air and paid television, and that it was not up to the EU to favour one type of broadcaster rather than another (UEFA, 2003).

Since 1994, Australia has used a form of regulation – known as anti-siphoning legislation – which enables the government to rule that certain events must be shown on free-to-air television. As in Europe, legislation of this type was not necessary before the arrival of pay-TV. The goal of the Australian legislation is more or less the same as that of the European Directive, that is both are rules aimed at strengthening national identity and culture which 'rely on the assumption that certain events are so important or even vital to the national interest that they must (or at least should) be shown on free-to-air television'. The so-called anti-siphoning scheme

'protects the access of Australian viewers to events of national importance ... by preventing pay-TV operators from siphoning off television coverage of those events before free-to-air broadcasters have had an opportunity to obtain the broadcasting rights' (Minister for Communications, 2004).

The list, which is drawn up at the Minister's discretion, is long and contains events as varied as the National Soccer League finals and international matches involving the Australian netball team. The main practical effect of the legislation seems to be that only the three commercial and the two public broadcasters are entitled to bid to show all the events on the list. In effect, this excludes pay-TV broadcasters from the market. The issue of protecting the national interest remains open, but it is certain that the bill creates major distortions in the television market in Australia; the result being that 'there is no "market" in broadcasting in Australia' (Fraser and McMahon, 2002). In the USA, there are also fears of free (over the air) sports programming being progressively 'siphoned' away by cable and pay-per-view television. In the last decades, several bills were introduced in the House and in the Senate, in an attempt to restrain the migration of sports programming to pay-TV or pay-per-view. All these attempts at passing anti-siphoning legislation failed (Cox, 1995).

Finally, what is the expected impact of a pay-TV ban, general or limited to outstanding events, on social welfare? If broadcasters cannot sell the event on a subscription or pay-per-view basis, they would have no other choice but to charge viewers indirectly through advertising. It is likely however that the value placed on sports programs by advertisers is lower than the amount sports fans would be willing to pay to watch the events. Thus the signal sent to broadcasters by advertisers understates consumers' preferences (Yoo, 2004). Moreover, with a ban on pay-TV, there is a risk that 'minority' sports – characterised by a small audience and a relatively inelastic demand – would not be broadcast at all, the advertising revenue being insufficient to cover the costs. Using a more elaborate pricing scheme, a pay channel would be able to extract the rent and produce the program with a profit (Cave, 2004). When measuring the impact of a pay-TV ban on welfare, both the changes in consumers' surplus and in producers' surplus have to be considered.

Hafner and Neunzig (1999) have studied the consequences of different regulatory options on welfare: free market, a general ban and a ban on specific events. In a free market environment, too many programs would be broadcast through pay-TV or pay-per-view. Some of the sports fans with a positive willingness-to-pay would be denied access to the programs. A general ban on pay-TV compared to a free television market would have positive as well as negative consequences on welfare. The net impact is however uncertain. The authors conclude that a selective ban on pay-TV is superior to a general ban and to a free broadcasting market. Premium events such as the football World Cup with a large audience, and whose broadcasting costs can easily be financed through advertising, should be offered on free television. Hansen and Kyhl (2001) compare free television to pay-per-view, considering that commercials reduce the utility of the programs ('viewers dislike the ads'). The results are only partially consistent with those of the previous study by Hafner and Neunzig. A ban reduces total surplus if broadcasting cannot be financed through pure advertising, which is straightforward. On the other hand, pay-per-view makes it possible to broadcast events attracting only a limited audience, the so-called 'minority sports'. Those events cannot generate a net profit under pure advertising support and they would simply not be transmitted if broadcasters had no other opportunity than indirect pricing.[4] Otherwise, if it is possible to cover the costs through advertiser finance, a ban on pay-per-view may increase or reduce total surplus, the latter being more likely. Thus Hansen and Kyhl's research outcome does not provide sufficient arguments to support a ban on pay-per-view. The introduction of a ban has however important distributional implications: consumers' surplus increases and the value of broadcasting rights sharply decreases.

OVERVIEW OF THE CHAPTERS

This overview attempts to outline the main issues in the debate over the sports–media long-standing relationship. The following chapters deal with the major current policy concerns relating to the commercialisation of sports broadcasting rights. What is the impact of marketing arrangements between content owners and media companies on fans, big-city and small-city clubs, and finally on consumer welfare? Do consumers in Europe and the USA receive a fair value for the fees they pay to broadcasters? And does the way programs are delivered to the viewers (free-to-air, pay-TV or pay-per-view) have a positive or negative influence on the deal the consumers receive? These are some of the central issues discussed in the following chapters. The volume, which reports on the current state of research in sports economics, focuses on the latter effect. The emphasis is clearly placed on team sport as it constitutes the bulk of the sports broadcasting rights market.

The chapter by Bill Gerrard deals with the issue of competitive dominance in European football. The author is Professor of Sport Management and Finance at Leeds University Business School and is actively involved as a consultant to the sports industry, teams and governing bodies. The starting point of his chapter is the increasing competitive dominance in European football at both the continental and domestic levels. In the domestic championships, there is a growing gap between a handful of top clubs and the rest of the league. Both the deregulation of the player transfer market – following the Bosman ruling – and the deregulation of the market for sports rights have contributed to the dominance of successful clubs located in large metropolitan areas. The situation in North America is different, as leagues have more or less limited the deregulation of the rights market and have adopted rules to promote competitive balance. After reminding us of the specifics of the sports industry – jointness, the important roles played by uncertainty of outcome, and the loyalty of fans – Gerrard examines the complex question of media rights valuation, and points out that market confidence in future revenues plays a key role in pricing. The final part of the chapter focuses on the main determinants of the value of team tournaments. As expected, property rights arrangements – in terms of their being sold collectively or individually – play a key role. This issue is complex, as we have to consider the segmentation of the market between those who only value the performance of their club (fans of the club) and those who place the value on the game as a whole rather that in a particular club (fans of the game). Gerrard strongly believes – and provides convincing arguments to support his view – that individual selling may ultimately hurt consumer interests.

Chapter 3, by Wladimir Andreff and Jean-François Bourg, compares the two basic forms of ownership of sports rights in European football – individual (or club) ownership and collective (or league) ownership – in terms of their impact on clubs' overall revenue and competitive balance. Andreff is Professor of Economics at the University of Paris I Panthéon-Sorbonne and is currently Honorary President of the International Association of Sport Economists and Vice-President of the French Economic Association. Bourg – also a leading French sports economist – is a member of the Center for Law and Sport Economics at the University of Limoges. The chapter begins with an overview of the different arrangements regarding the ownership of football broadcasting rights and revenue sharing adopted for European countries' domestic championships and for the Champions League. The issue is whether these arrangements – joint selling and revenue sharing – actually contribute to a better competitive balance. Through looking at five major national football championships, the authors found greater uncertainty – i.e. a better competitive balance – when media rights were pooled. However, a strong redistributive scheme at the national level has an unwanted side effect: the clubs (in the countries concerned) will be less competitive at the European level. The revenue sharing mechanisms that the leagues have designed for distributing (pooled) television rights reduce, but do not eliminate, the inherent advantage of big-city teams in terms of a larger market which is capable of generating higher gate receipts, and greater sponsorship and merchandising revenue. The degree of concentration of total revenue – as measured by the Gini coefficient – is actually higher in countries which have adopted individual selling (Spain and Italy) than in France and England, where joint selling is the rule; but the difference is surprisingly small. The comparisons between revenue concentration and competitive balance in the five major domestic championships produce the expected result: the more even the distribution of revenue, the more uncertain the outcome of the championship. Finally, the authors make five recommendations regarding the ownership of television rights and the usefulness of revenue sharing.

European public broadcasters have joined forces to form a joint purchasing group – the European Broadcasting Union – which negotiates rights for major sport events on behalf of its members. Chapter 4 by Adrian Fikentscher – who is a legal adviser at the Bavarian Broadcast – discusses this joint purchasing arrangement from the perspective of complying with European competition rules. The main argument for the joint purchasing arrangement is that it is the only way of acquiring rights directly from the property holder without having to pay a mark-up represented by a sports rights agency's profit margin. Joint purchasing minimises transaction costs and helps smaller members to purchase rights at an affordable price. The central part of the chapter discusses, firstly, a recent judgment by the Court of First Instance which annulled the (antitrust) exemption granted by the European Commission in 2000. The Court's main argument is that some of the rights remain unused. Effectively, EBU members reserve the rights when they do not intend to broadcast all competitions live. Fikentscher then discusses the general framework of joint purchasing. In order to determine whether joint purchasing is regarded as anticompetitive, the three following criteria have to be considered: the market power of the cooperating buyers (in the upstream and downstream markets), the fact that joint purchasing may counterbalance the bargaining power of a single seller (the property owner or its agent) and, finally, the fact that the buyers' benefits are passed on to viewers in the downstream market. In the final part of the chapter, Fikentscher examines the Eurovision joint purchasing system.

Chapter 5 by David Forrest (University of Salford), Robert Simmons (Lancaster University), and Batatunde Buraimo (University of Central Lancashire) helps us to better understand the characteristics of the demand for the English Premier League games by the broadcaster and the final consumer. A better understanding of the demand for sports rights is important because revenue from broadcasting rights now exceeds gate revenues for the leading teams and, furthermore, there has been little academic research on television demand. In the 1990s, Sky, the exclusive holder of live broadcasting rights, was allowed to choose the games it covered (given the constraints within the contract). Thus, Sky's selections reveal the strategy of the broadcaster and also the value it attributes to the games. Observing the selections made by Sky provides information on the demand functions of both broadcaster and viewers. Using a probit model, the authors show that broadcaster choice is consistent with the assumptions underlying the economics of sport: concentration of playing talent, the significance of the match, and uncertainty of outcome are the determining factors. The chapter concludes by providing an analysis of viewers' demand. A surprising conclusion is that the uncertainty of outcome appears to have no influence on the audience, which would mean that the determinants of demand for viewers and broadcasters are not the same.

Chapter 6 by Harry Arne Solberg, from Trondheim University in Norway, examines the risks of acquiring sports rights. The list of deals in which broadcasters suffered significant losses, or even went bankrupt after they bought expensive television rights, is long. Solberg's argument is precisely that the acquisition of sports rights is a risky business, notably when the rights cover an international event or tournament. Contracts often run over several years and decisions have to be made when key determinants of viewers' demand – the host country of the Olympic Games or FIFA World Cup for example – are not yet known. Solberg notes that information asymmetry and moral hazard are probably the reasons why rights owners are reluctant to share the risk with broadcasters. There are some indications of collusion between broadcasters to avoid fierce competition for sports rights, but also examples of channels placing bids not to win the contract but to force a competitor to pay the highest possible price. Solberg's analysis of the risks of buying sports rights for international competitions is illustrated by two case studies, the Champions League in the Scandinavian countries and the Euro 2000 and 2004 competitions.

In chapter 7 Michel Desbordes presents a case study of the 2002 football World Cup television rights bought by TF1, France's leading commercial free-to-air broadcaster. The author is Professor of Sports Marketing at Marc Bloch University, Strasbourg. Desbordes' argument is that sport telecasting is a risky business, the extremely high costs of premium sporting rights making it almost impossible for the broadcaster to make a profit. This would mean that joint selling and strong competition between buyers – the number of channels increased in the 1990s while the number of premium events remained constant – allow the property owners (mainly FIFA and EUFA as far as football is concerned) to retain the entire economic rent generated by these rights.

Why have most key sports rights migrated to pay television in Europe while they are still available free-to-air in the United States? This question is the starting-point of chapter 8 by Stefan Szymanski. The author, Professor of Economics at Tanaka Business School, Imperial College in London, is a leading sports economist and a consultant for government bodies and commercial organisations. In the USA, terrestrial television remains the main platform for televised sport, the market being dominated by the four major broadcast networks. By contrast, most of the premium European sports rights – essentially top national football championships – are almost always only available on pay-TV. After describing the structure of television markets, Szymanski shows how technological changes – development of cable networks, satellite television and digital television – have strengthened competition between broadcasters by allowing property owners to capture an increasing share of the economic surplus. Szymanski gives four possible reasons why major sports events can be viewed on free-to-air networks in the USA but not in Europe: a different sports culture on either side of the Atlantic, market size, sports leagues in the USA more willing to change the rules of the game to make matches more 'watchable', allowing commercial spin-offs and, finally, the fact that the European Union decided in the 1980s to open up the television market to competition. There is probably a fifth reason, not mentioned by Szymanski; namely the fact that football – the most popular sport in Europe – has fewer stoppages, making it harder to insert commercial breaks during the game. In Szymanski's view, the regulation of competition in the broadcasting market is the most plausible reason why sports rights have not migrated to pay-TV in the United States.

Andrew Zimbalist, the author of chapter 9, is Robert A. Woods Professor of Economics at Smith College in Northampton (Mass.), and a consultant for the sports industry, Players' Associations, leagues, cities and private companies. He examines the consequences for consumers of what he calls 'the steady trend towards cablisation' of major sport contests in the United States, the legality of contract arrangements, and the options open to government for action. A shift from free-to-air television can be observed in Major League Baseball, in the NBA, and in the NHL. The teams and leagues see advantages in the move to cable in terms of revenue stream benefits: advertising and transmission fees. The central part of the chapter questions the legality of pooled cable contracts and channel bundling. Zimbalist notes that the authorisation for rights pooling was granted to promote audiences and to favour revenue sharing. This is not consistent with shifting the telecasting of sport events from free-to-air television to cable. Channel bundling is also a restriction of consumer choice. Using a simple numerical example, Zimbalist shows that bundling – contrary to received opinion – does not necessarily leave the surplus unchanged in terms of simply redistributing it between the consumer and the producer, but reduces the total surplus and thus the welfare of society. Bundling is not welfare neutral, and the adverse effect on welfare is especially significant given that, in most communities, consumers cannot select their preferred bundle as there is no competition (and consequently no choice). The author then examines the consequences of vertical integration. When a team owns a regional sports network, the revenues do not have to be reported as team revenues, which places the team in a better position to receive subsidies or to negotiate players' salaries. Zimbalist demonstrates that vertical integration has a negative impact on viewers' welfare, increasing the price and reducing output. The final part of the chapter contains policy recommendations to reduce the adverse effects of bundling and monopoly power.

The final chapter is by Paul Staudohar, Professor of Business Administration at California State University, Hayward, who explores the relationship between baseball and broadcasting in an historical perspective. Radio came first and, at the beginning, rights were not sold but given away free; broadcasting being viewed as a free promotion for teams. The chapter shows how baseball played a pioneering role in the development of a symbiotic relationship between professional sports and the media. A majority of team owners assumed that radio would reduce gate receipts, and therefore broadcasting was not very common. It was not until the mid-1940s that radio broadcasts of Major League Baseball really took off. In the early years of television, owners were also skeptical, but then realised that telecasting would not affect attendances if used judiciously. Already in the early 1950s, baseball executives recognised the advantages of collective selling and rights pooling. Joint selling became possible in 1961, after Congress granted antitrust exemption to major team sports. In the final part of his chapter, Staudohar highlights some of the problems that teams and leagues have come across in managing broadcasting rights: the fact that baseball is less suited for television than American football or basketball, the relatively low ratings, the sharp drop in national television rights in 1993, which was a major factor causing the 1994 strike, followed by the cancellation of the rest of the regular season and the entire postseason, and the unequal distribution of local television rights which represents a threat to competitive balance. Staudohar concludes that the only way for smaller teams to compete effectively with the wealthier ones is to have a larger share of the local broadcasting revenue.

NOTES

1.   The American journalist and television commentator, Andy Rooney, made the following
     suggestions regarding the need for changing the sporting rules:

     > Hockey is losing fans. Too many games end up 1-0. There is a need for more scoring in
     > hockey and there's a very simple way to do it. Make the net 4 inches wider so it would
     > be easier to put the puck in the net ... Basketball is just the opposite of hockey. There's
     > too much scoring in basketball. They should raise the basket about three feet ... (CBS
     > News, November 14, 2004).

     In July 2005, the NHL Board approved a long series of rule changes expected to emphasise
     entertainment. The primary objective was to reduce the scope of defensive tools a team can
     employ. One of these new rules limits the size of goaltender equipment. Some sports such
     as volleyball, gymnastics and swimming changed more rapidly than others (football for
     example) to respond to television needs. The market, not the television, is the primary
     driver of change: if you do no adapt to viewers' taste, you will not appear on screen
     (Weingarten, 2003).
2.   With the exception of the Coppa Italia games, for which an exemption allowing for the
     collective selling of broadcasting rights was granted by the Italian Competition Authority.
3.   A French broadcaster, TPS, bought English Premier League broadcasting rights for the
     next three seasons for €25m. Canal+ is going to pay, on average, €600m per year over the
     next three years for exclusive French First Division broadcasting rights. If there were any
     doubts, this clearly confirms that national football championships are not close substitutes.
4.   Empirical works suggest that viewers' willingness-to-pay for television programs is several
     times higher than the value advertisers place on the programs (Yoo, 2004). Thus
     advertising-supported television doesn't allocate sufficient resources for programming, and
     the programs preferred by a small segment of the audience – 'minority sports' fans – are
     most likely to be neglected. It is not uncommon for some 'minority sports' to pay for
     program production in order to provide a better audience for their sport. Subscription
     pricing is a way to improve allocative efficiency in this case (Anderson and Gabszewicz,
     2006).

REFERENCES

Anderson, S.P. and J.J. Gabszewicz (2006), 'The Media and Advertising: A
     Tale of Two-Sided Markets', in V. Ginsburg and D. Throsby (eds),
     Handbook on the Economics of Art and Culture, New York, NY: Elsevier
     Science Ltd.
Baran, S.J. (2004), 'Sports and Television', in S.R. Rosner and K.L.
     Shropshire (eds), *The Business of Sports*, Sudbury, MA: Jones and Bartlett
     Publishers, 143–146.
Blociszewski, J. (1999), 'Television in Sport. What Future?', *Diffusion EBU*,
     Winter, 13–14.
Buchanan, J.M. (1965), 'An Economic Theory of Clubs', *Economica*, **32**
     (125), 1–14.
Cave, M. (2004), 'Competition in broadcasting – consequences for viewers',
     available at: http://www.ofcom.org.uk/consult/condocs/psb2/psb2/psbwp/
     wp1cave.pdf.

Cave, M. and R.W. Crandall (2001), 'Sports Rights and the Broadcast Industry', *The Economic Journal*, **111** (469), F4–26.

Collins, R. (2002), 'The Contemporary Broadcasting Market and the Role of the Public Service Broadcaster. A View From the UK', Paper presented at the Meeting on the Future of Broadcasting, March, Helsinki.

Cox, P.M. (1995), 'Flag on the Play? The Siphoning Effect on Sports Television', *Federal Communications Law Journal*, **47** (3), 571–591.

CSA – Conseil supérieur de l'audiovisuel (2000), 'Sport et télévision: état des lieux', *La lettre du CSA*, 126.

Department for Culture, Media and Sport (1999), *The future funding of the BBC: Report of the Independent Review Panel, Annex 8: Market Failure in Broadcasting*, London.

European Commission (1998), DG X, *The European Model of Sport*, Brussels.

European Commission (1999), First European Union Conference on Sports, Olympia (Greece), 20–23 May.

European Commission (2003), *COMP/C.2–37.398 – Joint Selling of the Commercial Rights of the UEFA Champions League*, Brussels.

European Commission, Press release (24 July 2003), *Commission Clears UEFA's New Policy Regarding the Sale of the Media Rights to the Champions League*, Brussels.

EU – European Union (2002), *Consolidated version of the Treaty establishing the European Community*, Official Journal of the European Communities, C 325, Luxembourg.

Fraser, D. and K. McMahon (2002), 'When Too Much Sport is Barely Enough: Broadcasting Regulation and National Identity', *Entertainment Law*, **1** (3), 1–52.

Goddard, J. and P.J. Sloane (2005), 'Economics of sport', in S.W. Bowmaker (ed.), *Economics uncut: a complete guide to life, death and misadventure*, Cheltenham and Northampton, MA: Edward Elgar.

Hafner, M. and A.R. Neunzig (1999), 'Regulating Television and the Case of Football World Cup', Discussion Paper 9803, Universität des Saarlandes (German version published in *Betriebswirtschaftliche Forschung und Praxis*, 2/99, 151–165).

Hansen, C.T. and S. Kyhl (2001), 'Pay-per-view Broadcasting of Outstanding Events: Consequences of a Ban', *International Journal of Industrial Organization*, **19** (3–4), 589–609.

Harbord, D. and M. Ottaviani (2001), *Contracts and Competition in the Pay-TV Market*, London Business School, Department of Economics, Working paper no. DP 2001/5.

Harbord, D. and S. Szymanski (2004), 'Football Trials', *European Competition Law Review*, 25, 117–121.

IOC – International Olympic Committee (2005), *IOC 2006 Marketing Fact File*, Signy (Switzerland), available at: http://multimedia.olympic.org/pdf/ en_report_344.pdf.

Kesenne, S. (2000), 'Revenue Sharing and Competitive Balance in Professional Team Sports', *Journal of Sports Economics*, **1** (1), 56–65.

Lambert, C. (2001), 'The Dow of Professional Sports', *Harvard Magazine*, **104** (1), September–October, available at: http://www.harvardmagazine. com/on-line/09014.html.

Levitt, A. (2004), 'Independent Review of the Combined Financial Results of the National Hockey League 2002–2003 Season', Westport, CT.

Mensching, J. (2003), 'Sport et télévision: Exclusivité et concurrence', Communication au Rendez-vous international du sport et de la télévision, septembre, Monaco.

Minasian, J.R. (1964), 'Television Pricing and the Theory of Public Goods', *Journal of Law and Economics*, **7**, 71–80.

Minister for Communications, Information Technology and the Arts (2004), 'Amendments to the Anti-siphoning Scheme', *News release*, 41, Canberra.

Reding, V. (2002), 'Sport and television: moving towards more balanced relations', Communication at the XIII international Sportel Symposium, October, Monte Carlo.

Reding, V. (2003), 'EU Media Policy: "Culture and Competition"', Paper presented at the Fifth Conference on Competition Law, Institute for European Studies of San Pablo-CEU University, March, Madrid.

Reimer, B. (2002), 'Altered images. TELEVISION, sports and cultural change', Paper presented at the Media and Transition Conference, MIT, May, Cambridge, MA.

Sandy, R., Sloane, P.J. and M.S. Rosentraub (2004), *The Economics of Sport: An International Perspective*, Houndsmill and New York, NY: Palgrave.

Scheuer, A. and P. Strothmann (2004), 'Le sport à la lumière du droit européen des médias: 1ère partie', IRIS *plus*, Observatoire européen de l'audiovisuel, Strasbourg.

Scully, G.W. (2004), 'The Market Structure of Sports', in S.R. Rosner and K.L. Shropshire (eds), *The Business of Sports*, Sudbury, MA: Jones and Bartlett Publishers, 26–33.

Senate Judiciary Committee (1999), 'Testimony of Paul Tagliabue, Commissioner, National Football League', June, Washington, DC.

Sloane, P.J. (2000), 'Government regulation of sport', Paper presented at the IEA Seminar on the Economics of Sport, October, London.

Szymanski, S. (2000), 'Sport and Broadcasting', Paper presented at the IEA Seminar on the Economics of Sport, October, London.

Szymanski, S. and S. Késenne (2004), 'Competitive Balance and the Revenue Sharing in Team Sports', *Journal of Industrial Economics*, **52** (1), 165–177.

The Economist (1996), 'Sport and Television: Swifter, higher, stronger, dearer', *The Economist*, 20 July, 17–19.

Toft, T. (2003), 'Football: Joint Selling of Media Rights', *Competition Policy Newsletter*, **3** (Autumn), 47–52.

Tonazzi, A. (2003), 'Competition Policy and the Commercialization of Sport Broadcasting Rights: The Decision of the Italian Competition Authority', *Economics and Business*, **10** (1), 17–34.

UEFA – Union of European Football Associations (2003), *Response to the Public Consultation on the Review of the Television Without Frontiers Directive*, July, Nyon, Switzerland.

Ungerer, H. (2003), *Commercialising Sport: Understanding the TELEVISION Rights Debate*, Paper presented at European Commission, Competition DG, 2nd October, Barcelona.

Veljanovski, C. (2000), 'Is Sports Broadcasting a Public Utility?', Paper presented at the IEA Seminar on the Economics of Sport, October, London.

Wachtmeister, A.M. (1998), 'Broadcasting of Sports Events and Competition law', *EC Competition Policy Newsletter*, **2** (June), 18–28, available at: http://europa.eu.int/comm/competition/speeches/text/sp1998_037_en.html.

Weingarten, G. (2003), 'The Reconstruction of Sport by Television', Paper presented at the Television in Transition Conference, MIT, May, Cambridge, MA.

Yoo, C.S. (2004), 'The Role of Politics and Policy in Television Regulation', *Emory Law Journal*, 53, 255–275.

Zimbalist, A. (1992), *Baseball and Billions: A Probing Look inside the Big Business of our National Pastime*, New York, NY: Basic Books.

2. Competitive Balance and the Sports Media Rights Market: What are the Real Issues?

Bill Gerrard

CURRENT PROBLEMS IN EUROPEAN CLUB FOOTBALL

European club football faces a number of threats currently. There is a trend for club tournaments, both domestic and European, towards greater competitive dominance. In the premier European club tournament, the UEFA Champions League (formerly the European Cup), the leading clubs from the 'Big Five' domestic leagues (i.e. England, France, Germany, Italy and Spain) dominate the final stages. In the five seasons, 1992/93–1996/97, the Big Five accounted for 65.0 per cent of the clubs reaching the last four (i.e. the semi-final stage or equivalent). In the next five seasons, Big Five clubs almost achieved a clean sweep of the semi-finals with 95.8 per cent of the last four places. Only one club from outside the Big Five reached the semi-finals of the Champions League during those five seasons – Dynamo Kiev from the Ukraine in the 1998/99 season.

The situation in domestic club football is less clear. Within the top divisions of the Big Five domestic league structures over the last ten years, there is no systematic tendency towards greater concentration of league titles. Although Manchester United has been very dominant within the FA Premier League in England over the period (although that dominance is now being challenged by Arsenal and, potentially, Chelsea), in the other Big Five leagues, there have been four or more different league champions. However, there is some evidence that there is a trend towards less competitive mobility in these leagues with the same clubs tending to finish towards the top of the league. There is also some tendency towards the league champions finishing with a higher points percentage in recent years indicating a growing gap between the top clubs and the rest of the league.

The reasons for increasing competitive dominance in European club football are largely due to the changing economics of European football and other professional team sports. Deregulation of the players' labour market through the removal of restrictions on the mobility of players following the introduction of free agency in professional team sports (e.g. the Bosman ruling in European football) has allowed players to respond to market incentives. Wealth-maximising players will move to those teams with the highest revenue potential and thus able to maximise their marginal revenue products (MRPs). The revenue potential of teams is primarily a matter of history and geography. The top players in any professional team sport will gravitate towards the big-market teams (i.e. teams with a history of sporting success located in large metropolitan areas) in the big-market leagues (i.e. countries with large populations, high per capita income and strong affinity to the sport).

Increasing commercialisation of sport combined with the deregulation of the rights markets (e.g. less cross-subsidisation of smaller-market teams through revenue redistribution such as sharing gate receipts and the collective selling of television rights) has significantly increased the opportunities and capabilities of professional sports teams to generate and retain more revenue. Coupled with deregulation of the players' labour market particularly the greater international mobility of players this has inevitably resulted in greater competitive dominance by the big-market teams. European club football is not unique in this process of cumulative causation. The North American major leagues have also faced similar economic forces although the experiences have differed across the leagues depending largely to the extent to which leagues have limited deregulation of the rights markets and/or enforced a hard salary cap.

Another related problem in European club football but common across professional team sports is the large number of teams that operate under conditions of financial distress, often severe with a high risk of insolvency. The widespread financial distress of professional sports teams is the result of a co-ordination problem endemic in the industry under conditions of deregulated players' labour markets. Teams pursuing sporting success engage in an 'arms race' in which the value of elite playing services is bid upwards through a competitive auction. Teams compete vigorously to sign the best talent and inevitably player remuneration and transfer fees (i.e. compensation payments for contracted players moving to another team) escalate. Team owners are persuaded by the coaching staff to sign another big cheque to get that 'must-have' player to achieve sporting success or avoid sporting failure.

The arms race is even more intense in leagues organised as merit-hierarchies with promotion and relegation as in European club football. The co-ordination problem becomes even more difficult if teams have weak corporate governance structures and processes that allow senior executives to operate with insufficient concern for financial prudence and risk management as the recent high-profile insolvency of Leeds United in England demonstrates clearly. Across European club football the player wages have grown significantly faster than club revenues as the advent of Bosman free agency shifted bargaining power significantly in favour of the top players. For example, in the two-year period 1997–1999, the wage-revenue ratio in the FA Premier League in England increased from 48 per cent to 58 per cent. In the Italian Serie A over the same two years the wage-revenue ratio rose from 58 per cent to 72 per cent. The comparable change in Spain was 44 per cent to 56 per cent. Wage growth has slowed subsequently but wage-revenue ratios remain at a non-sustainable level and show little sign of falling back towards the industry benchmark of 50 per cent, generally acknowledged as the level consistent with financial stability.

THE NATURE OF THE SPORTS–MEDIA INDUSTRY

The professional team sports industry has a peculiar economics compared to other industries. There are three particular economic peculiarities – the jointness of production, pro-competitive regulation, and expressive allegiance. The production of sporting contests in professional team sports requires joint production by independent teams. Team independence is a necessary requirement for contest legitimacy so that sporting contests are perceived to involve teams competing to win. It takes two teams to produce an individual sporting contest and many teams to produce a sporting tournament. This inevitably means that property rights are ill-defined. Suppose Manchester United plays Chelsea in the FA Premier League at the Old Trafford stadium in Manchester. Who owns the property rights to that sporting contest? Manchester United as the home club could claim property rights as the supplier of the venue but without the participation of the opponents, there would be no game. And some of the economic value of the game will be created by the fact that it is part of a tournament, the FA Premier League, with 18 other current members clubs plus past members all contributing to the status and significance of the tournament. Compare the economic value of the league game with the economic value of Manchester United versus Chelsea as a pre-season exhibition game organised jointly by the two clubs independently of the FA Premier League. There is a huge difference in the economic value of the two games entirely due to the value created by the FA Premier League as a whole not the two clubs themselves. By virtue of the prestige of the tournament, the FA Premier League ensures the perception of contest legitimacy in a way that an exhibition game can never do. A comparison of the economic value of tournament and non-tournament contests provides a market test of the property rights that a league possesses over all of the games played as part of a tournament.

A second economic peculiarity of the professional team sports industry is that regulatory mechanisms are in some respects pro-competitive not anti-competitive. To the extent that fans value uncertainty of outcome, there is additional economic value generated from tournaments if the participating teams are competitively balanced. Professional sports leagues have long recognised the importance of uncertainty of outcome to ensure the sporting and economic viability of tournaments. Leagues have created a variety of restrictions on rights markets and the players' labour market in order to maintain fair and balanced sporting competition. These regulatory mechanisms include salary caps, player drafts, transfer fees, sharing of gate receipts and collective selling of media/image rights. These regulatory mechanisms have also been used to try to maintain the financial viability of teams and leagues as well as sporting viability.

A third peculiarity of professional team sports is the expressive allegiance of fans (i.e. consumers) to the teams and players (i.e. the suppliers). The brand loyalty of fans to their teams is very strong and, indeed, for many fans these bonds are closer in intensity to family and friends, and religious allegiances rather than the economic trading allegiances. For many sports fans, team allegiances are passionate, lifetime attachments – the 'fanatics'. It is the passion and intensity of these team allegiances that makes professional team sports such a valuable advertising and sponsorship property. The degree of team loyalty in professional team sports implies that the market for team-fans (as opposed to general-sports fans) is highly segmented with little mobility. Teams only really compete for new entrants and the general-sports fans and even this competition is limited since fans are typically attracted to teams by geographical locality, family affinity and/or sporting success. Given such a segmented market, it follows that effective marketing by teams is better directed at enhancing and leveraging economic value from existing affinities. Another implication of the expressive allegiance of fans towards their teams is that teams are perceived as social assets with the private owners as stewards. This inevitably creates potential conflicts between team owners and the fans particularly over the relative weighting of sporting and financial performance in resource allocation decisions.

As well as its peculiar economics, the professional team sports industry is strategically complex. There is an intense competitive dynamic between four sets of strategic actors – teams, players, governing bodies and commercial media and sponsorship partners. All of the strategic partners are competing to maximise their share of the value created within the industry. In addition, the industry operates within a highly turbulent external environment subject to intense external pressures – political, economic, social and technological.

Yet despite its strategic complexity and turbulent external environment, the commercial structure of the professional team sports industry is relatively simple. Ultimately teams and leagues produce and sell events and image associations. Traditionally spectators could only view sporting contests by attendance at the stadium, generating gate revenues and other related event-day revenues such as car parking and catering. The modern alternative method of viewing sporting contests is through media broadcasts. Increasingly media revenues have become the biggest single income source in most professional team sports. Teams and leagues (and the players themselves) also produce and sell image associations through advertising and sponsorship, merchandising and other goods and services that utilise the team and/or league brand. Private and public organisations want to buy into the passion and excitement of sport as an unscripted human drama, creating a demand for sporting image associations as an advertising and sponsorship medium. Teams and leagues also cater for the demand of fans to purchase products that embody their sporting allegiances including replica sportswear and memorabilia.

The existing sports–media business model is based on teams and/or leagues selling the media and image rights for a specific sporting event to one or more media broadcasters and sponsors. The media broadcaster is responsible for the production and distribution of the programming that incorporates the sporting event. The media rights may include live coverage, full delayed or edited highlights. The rights may also be sold to different broadcast media – television, radio, mobile phones and the Internet. Television broadcasts are provided to the viewers via alternative delivery platforms – terrestrial, cable and satellite. There are also a variety of revenue models whereby television broadcasters monetise the value of their sports event programming. Free-to-air broadcasts are provided free at the point of delivery to the viewer by public-service broadcasters and commercial networks. Public-service broadcasters are funded by government grants e.g. the television licence fee in the UK provides funding for the BBC. Commercial network broadcasters such as ITV sell the advertising slots around their programming as well as sponsorship of programmes. The alternative revenue model is pay-TV in which viewers pay directly for the right to view either through subscription channels or pay-per-view programmes. Pay-TV represents the second enclosure movement in sport. The first enclosure movement involved the construction of stadia with gate turnstiles at which spectators had to pay to enter in order to view the sporting contest. Pay-TV provides an electronic turnstile at which television spectators must pay to view.

Sports media and image rights are intangible assets and inevitably there are severe valuation problems. It is difficult to determine fundamental valuations of sports media and image rights using discounted cash flow (DCF) analysis. As in other asset markets, there is a tendency to use an anchor-and-adjustment method. Previous media deals are used as the anchor benchmark to be adjusted for inflation, estimated market size and other deal-specific factors. As in any asset market, the anchor of current valuations is ultimately based on confidence about future cash flows. If there is a loss of confidence in the market, the anchor is itself adjusted as the market goes through a process of back-to-basics revaluation of asset values. In recent years the boom in the value of sports media rights fuelled by optimistic expectations of future revenue growth has been replaced by greater uncertainty caused by the shakeout and consolidation of the media industry, the advertising downturn particularly after 9/11 and general economic conditions. Within the sports media rights market, the non-premium rights have dropped substantially in value possibly due in part to the saturation of supply.

THE MEDIA VALUE OF TEAM TOURNAMENTS

There are four key drivers of the media value of team tournaments – the sporting quality of the tournament, the type of media coverage, the type and extent of fan allegiance and budget constraints. The sporting quality of team tournaments depends on contest legitimacy, playing talent, uncertainty of outcome and contest significance. Contest legitimacy is the requirement of open entry for all possible contenders to win a tournament with participants engaged in fair (i.e. within the laws of the game) and independent competition to win significant prizes such that contest outcomes are determined by playing skill and effort without external manipulation. Exhibition games have limited value for a variety of reasons – closed entry, insignificant prizes and restricted playing effort.

The value of team tournaments crucially depends on the quality of playing talent involved. Viewers and commercial partners will pay a premium for sporting contests involved the elite players in the particular team sport. But, as well as the level of playing talent, the value of a tournament depends on the distribution of that playing talent across teams. To the extent that fans value uncertainty of outcome, the media value of tournaments is enhanced by greater competitive balance. Conversely the media value of tournaments is diminished by competitive dominance. The media value of tournaments also depends on the significance of individual contests within the tournament in respect of determining the overall tournament outcome. Contest significance depends on the format of the tournament – round-robin (partial or full) or elimination or hybrid – as well as the prize structure. The principal types of prizes are the tournament championship, post-season qualification, and promotion and relegation. Sudden-death elimination tournaments ensure that individual contests are significant since one team is eliminated in every contest but round-robin tournaments can enhance contest significance by retaining credible contenders and scheduling more head-to-head confrontations between contenders.

As well as its sporting quality, the media value of a tournament depends on the type of media coverage. Viewers will pay a premium for live as-it-happens coverage compared to delayed coverage (either full delayed coverage or edited highlights). Broadcasters also seek to extract added value by providing various media enhancements to viewers such as match analysis, camera selection, and gaming opportunities. The type and extent of fan allegiance is another key driver of the media value of tournaments. There is an important distinction between team-fans and game-fans. Team-fans have an allegiance to one of the teams involved in a tournament. Typically these fans are prepared to pay a 'passion' premium to view their own team and their demand may be more price-inelastic. Game-fans have an allegiance to the particular team sport rather than the participating teams. Game-fans are interested in those games involving more playing talent and greater contest significance. Typically game-fans are expected to be more price-elastic.

The potential value surplus to be generated from the media broadcast of a team tournament equals the user value to viewers and commercial partners minus the resource cost of broadcasting the tournament. The actual value surplus captured by the league and teams depends on the degree of competition in the media industry, the structure and exclusivity of the rights package, and the allocation of the media property rights between the league and its constituent teams. There are two broad types of media property rights regimes within professional sports leagues – collective selling and rights individualisation. Collective selling allocates the media (and image) property rights of a tournament to the league. Rights individualisation, on the other hand, allocates the tournament media property rights to the individual teams. There has been a broad trend across professional sports leagues in recent years towards rights individualisation as part of the general switch in competition (i.e. anti-trust) policy towards greater deregulation. From this perspective, professional sports leagues have often been seen as anti-competitive cartels that operate against consumer interests by restricting supply in order to maintain monopoly prices.

However, the impact of rights individualisation on both user value to consumers and the actual value surplus to the leagues and teams is a complex issue. There are two key effects of rights individualisation – the effect on total tournament revenue and the effect on the inter-team distribution of revenue. Both of these effects may be negative and significantly so. Rights individualisation is likely to reduce total tournament revenue effects by removing the exclusivity premium that broadcasters are prepared to pay to be have sole possession of the media rights to live coverage of a tournament. In addition, rights individualisation tends to make it more difficult to supply game-fans with a demand to view the tournament as a whole rather than the participation of a specific team in the tournament. Rights individualisation is much more suited to a segmented team-fan market in which viewers demand only those games involving their team. Given the potential significant menu costs of supplying both team-fans and game-fans as well as the differing demand conditions and the associated difficulties of effective price discrimination, rights individualisation may significantly reduce or even eliminate altogether the total tournament revenue from game-fans. Of course, rights individualisation creates more scope for the monopoly supply of team games to team-fans since, by definition, teams are exclusive suppliers to their own fans. Hence there will be a positive impact on total tournament revenue to the extent that teams are able to extract greater supra-normal profits from their captive markets. It is rather paradoxical that the supposed deregulation of the sport media rights market should serve to enhance rather than restrict monopoly power.

The other revenue effect of rights individualisation is the inter-team distribution of revenues. Whereas collective selling provides a means of administering the distribution of media revenues between teams to help foster competitive balance, rights individualisation removes that administrative mechanism. Hence big-market teams will increase their revenues relative to the small-market teams. Admittedly it does not necessarily follow that rights individualisation entirely rules out revenue redistribution but it certainly makes it more difficult and costly to implement. In principle a league could administer a tax and subsidy system to optimise inter-team revenue distribution but such a system of taxes on big-market teams and subsidies to small-market teams creates obvious incentive problems as well as incurring potentially huge transactions costs. Indeed it is potentially possible that teams would have to negotiate a full set of bilateral agreements with every other team in the tournament in order to agree the split of media revenues (and potentially all other revenues) from any individual contest. The optimal tax and subsidy system would in principle have to be adjusted after every bilateral agreement. In reality teams are able to economise on transactions costs by league-wide agreements such as, for example, home teams being allocated the media property rights but there is obvious scope for protracted and costly negotiations.

If rights individualisation leads to a negative impact on total tournament revenue and/or inter-team revenue distribution, then this may have an overall negative impact on the sporting quality of the tournament. Lower total tournament revenue may lower the total amount of playing talent in the tournament particularly if there is an open international players' labour market. A more inequitable distribution of revenues across teams may also have a negative impact on sporting quality of the tournament by reducing the degree of competitive balance. Any significant loss of playing talent and/or competitive balance is likely to reduce the user value of team tournaments, setting in motion a possible process of cumulative causation that undermines the longer-term media value of the tournaments. All in all, unlike standard textbook industries, there is good reason to believe that rights market deregulation in the professional team sports industry may be against the consumer interest. Deregulation is certainly not unambiguous in its effects for the sports fan in the way collusive behaviour reduces the consumer surplus in other industries. At the very least there is a clear case for the competition policy to acknowledge the specificity of sport and give some consideration to the economic peculiarities of the professional team sports industry consequent on the jointness of production inherent in sporting contests.

SOME CONCLUDING COMMENTS

Economic theory demonstrates the possible impact of the corporate objectives of teams (i.e. wealth-maximisation or utility-maximisation), playing talent supply conditions, tournament structures including prize structures, and league regulations on the competitive balance of tournaments. But in order to assess the practical policy implications of the economic analysis of competitive balance, there is an urgent need to achieve a better understanding of the determinants of fan demand. This is a complex issue that requires a theoretical input from both economics and marketing, and an empirical input both from quantitative analysis such as econometric demand studies and qualitative analysis of fan behaviour. Future research needs to clarify the nature and behavioural significance of the concepts of uncertainty of outcome, competitive balance and contest significance. And, as suggested above, it is likely that differentiating between team-fans and game–fans will play an important role in the analysis of the demand behaviour of sports fans.

The professional team sports industry is very dynamic. Alternative sports–media business models are emerging and future research needs to consider these new business models. In particular value chains are becoming more vertically integrated with media ownership of teams (i.e. upstream vertical integration) and the development of league- or team-owned media channels (i.e. downstream vertical integration). Another departure in the sports–media business model is for the creation of a television airtime market in which leagues buy television airtime from broadcasters rather than selling television rights to the broadcasters. This is the business model that US Track and Field adopted when US domestic athletics was relaunched in the late 1980s. More recently ice hockey in Norway has also become a buyer of airtime rather than selling its own rights. And the business model will change dramatically as broadcasting is replaced by 'narrowcasting' when the internet becomes capable of delivering top-quality television images through broadband to integrated television-media-PC systems in a sufficient number of households. The Internet could potentially change the whole economics of the media industry by removing the need for a spatial concentration of viewers in order to create profitable broadcasting opportunities. The Internet allows narrowcasting to a spatially dispersed audience so that value of sports media rights will no longer be restricted by the spatial location of potential viewers. If team-fans have an Internet connection, they can view their team's games anywhere in the world provided there are sufficient other team-fans for the team with Internet connections to create a profitable opportunity for the team or league to supply the games on the Internet.

Rights individualisation and the new, emerging sports–media business models create both opportunities and threats for the professional team sports industry. These developments may exacerbate existing structural problems of competitive dominance of big-market teams and big-market leagues. These structural problems already represent a threat to the media value of team tournaments. It is vital that leagues and teams evolve appropriate regulatory mechanisms to avoid the sporting and financial viability of their tournaments being further undermined. Tournaments may have to be restructured to maintain competitive balance. Leagues may also have to enforce tighter financial restrictions on teams participating in their tournaments. It is a dual strategy already being adopted by UEFA in European club football. UEFA has restructured both the Champions League and the UEFA Cup through the introduction of league stages in both tournaments. UEFA has also sanctioned the creation of a Nordic League, an annual tournament involving the top teams from the Scandinavian domestic leagues. The Nordic League may represent the first step towards the creation of an intermediate tier of European club competition for the leading clubs in smaller-market leagues. To go along with tournament restructuring, UEFA has also introduced a club licensing system setting minimum requirements for all clubs participating in UEFA tournaments. The UEFA club licensing system includes a requirement that clubs produce an approved financial budget annually to prove their financial solvency during the tournament.

3. Broadcasting Rights and Competition in European Football

Wladimir Andreff and Jean-François Bourg

INTRODUCTION

The economic relationships between sports and the media are long-lasting ones, even though they have evolved significantly in the past 20 years. In particular, converging interests make some sports appealing to television in terms of audience while television brings into sports a major inflow of money. As a result, the broadcasting of sports events increasingly attracts television channels. The beginnings of the 'sports and the media' economy were surveyed long ago (Andreff *et al.*, 1987; Horowitz, 1974; Rader, 1984). In Europe, deregulation (phasing out the former public monopsony[1]) and a technological revolution (cable, satellite, and digital televisions adding to terrestrial television) have boosted the growth of the demand side of the sports broadcasting market since the 1980s. Sports broadcasting, primarily football broadcasting, has become a private good produced and consumed as such in a plentiful fully-fledged market economy, which has replaced the former administered shortage economy of sports broadcasting. In 2002, 106 million households were equipped with appliances able to download pay-TV football. In 2001–2002, the European television channels devoted 3.9 billion euros to the payment of football broadcasting rights out of an overall 5.5 billion euro bill for sports broadcasting (70 per cent). In 2000, broadcasts of football matches reached 61 per cent of the best sport audiences. Since public taxation and advertising could not grow much further as sources of football finance, pay-TV has paved the way to a new era in the relationships between television and football.

The importance of television rights has increased tremendously during the last decade, with the result that the money derived from broadcasting has become the major pillar of European professional sports finance today. Typically, the European football financing structure can be encapsulated in a so-called MCMMG model, in which professional sports primarily raise funds from Media Corporations Merchandising Markets on a global – international – scale (Andreff and Staudohar, 2000). Now the media are the leading source of finance providing nearly half the turnover of major European football clubs. Nevertheless, the emergence of the MCMMG model is not without its problems, because it entails a strong concentration of financial strength in a handful of clubs with a high media exposure while a great number of their competitors are comparatively severed from the same source of finance (Andreff, 2000). Thus, the question is to know whether such a financial concentration is likely to weaken economic competition in a given domestic football league and, by the same token, whether it is going to harm the championship's competitive balance. The belief that it would be so had been one of the backbones for those solidarity mechanisms which were introduced into European football, including the pooling and redistribution of television rights by the league. The basic issue is to assess how much this mutuality principle is efficient in maintaining an acceptable level of economic competition between clubs as well as promoting a more competitive balance than it would have been otherwise (in the absence of solidarity).

In this chapter, we analyse the five most significant first division national football championships in Europe. We have ranked them after considering two criteria: their share in the aggregated turnover (6.6 billion euros in 2000–2001) of all the professional football championships organised in the 51 UEFA member countries, and their ranking as regards their clubs' performances in European competitions (their 2002 UEFA coefficient). Together, the five reach 78 per cent of the aforementioned aggregated turnover and gather 82 per cent of the quarter finalists in the Champions League, from 1997 to 2003. These five countries are: England (English Premier League, 24 per cent of the aggregated turnover, third rank with the UEFA coefficient), France (Championnat de Ligue 1, 10 per cent, fifth), Germany (Bundesliga, 13 per cent, fourth), Italy (Lega Calcio serie A, 17 per cent, second), and Spain (Liga de Futbol, 14 per cent, first).

The purpose of the chapter is to compare the individual clubs' ownership and trade of television rights with television rights pooling by the league in European football. The latter – coined the RPL model here – is usually enshrined in a league organisation based on significant income redistribution: in France, 50 per cent of the overall clubs' turnover is redistributed within the league, in England 40 per cent, and in Germany 32 per cent (Ippolito *et al.*, 2002). The former – coined the ICO model – relies on a 'mind your own business' approach by the clubs, and only redistributes a minor share of the clubs' turnover, 18 per cent in Italy and 5 per cent in Spain. Our comparison first deals with the legal arrangements, and the redistribution schemes within the league in the case of television rights pooling, contrasting them with the no-redistribution of television rights system in the Spanish league, and the limited redistribution that has prevailed in the Italian league since 1999–2000. Then, the impact of television rights on the clubs' turnover is assessed, and the empirical relationships between the distribution of television rights and club turnovers, and the championship competitive balance is analysed. Some concluding recommendations as to television rights management in European football ensue from this empirical analysis.

FOOTBALL AND BROADCASTING RIGHTS: AN OVERVIEW OF EUROPEAN PRACTICES

Since the 1980s, the renewal in the organisation of the market for broadcasting rights has usually led to a supply-side cartel facing the de-bundling of the demand side into a number of different television channels. This dramatic change has triggered various consequences as regards football financing, the amount of television rights, and how television broadcasts are sold and the revenues are redistributed across the clubs.

Two Models of Television Rights Management

In our country sample, as well as across the 51 UEFA members, two core models of television rights management must be distinguished, although some country variants are gravitating around each of them. In the first model, exclusive and individual trade talks and television rights trading are run by the clubs themselves, which are the television rights owners (Italy, Spain) whereas, in the second model, exclusive and pooled television rights are negotiated and traded by the league as the rights owner (France), or are jointly managed by the (co-owning) clubs and the league, but the latter is supposed to trade them (England, Germany, see Table 3.1).

Table 3.1   The supply side on the television rights market for domestic championships in Europe, 2002–2003

League	Individual clubs
Austria, Belgium, Denmark, England, France, Germany, Holland, Norway, Scotland, Sweden, Switzerland, Turkey	Greece, Italy, Portugal, Spain

Sources: UEFA, Lega Calcio.

The individual club ownership (ICO) model

In Italy, the law (n°78 of March 29, 1999) unambiguously establishes the individual club ownership of television rights. The league is confined to pooling the match highlights of serie A and serie B championships, and the national cup knockout stage. In addition, a new regulation adopted in March 1999 – *regolamento organizzativo* (Ippolito *et al.*, 2002), has recognised the right of each serie A and serie B club to trade individually the pay-per-view and pay-TV rights. Before the enforcement of this regulation, the television rights for the whole championship were sold to a single broadcaster, but the law n°78 of March 29, 1999 had forbidden any monopoly (in fact monopsony) position in the television rights market. Thus, no single pay-TV channel is allowed to buy more than 60 per cent (183 out of 306) of all the serie A matches per year. Through the limitation imposed on the access of each broadcaster to football television rights, the Italian legislation has approved the individual trading by the clubs. On the other hand, an outbidding strategy conducted by the channels (Telepiù and Stream) to contract with top clubs has come out from such a limitation and has resulted in harsher competition between broadcasters. Football revenues have benefited from competition for television rights, increasing the volume of football broadcasts, and yielding a low (or no) profitability to the television channels.

In Spain, as early as 1993, the anti-trust authorities made up their minds about the league monopoly: it should not survive. A law passed on May 1997 prohibited the exclusive broadcasting of championship matches by a single pay-TV channel. Just as in Italy, this law has phased out television rights pooling and has triggered the merger of two broadcasters into a monopsony (Sky Italia). After several years of harsh competition and outbidding between Canal Satellite Digital and Via Digital had entailed financial losses, a strategic alliance of the two duopsonists came about with a buying cartel, Audiovisual Sport. The latter now jointly manages the pay-per-view service and hopes to benefit from its monopsonistic market power to curb the television rights inflation. The Spanish football league has reacted to this situation with a statement in favour of a return to pooling, while Real Madrid and Barcelona have successfully opposed it until now.

The rights pooling by the league (RPL) model

In order to avoid fierce competition for television rights revenues, the clubs can accept television rights pooling by the league so as to create a cartel on the supply side of the market. Then, a sort of collective bargaining process develops between the league and the television channels, who are forced by the cartel into severe outbidding, to the league's benefit. The benefit of outbidding to the league has even increased with the supply-side segmentation into various lots (packages), when free to air live matches, highlights, differed broadcasts, pay-TV, pay-per-view, video on demand and new media (Internet, etc.) are traded separately. However, television rights supply cartels have been sued in England, Germany and the Netherlands, and lawsuits have been brought at either the domestic or European anti-trust authorities (France) against the league's cartel. Nowadays, the big clubs aim to recover their property rights over broadcasts. The European Commission has passed on to the UEFA some grievances regarding television rights pooling that are likely to hinder competition.

In England, the Court in charge of competition policy concluded in 1999 that pooling does not infringe the competition rules as long as the league's purpose is to supply the best show whose required inputs are the best players. The clubs badly need large revenues for acquiring the most talented players, and only pooling benefits can achieve that. Thus, pooling has been declared in keeping with the public interest, provided that television rights are fairly redistributed. The same test case has prevailed in the Netherlands. In Germany, the federal Court of Justice decided in 1997 that football clubs are, at least, the 'natural' owners of their television rights. However, the Bundestag has inserted a clause departing from the competition rules, which states that the league is entitled to trade the domestic championship television rights, in spite of the opposed views of the major clubs (Bayern Munich, Borussia Dortmund, Leverkusen), which find individual trading more desirable. Even French football has not escaped a wave of disputes regarding the legal regime of broadcasting rights. Some prestigious clubs (Marseille, Lyon, Paris-Saint-Germain) have brought lawsuits at the *Conseil de la concurrence* and the European Court of Justice motivated by cartel practices that are assumed to monopolise property rights on the sport show, thus hindering the increase in the value of these rights and *de facto* despoiling the clubs.

The European Commission recognised, in 2002, the benefits of pooling the Champions League television rights if it were to preserve the competitive balance through revenue redistribution, and if the clubs had the freedom to individually trade some rights (highlights, differed broadcasts, Internet, mobile phones, or live matches in case the UEFA agency failed to trade them), as early as 2003–2004. Moreover, those pooled rights are compulsorily to be sold to a number of different broadcasters.

The Criteria Used for the Redistribution of Television Rights

Different criteria can be used for redistributing television rights within a league. All depends on the geographical area of competition (domestic or

European) and the model of television rights management. The current trend is one of liberalising the redistribution criteria.

The domestic championships

The redistribution rules regarding the revenues that flow from television channels into football are directly affected by how much the league behaves as a cartel (Table 3.2). Solidarity and mutuality are stronger when the league is the only owner and manager of television rights (France). They are non existent when the league does not proceed to any redistribution (Spain).

The pooling system seems to have declined (Table 3.3) in some countries, in the past few years, under the pressure of the major clubs. The leagues are changing the redistribution mechanism from one season to the other, 'liberalising' it, *i.e.* using a redistribution scheme in which each club's share is more directly proportional to its sporting results, past achievements, audience attractiveness, and its own television revenues. The individual ownership and trading of television rights generate sizeable consequences. In the ICO model, a better endowment of a club is even less due to its sporting results than in the RPL model.

Table 3.2   The criteria used for the television rights redistribution in the main European football leagues (first division, 2001–2002)

Countries	Free to air rights	Pay-TV rights	Pay-per-view rights	International rights
England	50 per cent equal shares, 25 per cent sporting merit, 25 per cent television appearances			100 per cent equal shares
France	73 per cent equal shares, 27 per cent sporting merit and relegation indemnity			
Germany	50 per cent equal shares, 50 per cent sporting results		67 per cent home club, 33 per cent visitor club	50 per cent equal shares, 50 per cent sporting results
Italy	75 per cent equal shares, 25 per cent inverse relation to the value of individual TV contracts	82 per cent home club, 18 per cent visitor club		
Spain	No redistribution within the league			

Source: Lega Calcio.

The revenues paid every year by pay-TV channels to Real Madrid (78 million euros), Barcelona (73 million euros), Juventus (54 million euros) or

Milan AC (49 million euros) are in fact exclusively linked to their commercial attractions (in terms of television payers), and are guaranteed over four or five seasons. On the other hand, in the RPL model, the club which obtains the highest television revenues usually is the winner of the domestic championship: Bayern Munich (24 million euros in 1999–2000), Lyon (15 million euros in 2001–2002) or Manchester United (14 million euros in 1998–1999). From one model to the other, the distribution of television rights appears to be more or less uneven, stable, and independent from the uncertainty of the championship outcome.

Table 3.3   *The share of television rights pooling in France, Germany and the Champions League (in per cent of overall distribution criteria)*

Seasons	Solidarity	Sporting result	Media performance	Total
France				
1998–1999	91.0	9.0	0	100
2001–2002	73.0	27.0	0	100
2003–2004*	50.0	30.0	20.0	100
Germany				
1998–1999	65.0	35.0	0	100
2001–2002	50.0	50.0	0	100
Champions League				
1998–1999	22.0	54.5	23.5	100
1999–2000	23.5	31.0	45.5	100
2001–2002	25.0	25.0	50.0	100

Note: * Prospect.
Sources: Ligue de Football Professionnel and UEFA.

Finally, a declining or absent solidarity intensifies the segmentation of the international market for player transfers. Two-thirds of the 70 most important transfers in the whole football history had been achieved by two countries (Italy, Spain), and only seven clubs, representative of ICO model.

The Champions League
This major European competition magnificently highlights the evolving trade-off between the two models of television rights management. The UEFA cannot ignore two constraints in fixing the criteria of revenue distribution. The first one is that the revenue distribution has to fit in with the mutuality principle without which UEFA would be considered as an anti-competitive arrangement conflicting with the Treaty of Rome. The second constraint is to privilege the major clubs with high sporting potential and media attractive-

ness in order to dissuade them from joining a closed Superleague based on pure commercial interests.[2] The rather tricky outcome is an evolving distribution scheme (Table 3.3). The fixed revenue share, independent of sporting results and media performance, is no more than a quarter of overall television rights. On the other hand, the financial impact of sporting uncertainty has been reduced from 54.5 per cent in 1999 to 25 per cent in 2002 while the share which depends on performance in the domestic television market has reached 50 per cent of overall revenues.[3] Consequently, the gap between the most endowed and the least endowed clubs has been fluctuating from 6.7 in 1999 to 11.1 in 2001, and back to 7.2 in 2002.

A specific feature of the European model of professional sports is that it connects two levels of competition, domestic and European. The major clubs that are capable of participating at both levels definitely have a strong economic advantage compared with the clubs that are confined to the domestic championships. The revenues that the former draw from the Champions League distort the domestic championship economic balance, since these revenues are bigger than the overall turnover of most domestic competitors – in 2001–2002, Juventus Turin (25 million euros), Bayern Munich and Manchester United (31 million euros), Real Madrid (36 million euros) – and it is even more so in smaller domestic championships – Porto and Galatasaray (10 million euros), Panathinaïkos (13 million euros). This imbalance lasts for years because roughly the same clubs qualify every year for the European cups. The outcome is a sort of self-sustaining sporting and financial hierarchy that enables the major clubs to invest in the most talented players and, thus, maintain their supremacy. The selective access to the Champions League, through qualification, determines the number of clubs per country (from 0 to 4) and the distribution of television rights and, eventually, translates into an economic segmentation across domestic championships. From 1998–1999 to 2001–2002, the clubs from our five sampled countries attracted 74 per cent of overall Champions League revenues, which means an additional income of 273 million euros to Spanish clubs, 264 million euros to German clubs, 220 million euros to English clubs, 206 million euros to Italian clubs, and 168 million euros to French clubs. All the clubs affiliated to the other 46 UEFA national member federations received 393 million euros together (26 per cent of all the distributed money).

The Resulting Distribution of Television Rights across the Clubs

An individual negotiation of television rights, club by club, is assumed by economic theory to yield a lower revenue than a league pooling, in particular if the demand side concentration of pay-TV broadcasters diminishes economic competition before the renewal of current contracts (Table 3.4). In the long run, where the supply side was a cartel, television rights did increase (they have been multiplied by 11 in Germany, 19 in France, and 43 in England, from 1992 to 2002) more than if they had individually been traded by each club (multiplication by eight in Spain, and nine in Italy). On the other hand, the UEFA pooling of the Champions League television rights has fuelled a substantial rise in distributed revenues: 88 million euros in 1994–1995, 135 million euros in 1998–1999, and 523 million euros in 2002–2003. Thus, both the past experience and economic analysis converge into the contention that solidarity is more efficient than individual strategies. That is the reason why pooling is now envisaged by UEFA for the UEFA Cup television rights.

Table 3.4   *The growth of broadcasting rights in European football first division, million euro*

Countries	1991–1992	2001–2002	Growth
England	21	907	x 43
Italy	55	486	x 9
France	21	397	x 19
Germany	36	384	x 11
Spain	30	237	x 8

Sources: Eurostaf, Deloitte & Touche.

Table 3.5   *The share of broadcasting rights in clubs' turnover (first division, per cent)*

Seasons	Italy	Spain	France	Germany	England
1996–1997	32	20*	32	--	20
1997–1998	37	51	42	--	27
1998–1999	35	--	42	29	29
1999–2000	56	51	56	29	31
2000–2001	54	--	51	45	39

Note: * in 1995-1996.
Sources: Lega Calcio, Ligue de Football Professionnel, Premier League, Eurostaf, Deloitte & Touche.

A second result of the evolving relationships between football and TELEVISION is that the broadcasting rights share in the overall clubs' turnover has become their major source of finance. In the so-called MCMMG model emerging in the last few years (Andreff and Staudohar, 2000), in particular in European football, the share of TELEVISION rights was expected to reach as much as 40–50 per cent of the overall club receipts. This expectation was roughly met in the five European football leagues we examine (Table 3.5), in 2000–2001. Now, European football is financially TV-addicted, and probably TV-dependent.

Football broadcasting is now one of the main TV-watchers' preferences, as shown in a number of polls as well as by the measured real audience. The time spent watching football programmes has increased markedly in Europe, from 10 per cent of all television programmes in 1982 to 30 per cent in 2002. The growth in the supply of football broadcasting has kept pace with this growing demand: for example, 52 per cent of all Canal Plus subscribers in France subscribe primarily in order to watch football programmes. Thus, the rationale for match broadcasting is now audience maximisation. The choice made by television channels between different match broadcasts is determined neither by an attempt to equalise the clubs exposure, nor by what is at stake in the matches. The same rationale prevails in all European countries. From 1984 to 2001, out of 785 match broadcasts by Canal Plus, 292 involved Olympique de Marseille (OM) or Paris-Saint-Germain, while Mulhouse and Rouen matches were broadcast only twice. Although its ranking in the championship was thirteenth in 1999–2000, fifteenth in 2000–2001, and ninth in 2001–2002, Marseille every year came first in the number of matches broadcast. This can be explained by the fact that Olympique de Marseille attracts 20 per cent of the overall First Division pay-per-view audience. In 2002–2003, 89 per cent of all Canal Plus and TPS first choices concentrated on OM. Given its share in the league's turnover and the channels' choices, Marseille was – still is – claiming 50 million euros per year (four times its current revenues from the league), assuming that this would be its revenue if the club were trading its television rights individually.

The previous examples show that competing broadcasters – once they have paid expensive rights – want to recoup their costs with pay-TV revenues based on broadcasting the most notorious clubs rather than the matches with the most interesting sporting stakes. We note that the top ranked clubs are not necessarily the most broadcast. Television channels preferably, or exclusively, buy the matches of prestigious clubs and, by the same token, deepen the hierarchy of club revenues in proportion with their television revenues (and indirectly through sponsoring contracts influenced by the club television exposure). The pay-TV revenue concentration is high in Italy with 100,000 subscribers to AS Roma, 90,000 to Juventus Turin, but only 900 to Chievo Verona and 700 to Piacenza (in 2001–2002). In Spain, the pay-per-view matches of Real Madrid and Barcelona reach 70 per cent of the league's pay-per-view turnover; in 1998–1999, there were on average 171,123 pay-per-view audience watching Real Madrid matches, 133,191 for Barcelona matches, 47,087 for Atletico Madrid matches and 30,044 for Atletico Bilbao matches.

The notion of a championship competitive balance (Fort and Quirk, 1995; Rouger, 2000; Bourg, 2003) enables us to compare the degree of uncertainty in five different domestic football championships (see below). The hierarchy going down from the most to the least uncertain championship, is as follows: from France, Germany and England (pooling and significant revenue redistribution) to Spain and Italy (individual trading and little or no revenue redistribution). The economic organisation of a championship is built up on more or less solidarity according to the regulation of broadcasting rights (Table 3.6). However, the European system of open leagues interlocking domestic and European competitions does not facilitate the enforcement of regulation measures. A nearly optimal revenue distribution at the domestic level – such as that of the French First Division – is not optimal at all as regards the competitiveness of French clubs qualifying for the European cups (Table 3.9). The more homogeneous economic strengths within the French league actually makes it possible for a greater number of different clubs to win, but the league's regulation is a handicap for the French major clubs in European cups, because it does not provide them with enough financial means to invest in the most talented players. This hinders their capacity to win a European competition. On the other hand, the top four Spanish and Italian clubs do participate very often to the Champions League and benefit from individual trading of television rights while they concentrate over 50 per cent of their league overall turnover, so that both their domestic and European domination on the pitch is long-lasting.[4]

BROADCASTING RIGHTS, ECONOMIC COMPETITION AND COMPETITIVE BALANCE

The problem is now to use available data about broadcasting rights in European football in order to assess the influence of television rights distribution on the statistical distribution of club turnovers, on club ranking in the championship, and on the competitive balance. In particular, it is of interest to compare the individual club ownership (ICO) and the television rights pooling by the league (RPL) models in this respect. We had intended to make a comparison of five different top division national championships in Europe. Unfortunately, most football leagues are not willing to disclose the financial data, namely the television rights revenues, broken down by club. Only the Italian Lega Calcio has made all the requested data available to us.[5] On the other hand, we have not been able to collect any of the required data for the German Bundesliga, which is nearly excluded from our sample. Thus, we are left with two championships having adopted the ICO model, Spain and Italy (where 82 per cent of pay-TV rights, pay-per-view rights and international rights are retained by the home club), and two championships representative of the RPL model, England and France. The data is comprehensive for Italy, very scarce for Spain and in between for England and France (see Annexes A, B, C, D).

Our rather simple methodology consists first in calculating the Gini coefficient of turnovers and television rights in order to provide a single-number picture of the unevenness in the distribution of economic strengths in a championship. The Gini coefficient is calculated as:

$$G = 1 - \Sigma \left[F_i \ (nx) + F_{i-1} \ (nx) \right] . f_i \ (x)$$

where F stands for the cumulative frequency of the values taken by the variable and f for the relative frequency. The figure obtained for the Gini coefficient can obviously be compared with the usual index of the competitive balance showing how well balanced the sporting strengths are in a championship. The competitive balance, according to a widely accepted definition in Quirk and Fort (1992), is the ratio between the percentage of actual wins and the theoretical standard deviation:

$$\sigma_w = 0.5 \ \sqrt{m},$$

where m is the overall match number. The lower this competitive balance index, the less uneven is the distribution of sporting strengths across the clubs, the fiercer the sporting competition is supposed to be within the league, and the more uncertain is the championship outcome.

Then we turn to three club rankings each season: 1/ the club ranking in relation to its performance in the championship; 2/ the club ranking in relation to its turnover; and 3/ the club ranking in relation to its television rights revenues. Since our sample is small (18 to 20 clubs per year), we are compelled to rely on a simplified econometric methodology, *i.e.* the calculation of Spearman rank correlation coefficients.[6]

The Spearman rank correlation is calculated as follows:

$$r_S = 1 - \frac{6 \sum_i d_i^2}{n(n^2 - 1)}$$

where d_i stands for the difference between the two rankings of a country, according to two variables, and n is the sample size. The Spearman table for coefficients of rank correlation helps us to understand whether a calculated correlation is significant or not. Then we can conclude a concordance (a positive coefficient close to one), or a discordance (a negative coefficient close to one), or no relation (a coefficient close to zero) between the ranks of the two variables. If the coefficient of rank correlation is not significant, then the two variables are independent. The first relationship we are looking for is to know whether the club turnover is correlated (concordant) with broadcasting rights collected by the club. In other words, does an uneven access to television rights translate into an uneven distribution of club turnovers, and to what extent? The second relationship – if successfully tested – would follow up the above-mentioned comparison between the Gini coefficient and the competitive balance index. It is the one between the club ranking in the championship and the ranking as to broadcasting rights.

The Relationship between the Club's Broadcasting Rights and Turnover

The calculation of Gini coefficients shows (Table 3.6) as expected, that the inequality of the television rights distribution across the clubs is quite high in post-1998–1999 Italy whose system resorts less to mutuality (thus closer to ICO model) than in England, France, and Italy itself in 1998–1999 – where the solidarity mechanism was more comprehensive.

A similar picture appears when looking at the top four clubs' market share in terms of television rights, since this share simply describes the upper part of the concentration measured with the Gini coefficient. In 1998–1999, the four Italian clubs (Juventus, Inter, Milan AC, Lazio Rome) attracting the biggest share of television rights, had concentrated 33.1 per cent of the market, as against only 27.6 per cent attracted by the first four English clubs (Arsenal, Manchester United, Chelsea, Leeds United). However, the top four French clubs (Girondins de Bordeaux, Olympique de Marseille, Olympique Lyonnais, AS Monaco) gathered 34.5 per cent of total television rights in 1998–1999, a bigger share than the four top Italian clubs, which means that the initial attractiveness of French clubs to television broadcasters is the most uneven, insofar as the French very comprehensive redistribution mechanism is not able to compensate for the initial inequality between clubs.

In 1999–2000, after the switch to individual trading, the top four Italian clubs (Juventus, Inter, Milan AC, AS Roma) gathered 42.7 per cent, and this percentage remained over 40 per cent in the following years. However, the values of the Gini coefficient and the four top market shares do not exhibit an extraordinary level of television rights concentration (it would have been the case had the Gini coefficient exceeded 50 per cent). A low concentration is

The Economics of Sports and the Media

clearly explained by the very existence of solidarity redistribution in England, France and Italy 1998–1999.

Table 3.6   The relationship between the club's broadcasting rights and turnover

Index	Year	Spain	Italy	Germany	England	France
Share of clubs' overall turn-over redistributed within the league[a]	2000–2001	5.3%	17.8%	31.7%	39.9%	50.3%
Turnover Gini coefficient	1997–1998	---	---	---	0.382	0.277
	1998–1999	---	0.359	---	0.309	0.325
	1999–2000	0.450	0.391	---	---	0.304
	2000–2001	---	0.410	---	0.361	0.316
	2001-2002	---	0.473	---	---	---
Ratio highest/lowest turnover	1998–1999	---	6.1	---	8.2	5.3
	1999–2000	27.0	6.8	---	11.5	5.4
	2000–2001	19.5	9.3	7.4	5.8	5.4
Top 4 clubs market share (in terms of turnover)	1997–1998	---	---	---	45.3	39.5
	1998–1999	---	45.5	---	39.4	43.9
	1999–2000	56.0	48.6	---	---	42.3
	2000–2001	---	50.8	48.3	42.2	43.8
	2001–2002	---	56.6	---	---	---
TV rights Gini coefficient	1998–1999	---	0.211	---	0.134	0.205
	1999–2000	---	0.430[b]	---	---	---
	2000–2001	---	0.404[b]	---	---	---
	2001–2002	---	0.429[b]	---	---	---
Ratio highest/lowest TV rights	1998–1999	---	2.7	---	2.2	4.4
	1999–2000	---	4.2	---	2.3	---
	2000–2001	5.3	6.3	2.6	2.3	1.8
Top 4 clubs market share (in terms of TV rights)	1998–1999	---	33.1	---	27.6	34.5
	1999–2000	---	42.7	---	---	---
	2000–2001	---	41.3	---	---	---
	2001–2002	---	44.0	---	---	---

Notes:
a   In Germany and Spain the turnover includes earned transfer fees.
b   Calculated on the non-pooled share of television rights.
Sources: Lega Calcio, Deloitte & Touche, Sport Finance and Marketing.

Even in post-1998–1999 Italy, when the outcome of the club competition for television rights is less alleviated by redistribution, the Gini coefficient, though higher, is still below 50 per cent. Notice that in post-1998–1999 Italy, a solidarity mechanism still remains on 75 per cent of free to air television rights. The ratio between the highest and the lowest television rights revenue tells the same story. In 2000–2001, in Spain and Italy, it reaches at least twice its level in England, France and Germany. *The redistribution of television rights in the RPL model purposely fills the gap between the clubs most exposed and least exposed to television.*

Turning now to the turnover distribution, the most striking observation is a Gini coefficient which is two to three times higher than its value in relation to television rights in England and France. Therefore, even though the solidarity mechanism at work through the television rights redistribution does actually narrow the range of television rights revenues across the clubs, it is *not enough to compensate for the uneven distribution of clubs' turnover* due to other sources of finance (think of the Manchester United merchandising revenues or the money poured into top clubs by some financial and industrial tycoons and media corporations). In 1998–1999, the market share of the four top clubs, in terms of turnover, is 39.4 per cent in England, and 42.3 per cent in France, much more than the same concentration ratio for television rights. The ratio between the highest and the lowest turnover is markedly higher than the ratio between the highest and the lowest television rights, in these two countries.

On the other hand, Spain and Italy exhibit a higher turnover Gini coefficient than England and France, but the inter-country gap is narrow compared to the television rights gap. A narrowing gap across the four countries is also reflected in the four top clubs market share and the ratio of the highest to the lowest turnover (except in Spain as to the last index). Therefore, *the concentration of the overall turnover is higher, the revenue distribution is more uneven and, supposedly, economic competition is lower in the Spanish Liga de Futbol, and then in the Italian Lega Calcio*, than they are in the English Premier League and the French Championnat de Ligue one. However, in the latter countries, revenue concentration, though lower, remains non-negligible, even after the redistribution of television rights which, of course, slightly alleviates turnover inequalities that would have been wider otherwise; but this redistribution is not significant enough to level off the economic playing field within the league.

Next, we estimate the Spearman rank correlation between the clubs' ranking in relation to their television rights revenues and their turnover ranking. Unfortunately, the data is available only for six 'country-years' (Table 3.7). The results show a strong rank correlation (concordance) between the turnover and television rights every year in any country, whether it be in the model of individual club ownership or in the model of rights pooling by the league. Here we simply find a proof that the MCMMG model of professional sports finance is relevant for European football. Since the relationship between television rights revenues and turnover is extremely significant (at a one per cent threshold), one can conclude that television rights have become the major determinant of the clubs' turnover in European football. *Now, the major football clubs are TV-dependent for their finance in Europe.* On average, the higher a club is ranked as to its financial attractiveness to television rights, the higher is its ranking in terms of turnover. The economic (financial) strength of a club depends heavily on its access to television broadcasting rights. The economic hierarchy across the clubs derives significantly from the hierarchy as to their access to the media, in particular to television channels.

Table 3.7   Rank correlation between club turnover and television rights[a]

Model RPL		Model ICO			
England 1998–1999	France 1998–1999	Italy 1998–1999	Italy 1999–2000	Italy 2000–2001	Italy 2001–2002
0.898 [b]	0.734	0.926 [b]	0.926 [b]	0.936 [b]	0.812 [b]

Notes:
a   Calculated from Annexes A, B, C.
b   Significant at a 1 per cent threshold.

On the other hand, the fact that club turnover is strongly correlated with television rights is useful to offset the missing television rights data in our calculation below. It means that we can take – with some caution – turnover as a proxy for television rights.

Table 3.8   Overall value of television rights in national championships* (million euros)

Country/season	Number of clubs	Value of TV rights	Average per club
England 1998–1999	20	224.2	11.2
France 1998–1999	18	114.5	6.4
France 2001–2002	18	389.2	21.6
Italy 1998–1999	18	196.8	10.9
Italy 1999–2000	18	404.2	22.5
Italy 2000–2001	18	434.4	24.1
Italy 2001–2002	18	418.1	23.2

Note: * International rights excluded.
Sources: Lega Calcio, Sport Finance and Marketing, Ippolito *et al.* (2002).

In the short term, it must be noted that the ICO model seems to be more efficient than the RPL model as far as the money raised from television channels is concerned (Table 3.8). This empirical evidence conflicts with the economic common sense that a (league) cartel negotiation with television channels should yield higher rights than an individualised negotiation by each club. In 1998–1999, the French very comprehensive redistribution system raised a lower value of television rights (6.4 million euros per club on average) than the English Premier League (11.2 million euros per club on average); of course, the different quality of the products affects that as well. In Italy, where the product quality can be assumed to remain nearly the same, from 1998–1999 to 2001–2002, the switch from a pooling system in 1998–1999 to individual television rights trading in 1999–2000, translates into a sharp increase of television rights, from 10.9 to 22.5 million euros per club on average. A second increase in 2000–2001 is followed by a slight fall in 2001–2002. It remains to be seen whether the ICO model will have a self-sustaining effect of raising television rights in the long run, as compared to the former RPL model. One of the most interesting observations to follow up in the coming years is the value of television rights in Italian football.

The relationship between television rights and turnover would have been even more crystal clear had we been able to test it with more detailed data about the amounts of money flowing to a clubs' hands from the Champions League. However, it appears that participating in UEFA competitions inflates a club's television rights and consequently increases its overall turnover. For example, in 1999–2000, 12 of the 16 wealthiest European football clubs were playing in the Champions League (the four exceptions were Juventus, Inter, AS Roma and Leeds United). The UEFA shared 216 million Swiss francs (SF) across 24 clubs (from SF3 to 20 million per club) in 1998–1999, SF615 million across 32 clubs (from SF5 to 46 million each) in 1999–2000, SF734 million (from SF6 to 71 million per club) in 2000–2001, and SF768 million (from SF8 to 55 million each) in 2001–2002. In comparison, the 18 clubs participating the whole year to the Italian Calcio serie A have shared 160 million euros – roughly SF242 million – of television rights (European cups excluded) in 1998–1999, 377 million euros (SF569 million) in 1999–2000, 413 million euros (SF624 million) in 2000–2001, and 398 million euros (SF587 million) in 2001–2002.

The Relationship between Broadcasting Rights, Turnover and the Competitive Balance

Let us compare now the turnover Gini coefficient and the competitive balance index. The lower the former, the harsher the economic competition between the clubs is assumed to be. The lower the competitive balance, the more uncertain the sporting result. From Table 3.9, it is obvious that *the lower the concentration of economic strengths (the higher the economic competition) in the league, the better is the competitive balance index* (the more uncertain is the outcome of the sporting competition).

Table 3.9   Uneven economic strengths and competitive balance in European football

Index	Year	Spain	Italy	England	Germany	France
Turnover Gini	1997–1998	---	---	0.382	---	0.277
coefficient	1998–1999	---	0.359	0.309	---	0.325
	1999–2000	0.450	0.391	---	---	0.304
	2000–2001	---	0.410	0.361	---	0.316
Competitive balance	1997–1998	1.0512	1.6890	1.7328	1.4753	0.9075
	1998–1999	1.4443	1.3845	1.5613	1.5591	1.4576
	1999–2000	1.4298	1.8150	1.3179	1.1721	1.3517
mean 95/96–99/00		1.4197	1.5579	1.5028	1.3612	1.2979
mean 90/91–94/95		1.4194	1.6194	1.4397	1.3724	1.3731
mean 85/86–89/90		1.5638	1.4084	1.4843	1.4036	1.2334
mean 80/81–84/85		1.3996	1.4015	1.3656	1.5561	1.4082
Number of championship winners, 1993–2002		5	4	3	4	8
Number of championship won by the best 2 clubs in 1993–2002		7	8	9	8	4
Number of quarter finals in Champions League, 1997–2003		15	8	11	10	2
UEFA country ranking 2003		1	2	3	4	5

Sources: UEFA, leagues.

Among the four countries, on average, France exhibits both the lowest turnover Gini coefficient – partly lowered by the television rights solidarity mechanism – and the lowest competitive balance index. Then comes England for both ratios. On the other hand, Spain and Italy display a more uneven turnover distribution which is associated with a less uncertain championship outcome, reflecting a more uneven distribution of the sporting strengths on the pitch. This comparison strongly suggests that (in contrast to the Rottenberg (1956) invariance principle), reinforcing the revenue distribution between clubs, whether through television rights or other mechanisms, ought to improve the competitive balance within the Italian Lega Calcio; and in Spain, the introduction of some television rights distribution would probably upgrade the competitive balance in the Spanish Liga as well.

The previous comparison features a sort of hierarchy across the four observed domestic championships. The Italian and Spanish championships are the most uneven, the least uncertain. On the other hand, after top ranking in these championships, the strongest domestic clubs perform better than any one else in European competitions. Together, these two countries have produced 23 quarter finalists in the Champions League (as against 13 for both England and France) between 1997 and 2003. They are respectively ranked first and second in the UEFA country ranking in 2003. While a stronger concentration of sporting strengths is detrimental to the competitive balance of the domestic championship, for the strongest clubs this imbalance pays off, since it enables them to skim off the best of the television rights in the Champions League (and other UEFA competitions). The opposite French story is the one of a more balanced domestic championship, which is eventually a handicap for the French top clubs since they are not strong enough to win a European competition. Rather paradoxically, in European football, *a worse domestic competitive balance seems to be a good precondition, or even a required launch pad, for achieving the best sport performances in European cups*. The question of uneven economic distribution and downgraded competitive balance then moves up to the European level, and is beyond the scope of the present chapter.

The calculation of the Spearman rank correlation (Table 3.10) verifies a significant relationship between club ranking in the championship and the turnover ranking. In nine cases out of 13, the relationship is extremely significant (at a 1 per cent threshold). *The wealthier a club, the higher its probability to reach a ranking at the top of the championship; and the other way round, a top-ranked club has a higher probability to be wealthy* than if it is lower ranked in the championship. The Italian Lega Calcio, with a rather high correlation coefficient (between 0.79 and 0.66), is the best exemplification that, in the ICO model, the club ranking and its turnover are tightly linked. The Spanish lower correlation (however significant at 5 per cent) is probably unusually low, since the 2000 champion (unusually) is Deportivo La Coruna (the fifth turnover the same year) instead of Real Madrid or Barcelona (together seven wins from 1993 to 2002). The season 1999–2000 is not really representative of the most common way of life in the Spanish Liga, so that we cannot definitely conclude anything about the ICO model in this case. The relationship is also significant at the (usual) 5 per cent threshold in England 1996–1997 and France 1999–2000. It is not significant in France, 2000–2001: the champion, FC Nantes, is only the sixth in turnover in the league this year. The French result, with two seasons of weaker correlation between ranking and turnover, after two seasons of very significant correlation, is of interest. It confirms our conclusion about the great uncertainty of the French championship outcome being due to a less uneven distribution of wealth (turnover) and a better competitive balance. The somewhat fluctuating Spearman value in England, from 1997 to 2001, supports the same conclusion.

Table 3.10   Rank correlation between club ranking, turnover and television rights

R2 values	England			
	1996–1997	1997–1998	1998–1999	2000–2001
ranking/turnover	0.541**	0.629*	0.836*	0.602*
ranking/TV rights	---	---	0.970*	---

	France			
	1997–1998	1998–1999	1999–2000	2000–2001
ranking/turnover	0.763*	0.620*	0.492**	0.261
ranking/TV rights	---	0.942*	---	---

	Italy			
	1998–1999	1999–2000	2000–2001	2001–2002
ranking/turnover	0.787*	0.779*	0.771*	0.664*
ranking/TV rights	0.688*	0.812*	0.695*	0.507**

	Spain
	1999–2000
ranking/turnover	0.465**

Note: * significant at a 1 per cent threshold; ** at a 5 per cent threshold.

The paucity of television rights data makes it difficult to test the correlation between ranking and television rights revenues. In Lega Calcio, club ranking in the championship is very significantly correlated (at a 1 per cent threshold) with television rights revenues, three years out of four; the fourth year the relation is still significant (at a 5 per cent threshold). Thus, *when there is less television rights redistribution across the clubs, the more a club is television exposed, the higher its probability to be top-ranked in the championship; and the other way round, the better its ranking, the higher is its probability to attract substantial television revenues.* This is exactly the relationship which is expected by the ICO model. The limited data for the

Spanish Liga in 1999–2000 shows that Real Madrid (ranked fifth) and Barcelona (second) received eight times more television rights than Numancia (ranked twentieth) while the champions La Coruna attracted six times more television rights than Numancia. More data is needed to actually test the relationship between ranking and television rights in ICO model. However, if we consider turnover as a proxy for television rights, we have already some food for thought about the existence of such a relationship.

A more interesting result is with testing the RPL model. In 1998–1999, in England and France, the correlation between ranking and television rights revenues is extremely significant. The club ranking shows an even stronger correlation with the television rights rank than with the turnover rank. This means that, once the 50 per cent equal share (£3,544,000 in 1998–1999) is distributed to all clubs in England, the 25 per cent sporting merit and the 25 per cent television appearances shares are strictly proportional to the club ranking. Therefore, the English television rights redistribution mechanism not only improves the competitive balance, but it does not disturb the club's incentive to win and to put an attractive squad on the pitch, since the television reward for each club is practically determined by its ranking and television appearances. With the available data, it appears to be an *efficient redistribution mechanism that does not disturb the relationship between television revenues and sport (and audience) performances*. The French data calls for the same comment, in 1998–1999, when television rights were distributed as follows: 72.3 per cent equal shares, with a minimum 8.23 million euros per club, 27.7 per cent sporting merit and relegation indemnity, in the first division. The French results should come closer to the ones exhibited by the English Premier League, since a new division of television rights had been adopted in the new 2002 Charter of French football professional clubs[7] in which the distribution was defined as: 50 per cent equal shares, 30 per cent sporting merit, 20 per cent fame[8] (Ippolito *et al.*, 2002).

THE DIFFERENT PRACTICES OF TELEVISION RIGHTS MANAGEMENT IN EUROPEAN FOOTBALL: RECOMMENDATIONS

Our main findings can be summarised in the form of stylised facts contrasting the ICO and RPL models (Table 3.11). When more detailed data is available, these stylised facts will have to be tested further and more carefully.

At the present stage of analysis, we can derive a few recommendations regarding management practices in European football as far as the redistribution of television rights within a league, and its impact on economic concentration and the competitive balance are concerned. The most crucial issue is more about how television rights are traded, by the league or by the clubs, than the legal question of their ownership. From the English example, and as against the Spanish and Italian experiences, collective trading (pooling) must prevail over individual trading.

Table 3.11   Summary of stylised facts: ICO and RPL models

MAIN FEATURES	ICO	RPL
Definition: TV right redistribution	**limited**	**significant**
Economic concentration	*higher*	*lower*
Turnover Gini coefficient	higher	lower
Highest/lowest turnover	higher	lower
Top 4 clubs market share	higher	lower
Assumed competition intensity	*lower*	*higher*
Competitive balance	*worse*	*better*
European level sport performance	*better*	*worse*
Value of TV rights (short term)	higher	lower
Value of TV rights (long term)	lower	higher
TV rights concentration	*higher*	*lower*
TV rights Gini coefficient	higher	lower
Highest/lowest TV rights	higher	lower
Top 4 clubs market share	higher	lower

First Recommendation

Our first recommendation is to support television rights pooling – keep it where it still works, restore it where it has been dropped – since, all in all, it maintains some cohesion in the championships, it is a barrier to clubs' opportunistic temptations,[9] it improves the competitive balance and, therefore, it must be collectively more profitable in the long run. Top clubs increasingly dislike bad results on the pitch and attempt to circumvent their economic consequences with individualistic and selfish behaviour. When the access to the television market is based on sport performance criteria, even a well-managed club can suffer from a demotion in the lower division or a failure to qualify for a European cup. For instance, in France, a club's television rights are roughly reduced by four fifths in the event of demotion to the second division, and the club which does not qualify for a European cup incurs a loss of earnings in the range of 20 to 40 million euros. A sub-optimal solution is likely when regulation is the least comprehensive, since the clubs have strong incentives to adopt opportunistic and selfish behaviour which endangers the competition in deepening the dual sporting and economic gap between the top wealthy clubs and the smaller and poorer ones (Bourg and Gouguet, 1998, 2001).[10]

The demand side concentration (of television channels) will have a more significant impact in those championships where the clubs individually trade their television rights. Outbidding will only be geared towards those teams whose matches generate high pay-per-view television revenues. The segmentation of domestic championships would probably deepen. Moreover, no football club could bear diminishing television rights, when it achieves a large turnover (the football TV-dependence); it could not afford the present share of wages in its expenses without the godsend of television. A downward trend in television rights would mainly affect small clubs since their matches were – are – less appealing to broadcasters. Therefore, television rights pooling is a badly needed safety net and a barrier against the impoverishment of small clubs. After some problems created by television rights individual trading in Italy, in 2002–2003, the top six clubs have agreed to pay back 6 million euros out of their television revenues to the other 12 serie A clubs, they have given up the 18 per cent of television rights and gate receipts they were entitled to as visitor clubs, and the small clubs have been allowed to start up Plus Media Trading with a view to broadcasting their own matches.

Second Recommendation

Our second recommendation advocates, at least, a minimum enforcement of the mutuality principle and television rights redistribution by the league, without which domestic championships would not be sustainable in the long run. We have demonstrated above that a club's sports performance is correlated with its economic strength and financial capacity. The 'liberalisation' tendency in European football is worrying in the face of the relationship between a worsening competitive balance and the increased economic concentration of a championship. A more egalitarian television rights distribution is to be preferred, since a more competitive championship requires regulated economic competition (Rouger, 2000). The legal arrangement of television rights pooling is useful, but not enough. Redistribution should aim at providing more homogeneous competition and thus should not rely only on ranking, media exposure and the number of pay-television subscribers, otherwise the incentives in favour of even more individualistic behaviour of the major clubs would be strengthened.

Third Recommendation

Our third recommendation is to set some limits on domestic regulation. We have shown that a revenue redistribution close to or higher than 50 per cent, as in France, is counter-productive to the French clubs qualifying for European competitions, in particular in a European context where distortions to free and fair competition do exist, such as uneven taxation and social security contributions, or the still forbidden access to a stock exchange quotation for clubs in some countries. While being relevant at a domestic level, the very egalitarian French redistribution system is the closest to the North American model, namely to the National Football League, and it is the one which preserves the best competitive balance and the strongest outcome uncertainty of the championship. On the other hand, in Italy and Spain, the more uneven distribution of turnovers and television revenues hinders a genuine solidarity within the league. The French RPL model would be the best practice in a closed league, with clubs participating to only a single (domestic) level of competition. The Italian–Spanish ICO model is more efficient in providing plentiful financing to the major clubs, enhancing their economic and sporting competitiveness at the European level. The dilemma is that each model fits with just one (domestic or European) level of competition. What could be the efficient compromise between the French RPL and the Italian ICO models? Until now, no theoretical or empirical analysis has determined the most efficient competitive balance from the viewpoint of fans' expectations, media stakes and sponsors' interests. A perfect competitive balance, of course, is an unrealistic hypothesis; all squads being of the same strength, a ranking would be meaningless and the attractiveness of such a championship would be debatable. However, the evolving competitive balance that we have observed in our sampled championships seemingly does not affect the fans' attitude in the short term, since the fan attendance in European football stadiums and arenas is still growing.

In spite of the aforementioned dilemma, determining fair television rights redistribution criteria is now at stake, including at the European (UEFA) level. These criteria could only come out from a negotiation involving all the vested interests, *i.e.* the clubs, the domestic leagues, the players' unions, and the European Commission. Would the English redistribution scheme (50 per cent equal shares, 25 per cent sporting merit, 25 per cent television appearances) be the most efficient regulation of a domestic championship in Europe? We have seen that, despite significant revenue sharing, the English system does not demonstrate the highest efficiency in terms of both the competitive balance and the rotation of championship winners. Does this mean that the degree of mutuality would have no impact on the distribution of talented players? Such is a main train of thought among sports economists (Fort and Quirk, 1995; Vrooman, 1995). Some go even further, suggesting that mutuality can even entail negative consequences for the competitive balance (Hoehn and Szymanski, 1999). In the case of profit maximising club owners, revenue sharing has seemingly no influence on sports performance; the shared revenues are simply used to bail out the clubs, under the assumption that revenue sharing does not depend on ranking, *i.e.* revenues are pooled by the league (Késenne, 2000). When revenue sharing is influenced by the club's own revenues (gate receipts, local media revenues), the mutuality principle has no impact on the competitive balance. Therefore, under the profit maximising assumption, various economists do not advocate revenue sharing as a recipe for improving the competitive balance. Revenue sharing simply increases the financial wealth of club owners. Thus, the economic regulation of a championship can be efficient if, and only if, clubs are win maximising, under a minimal profit constraint (Késenne, 1996). Club owners will use the shared revenues to recruit talented players and obtain better sporting results. It is crystal clear that the assumptions about the owners' objectives are crucial in this respect (Lavoie, 2003). In Europe, clubs are very obviously behaving as win maximisers with a minimal profit constraint, so that a mutuality principle based on television rights redistribution would improve both the economic and competitive balances of domestic championships.

Fourth Recommendation

Our fourth recommendation aims at hedging the risk which ensues from diminished television rights that will occur at the end of the current contracts (between 2003 and 2005, from one country to the other). In all European countries, those pay-TV channels that rely heavily on football are now in the red or going bankrupt, and thus they are compelled to merge or withdraw. The survival of these channels is endangered by the cost of football, and a concentration process seems inevitable. From the early 1980s to the late 1990s, a supply-side monopoly was facing harsh competition on the demand side of the television rights market. In the early twenty-first century, this market structure is phased out. The league monopoly, in terms of television rights ownership and more basically in terms of pooling, is questioned by the major clubs. Such a dispute can fuel more competition between the clubs and favour the broadcasters. A decreasing number of buyers on the demand side is already resulting from the mergers of cable and satellite television networks (Stream and Telepiù in Italy, Via Digital and Canal Satellite in Spain) and bankruptcies (Kirch in Germany, ITV Digital in England). Consequently, competition fades away. In this new market context, the demand side (television channels), and no longer the supply side (leagues or clubs), will be able to determine the price. Terrestrial channels, either private or state-owned, being watched for free, do not seem capable of competing with pay-television broadcasters. In the face of a double threat emanating from a return to a demand monopsony in the television rights market and from the perverse results of individual trading, the creation by the league or by the club of its own television broadcaster, producing broadcasts and pooling the rights, might be an alternative solution. It is envisaged in Italy from 2005 on.

Fifth Recommendation

Our fifth recommendation is more general. The European professional football economy should transform itself from a media industry into an overall leisure industry. Football management cannot remain so TV-dependent any longer. The clubs are trapped in the perspective of reaching a television rights demand ceiling, or even suffering a decline in broadcasting contracts. A new model of football club management should be built on two pillars in the future. The first one is a strategy that diversifies the sources of finance in order to reduce the clubs' dependence on television broadcasters.[11] The second one is to curb wage inflation (growing now at an annual rate of 20 to 40 per cent) which is facilitated by the players' free mobility in the European market since the Bosman case and is financed by the television godsend. European football has probably entered a stage in which football broadcasting is evolving and transforming itself into a maturing product, advertising expenditures are shrinking, pay-TV networks are merging, the growth in the number of television subscribers is slowing down, audiences are stagnating, and the major clubs are calling television rights pooling into question. All these trends may converge into a television rights decreasing slope, and may undermine the RPL economic model of professional football management that prevailed in 1985–2003, based on steadily increasing television rights and a major role of television channels in football finance. The recent wave of acquisitions and mergers in the broadcasting business demonstrates the willingness to rationalise production costs and yield profits. With fewer buyers in the market for football broadcasts, competition for acquiring television rights weakens, paving the way to production cost decreases and the erection of new barriers to entry in this business.

CONCLUSION

We do not conclude that there is a best practice for managing television rights which could be defined and recommended to European football. At the moment, comparing the individual club ownership and trading model and the 'rights pooling by the league' model, both the empirical evidence and the statistical and econometric testing show an overall advantage in favour of the latter. Therefore, our recommendations gravitate around the RPL model, not without some emendations such as a limitation on domestic championship regulation, a strategy of hedging against diminishing television rights in the future, and a diversification in the structure of football finance to make it less TV-dependent.

NOTES

1. In standard microeconomics, a demand-side monopoly (a single buyer) is named a monopsony, a demand-side duopoly is a duopsony, and a demand side oligopoly, an oligopsony.
2. The project of a European Superleague put forward by Media Partners in 1998 was relying on the distribution of 2 billion euros across 36 clubs. In 2002–2003, UEFA has distributed 523 million euros to 32 clubs. The initiative for a European Golden Cup in 2003 had envisaged a 110 million euro prize to the winner.
3. For instance, 26 million euros were allocated to the winner of the 2001 Champions League from the television market pool, a higher amount than both its solidarity and sporting result shares (21 million euros together).
4. For example, Juventus Turin (26 wins in the Italian championship) and Real Madrid (28 wins in the Spanish championship) qualified every year for the European cups since the latter were created in 1955.
5. We would especially thank Dr. Marco Brunelli for his extremely open-minded response to our request. For the English Premier League, the data comes from the *Deloitte & Touche Annual Review of Football Finance*, for the French Championnat de Ligue one from Eurostaf 2002, and for Spain from the newspaper France Football.
6. This methodology is recommended (Saporta, 1978) as a way of testing the dependence or independence between two variables on the basis of small samples, because this method does not depend on the underlying distribution of variables (namely it does not depend on the assumption of a Gaussian distribution). Moreover, with this methodology, we can avoid disclosing club names and the money value of any variable.
7. Signed by the 34 French professional clubs, on 1 February 2002.
8. The fame itself combines the championship ranking in the past 5 years, the average attendance in the away games, and the result of a survey carried out by an independent agency.
9. We refer, for example, to 'secret and illegal' contracts that have been signed, then cancelled, by Bayern Munich with Kirch in Germany, or the contract signed by the *Club Europe* (the top six French clubs) with Canal Plus.
10. Several econometric tests have demonstrated, in English professional football, a correlation between wages and sport performances (49 per cent from 1960 to 1969, 94 per cent from 1990 to 1999) and between sport performances and revenues (78 per cent from 1960 to 1969, 92 per cent from 1990 to 1999), which has strengthened in recent decades (Hoehn and Szymanski, 1999).
11. A front runner on the path toward such a more balanced revenue structure unquestionably is Manchester United: 36 per cent from gate receipts, 24 per cent from television rights, 17 per cent from merchandising, 17 per cent from sponsoring, and 6 per cent from catering and conferences, in 2001–2002. Real Madrid is conducting a similar strategy in recruiting only star players which fit with its global (world) marketing.

REFERENCES

Andreff, W. (2000), 'L'évolution du modèle européen de financement du sport professionnel', *Reflets et perspectives de la vie économique*, **39** (2–3), 179–195.

Andreff, W., Nys, J.F. and J.F. Bourg (1987), *Le sport et la télévision. Relations économiques: pluralité d'intérêts et sources d'ambiguïtés,* Paris: Dalloz.

Andreff, W. and P. Staudohar (2000), 'The Evolving European Model of Professional Sports Finance', *Journal of Sports Economics*, **1** (3), 257–276.

Bourg, J.F. (2003), 'Professional Team Sports in Europe: Which Economic Model?', in R. Fort and J. Fizel (eds), *International Perspectives on Sports Economics*, New York, NY: Praeger.

Bourg, J.F. and J.J. Gouguet (1998), *Analyse économique du sport*, Paris: Presses Universitaires de France.

Bourg, J.F. and J.J. Gouguet (2001), *Economie du sport*, Paris: La Découverte.

Fort, R. and J. Quirk (1995), 'Cross-subsidization, Incentives and Outcomes in Professional Team Sports Leagues', *Journal of Economic Literature*, **33** (3), 1265–1299.

Hoehn, T. and S. Szymanski (1999), 'The Americanization of European Football', *Economic Policy*, 28, 205–240.

Horowitz, I. (1974), 'Sports Broadcasting', in R.G. Noll (ed.), *Government and the Sport Business*, Washington, DC: The Brookings Institution.

Ippolito, M., Karvounaridis-Karydis, K. and N. Lainé (2002), 'Football Television Rights: Mutuality and Anti-Competitive Effects. The Case Studies of France, Italy and Greece', International Master in Humanities, Management and Law in Sport, CIES, Neuchâtel.

Késenne, S. (1996), 'League Management in Professional Team Sports with Win Maximising Clubs', *European Journal of Sport Management*, **2** (2), 14–22.

Késenne, S. (2000), 'Revenue Sharing and Competitive Balance in Professional Team Sports', *Journal of Sports Economics*, **1** (1), 56–65.

Lavoie, M. (2003), 'Faut-il transposer à l'Europe les instruments de régulation du sport professionnel nord-américain?', *Revue Juridique et Economique du Sport*, 67, 11–34.

Quirk, J. and R. Fort (1992), *Pay Dirt: The Business of Professional Team Sports*, Princeton, NJ: Princeton University Press.

Rader, B.G. (1984), *In Its Own Image: How Television Has Transformed Sports*, New York, NY: The Free Press.

Rottenberg, S. (1956), 'The Baseball Players' Market', *Journal of Political Economy*, **64** (4), 242–260.

Rouger, A. (2000), *La régulation des championnats de sports collectifs professionnels. Entre équilibre compétitif et équilibre concurrentiel*, Thèse de doctorat en Sciences Economiques, Université de Limoges.

Saporta, G. (1978), *Théories et méthodes de la statistique*, Paris: Technip.

Vrooman, J. (1995), 'A General Theory of Professional Sport Leagues', *Southern Economic Journal*, **61** (4), 339–360.

APPENDIX

Table 3.A.1 England's Premier League: championship ranking, turnover ranking, television rights ranking

Clubs	Champ.[a] 96–97	Turn.[b] 1996	Champ. 97–98	Turn. 1997	Champ. 98–99	Turn. 1998	TV rights 98–99	Champ. 00–01	Turn. 2000
A	1	1	2	1	1	1	2	1	1
B	2	5	1	5	2	3	1	2	3
C	3	3	3	3	7	4	6	3	6
D	4	2	13	2	12	5	11	11	7
E	5	7	7	7	6	8	5	8	9
F	6	11	4	6	3	2	3	6	2
G	7	14	14	12	13	15	13	--	--
H	8	19	16	16	16	19	15	--	--
I	9	15	10	10	10	12	12	13	12
J	10	20	9	15	8	13	10	14	13
K	11	6	5	8	4	7	4	4	4
L	12	4	15	4	11	6	9	12	5
M	13	9	6	13	19	14	16	--	--
N	14	8	18	9	14	11	14	15	11
O	15	12	--	--	9	9	8	16	20
P	16	13	8	11	5	10	7	17	10
Q	17	16	11	14	15	16	17	18	14
R	18	17	12	17	17	20	19	10	16
S	19	18	--	--	--	--	--	7	8
T	20	10	--	--	20	17	20	--	--
U	--	--	17	19	--	--	--	--	--
V	--	--	19	20	--	--	--	--	--
W	--	--	20	18	--	--	--	--	--
X	--	--	--	--	18	18	18	9	18
Y	--	--	--	--	--	--	--	5	19
Z	--	--	--	--	--	--	--	19	15
a	--	--	--	--	--	--	--	20	17

Notes:
a   Championship.
b   *Turnover.*

Table 3.A.2 France's Championnat de Ligue one: championship ranking, turnover ranking, RV rights ranking

Clubs	Champ.[a] 97–98	Turn.[b] 1997	Champ. 98–99	Turn. 1998	TV rights 98–99	Champ. 99–00	Turn. 1999	Champ. 00–01	Turn. 2000
A	1	4	6	3	6	5	3	15	7
B	2	10	10	8	11	11	11	13	14
C	3	2	4	5	4	1	6	11	3
D	4	3	2	1	2	16	1	14	4
E	5	6	1	6	1	4	2	4	5
F	6	5	3	4	3	3	5	2	2
G	7	9	14	16	12	8	13	12	17
H	8	1	11	2	8	2	4	10	1
I	9	11	13	15	13	10	15	8	15
J	10	15	15	13	14	17	16	--	--
K	11	8	7	7	7	13	7	1	6
L	12	14	8	14	9	18	12	--	--
M	13	7	12	9	10	9	9	18	11
N	14	16	5	11	5	14	10	6	9
O	15	12	18	12	18	--	--	17	18
P	16	13	--	--	--	--	--	9	16
Q	17	17	--	--	--	--	--	--	--
R	18	18	--	--	--	--	--	--	--
S	--	--	9	17	15	15	18	--	--
T	--	--	16	18	16	--	--	--	--
U	--	--	17	10	17	--	--	--	--
V	--	--	--	--	--	6	8	16	8
W	--	--	--	--	--	7	14	5	12
X	--	--	--	--	--	12	17	7	13
Y	--	--	--	--	--	--	--	3	10

Notes:
a   Championship.
b   Turnover.

Table 3.A.3 Spain's Liga: championship and turnover ranking

Clubs	Championship 1999–2000	Turnover 1999	TV rights 1999–2000
A	1	5	3
B	2	2	1
C	3	4	4
D	4	7	5
E	5	1	2
F	6	15	n.a.[*]
G	7	11	n.a.[*]
H	8	13	n.a.[*]
I	9	18	n.a.[*]
J	10	8	n.a.[*]
K	11	6	6
L	12	19	n.a.[*]
M	13	12	n.a.[*]
N	14	10	n.a.[*]
O	15	16	n.a.[*]
P	16	20	20
Q	17	14	n.a.[*]
R	18	9	7
S	19	3	n.a.[*]
T	20	17	n.a.[*]

Note: * not available.

Table 3.A.4 Italy's Lega Calcio serie A: championship ranking, turnover ranking, television rights ranking

Clubs	Champ.[a] 98–99	Turn.[b] 1998	TV rights 98–99	Champ. 99–00	Turn. 99–00	TV rights 99–00	Champ. 00–01	Turn. 2000	TV rights 00–01	Champ. 01–02	Turn. 2001	TV rights 01–02
A	1	2	3	3	1	3	6	2	3	4	2	3
B	2	3	4	1	3	5	3	3	5	6	5	5
C	3	7	7	7	6	6	10	7	6	17	18	6
D	4	5	6	5	7	7	4	6	8	10	6	7
E	5	6	5	6	5	4	1	4	4	2	3	4
F	6	1	1	2	2	1	2	1	1	1	1	1
G	7	9	10	8	9	8	12	9	9	14	7	8
H	8	4	2	4	4	2	5	5	2	3	4	2
I	9	8	9	11	8	11	9	10	12	7	8	9
J	10	13	12	14	17	15	18	17	13	18	12	11
K	11	17	18	16	11	9	--	--	--	18	--	--
L	12	15	16	17	12	16	--	--	--	--	--	--
M	13	14	14	18	15	18	--	--	--	12	17	18
N	14	16	17	10	18	17	11	18	18	8	16	17
O	15	11	15	--	--	--	--	--	--	--	--	--
P	16	12	8	--	--	--	--	--	--	--	--	--

Table 3.A.4 (continued)

	Q	R	S	T	U	V	W	X	Y	Z
	17	18	–	–	–	–	–	–	–	–
	10	18	–	–	–	–	–	–	–	–
	11	13	–	–	–	–	–	–	–	–
	–	–	9	12	13	15	–	–	–	–
	–	–	13	16	14	10	–	–	–	–
	–	–	14	13	12	10	–	–	–	–
	16	13	13	14	15	7	8	17	–	–
	14	13	13	16	15	12	11	8	–	–
	14	17	17	15	16	10	11	7	–	–
	14	15	15	16	–	11	9	13	–	5
	–	14	14	13	–	9	11	10	–	15
	–	16	16	12	–	10	13	14	–	15

Notes:
a Championship.
b Turnover.

70

4. Joint Purchasing of Sports Rights: A Legal Viewpoint[1]

Adrian Fikentscher

This first part of this chapter provides an overview of pricing structures for premium sports rights and explains the non-economic value of acquiring such rights. The second part discusses the legal framework of joint purchasing of sports rights by the EBU, considering in particular the new guidelines on the applicability of Article 81 of the EC Treaty to horizontal cooperation agreements which were adopted by the Commission in 2001 (OJ [2001] C 3/2 4 CMLR 819; referred to below as: 'Horizontal Guidelines').

PRICING STRUCTURES FOR PREMIUM SPORTS RIGHTS. WHERE IS THE VALUE?

Overview of Price Developments

The cost of sports rights has increased enormously in recent years. The main reasons are the introduction of private television channels and the rise of pay-television.

Figure 4.2 does not yet include those additional costs for the Football World Cups 2002 and 2006 that arise for television broadcasters who acquired the broadcasting rights from Kirchsport (now Infront). In addition to the price paid by Kirchsport to FIFA, the broadcasters had to pay an additional 400 million Euros. Since the rights for the 2006 Football World Cup have not yet been sold in every country, it is to be expected that Infront will make a profit of up to 1 billion Euros from the sale of television rights for the Football World Cup of 2002 and 2006.[2] This would amount to a profit margin for the agency of more than 50 per cent.

Figure 4.1   Football World Cup – television rights costs

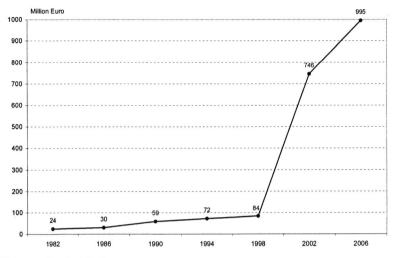

Note: * not yet final.
Source: CSA/EBU.

Figure 4.2   European Football Championship – television rights costs

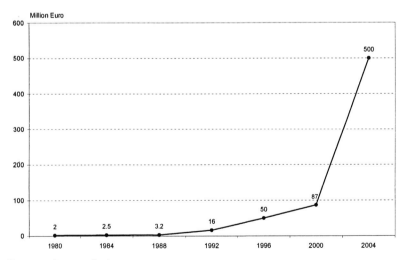

Note: * not yet final.
Source: CSA/EBU.

Where is the Value? A Public Broadcaster's View

For public broadcasters costs for major sports events, like the Olympic Games, cannot normally be recovered from market revenue. For example, the advertising and sponsorship revenue of the German EBU members ARD and ZDF for the 2002 Football World Cup recovered only the production costs that had to be paid in addition to the rights costs. At the same time, however, major sports events are at the core of the public broadcasting remit. It is a must for public service broadcasters to offer live transmission of certain major sports events. The audience expects the public broadcasters to transmit the Olympic Games, the Football World Cup, and the European Football Championship. People know that they can expect public broadcasters to cover events such as the Olympic Games more extensively than private broadcasters and to also show parts which are of interest to only a minority of sports enthusiasts. This expectation also arises from the wide coverage of different sports by public broadcasters throughout the year. Public broadcasters do not show just football, but a great number of different sports, from athletics to water polo, from cycling to table tennis. Ultimately, it is the public remit that requires public service broadcasters to invest a more or less substantial part of the licence fee revenue in major sports events. And not only the licence fee paying public expects this, but sometimes also the politics put pressure on the public broadcaster to acquire the broadcasting rights to a major sporting event. In the case of the 2002 Football World Cup German politicians of all political colour urged ARD/ZDF to buy the broadcasting rights from the Kirch group, some of them even considering a reduction of the licence fee otherwise.[3]

This pressure on the public broadcasters is well known to sports rights agencies who, therefore, take almost no risk when bidding exorbitant prices to acquire major sports events from the rights holder. Their financial calculation takes not only into account expected revenue from pay-TV broadcasting, but builds on the need for public broadcasters to acquire the rights to major events such as the Olympics or the Football World Cup.

It is a natural consequence that public broadcasters organise themselves in a joint acquisition group. It is the only way to acquire broadcasting rights directly from the rights holder at a fair market price without having to pay in addition for the profit margin of the sports rights agency. This is true at the European level, e.g. Eurovision, as well as at the national level, e.g. in Germany ARD and ZDF. The Eurovision joint buying system enables its members to have access to exclusive broadcasting rights to major international sports events at the lowest possible cost by:

- meeting the demand of the rights holder for Europe-wide transmission;
- keeping the transaction and rights costs low, in particular to avoid agency costs (countervailing power effect);
- providing for the best know-how;
- helping smaller members to acquire rights at an affordable price (solidarity effect).

In accordance with these aims, the EBU acquires the rights for its members and on behalf of its members. It is important to note that the EBU does not acquire rights for *resale* to its members. It is the members themselves who determine the offer presented by the EBU to the rights holder and it is the members which make the payment to the rights holder. The EBU acts merely for formal and practical reasons as the contractual partner of the rights holder, and there is not the slightest profit margin.

LEGAL FRAMEWORK FOR THE JOINT PURCHASING OF SPORTS BROADCASTING RIGHTS

For a legal analysis of the joint purchase of sports broadcasting rights I shall start with the latest judgment by the Court of First Instance (CFI) on the joint purchasing of sports broadcasting rights (A), then turn to the general legal framework of joint purchasing on the basis of the Horizontal Guidelines (B), before I come back to the Eurovision system by analysing it in the light of the general legal framework (C).

The CFI Judgment of 8 October 2002

On 8 October 2002, the Court of First Instance decided on the exemption accorded by the Commission for the Eurovision joint acquisition system of EBU (T-185/00, T-216/00, T-299/00 and T-300/00). The Court annulled the exemption which the Commission had granted on 10 May 2000 (what I shall call from now on the 2000 exemption). On the basis of the Commission's assumption that the Olympic Games and the Football World Cup could be regarded as separate markets it found the joint acquisition to be a restraint on trade under Article 81(1) of the Treaty which could not be exempted by Article 81(3) of the Treaty because the Eurovision sublicensing system could not prevent the possibility of eliminating competition in respect of a substantial part of the relevant products.

The main holdings:

1. The Court did not object to the statement by the Commission that there are two markets concerned, an upstream market for the 'acquisition of television rights' and the downstream market for the 'transmission of purchased sports rights' (Para. 53).

2. The Court accepted that the Commission had not defined the relevant product markets, and followed the Commission's *assumption* that the Summer Olympics and the Football World Cup could be regarded as separate markets (Para. 54).

3. The Court furthermore followed the Commission in its assessment of the restrictive effect of the Eurovision joint purchasing system. It noted two types of restrictions, one being the elimination of competition between the members of Eurovision in both the upstream and the downstream markets, and the other the foreclosure effect with regard to third parties, since the rights are sold on an exclusive basis.

4. The Court accepted that sports rights are normally granted on an exclusive basis for the purpose of guaranteeing the value of a given sports programme in terms of viewing figures and advertising revenue to the sports broadcaster (see Para. 60).

5. In this context, the Court also confirmed that the legitimacy of the joint acquisition can cover exclusive rights and that the Eurovision member has a priority right to choose which parts of the broadcasting rights purchased it wishes to broadcast live. The Court stated that 'it proves necessary, for reasons linked to exclusive transmission rights for sporting events and the guarantee of their economic value, for EBU members to reserve for themselves [exclusive] live transmission of the programmes acquired by the EBU' (Para. 73).

6. But with regard to the Summer Olympics and the Football World Cup under Article 81(3) of the Treaty the Court criticised the fact that Eurovision members reserve rights for live transmission 'when they do not intend to broadcast all those competitions live' (Para. 73). It objected to the corresponding clause in the sublicensing rules which reserved live transmission rights for Eurovision members as long as they transmitted more than the majority of principal competitions in an event or the majority of time during which the principal competitions take place.

7. The Court did not address the question of EBU membership, which it had discussed six years earlier when it annulled the Commission's exemption of the Eurovision system of 1993, claiming that the Commission should have clarified the membership criteria (see Judgment of the Court of First Instance of 11 July 1996, joined cases T-528/93, T-542/93, T-543-/93 and T-546/93). Since the 2000 exemption by the Commission considered that the only relevant criterion in connection with the joint acquisition of EBU is its market power and not who are its

individual members, the Court was correct not to mention this issue at all.

To summarise: on the basis of the very narrow market assessment by the Commission the Court's main objection related to alleged abusive behaviour by Eurovision members with regard to those rights that are fully or partly unused by them. The joint acquisition of exclusive sports rights itself was not challenged.

Joint Acquisition Under the Horizontal Guidelines

The negative decisions of the CFI in 1996 and 2002 concerning the Eurovision joint purchasing system did not hold or even as much as imply that the joint acquisition is, in general, to be regarded as anti-competitive. This is fully in line with the appreciation under national competition law as well as by the Commission. Joint purchasing cooperation agreements have a long tradition, particularly in the field of food and commodities. In these markets it is acknowledged that joint purchasing enables small and middle-sized corporations to negotiate with monopolist suppliers for a fair market price and to compete with large corporations (Whish, 2001, p. 521, Emmerich, 2001, p. 77). Joint purchasing therefore serves two economic purposes relying on the concept of the countervailing power: (1) the economies of scale and the increasing demand power make it possible to counterbalance the bargaining power of the supplier; (2) as a consequence, the members of the joint purchasing group find it possible to compete on the purchasing market with larger competitors.

This concept of countervailing power is also acknowledged by the Commission in the Horizontal Guidelines.

The Horizontal Guidelines state that horizontal cooperation agreements between competitors may lead to competition problems, but that, on the other hand, they can lead to substantial economic benefits, '*inter alia* by sharing risks, saving costs, pooling know-how and launching innovation faster, particularly for small and medium-sized enterprises' (Para. 3). Specifically with regard to purchasing agreements, the Horizontal Guidelines state:

> Purchasing agreements are often concluded by small and medium-sized enterprises to achieve volumes and discounts similar to their bigger competitors. These agreements between small and medium-sized enterprises are therefore normally pro-competitive. Even if a moderate degree of market power is created, this may be outweighed by economies of scale provided the parties actually bundle volume (Para. 116).

The question of whether or not purchasing agreements fall within Article 81 of the Treaty depends, according to the Horizontal Guidelines, on the market power of the cooperating competitors and on their nature. A market share below the threshold of 15 per cent will unlikely establish sufficient market power. On the other hand a market share above the threshold does not automatically indicate that a negative market effect is caused by the cooperation, it requires only a more detailed assessment of the impact of joint buying agreement, involving factors such as the market concentration and possible countervailing power of strong suppliers (see Para. 130, 131).

Furthermore, Article 81(1) of the Treaty normally only applies when *competitors* cooperate in joint purchasing agreements, joint purchasing agreements between non-competitors do not normally fall within the scope of the cartel clause (see Para. 24). Where upstream competing purchasers cooperate who are not active on the same relevant market downstream (e.g. in different geographical markets), Article 81(1) of the Treaty will only apply if the parties have a very strong position in the buying markets which could be used to harm the competitive position of other players in their respective selling markets (Para 123).

When assessing the effects of a joint purchasing agreement, two particular aims of the Horizontal Guidelines are to be taken into account: to protect the seller from selling under market price and to protect the consumer from not receiving the benefits of joint purchasing. In this context it is therefore worth noting that the competitor is protected only insofar as the seller or the consumer is negatively affected by joint acquisition. As the Guidelines state:

> Lower purchasing costs resulting from the exercise of buying power cannot be seen as pro-competitive if the purchasers together have power on the selling markets. In this case, the cost savings are probably not passed on to consumers. The more combined power the parties have on the selling markets, the higher is the incentive for the parties to coordinate their behaviour as sellers (Para. 128).

In other words: the pro-competitive effect of joint acquisition on the upstream market may have negative effects on the downstream markets, if the members of the joint purchasing group have together power on the selling market.

> Power on the selling market may be created or increased through buying power which is used to foreclose competitors or to raise rivals' costs. Significant buying power by one group of customers may lead to foreclosure of competing buyers by limiting their access to efficient suppliers. It can also cause cost increases for its competitors because suppliers will try to recover price reductions for one group of customers by increasing prices for other customers (Para. 129).

In other words: the advantage created for the joint purchasing group on the upstream market may not lead to increased selling power on the downstream selling market.

In the case law of the European Courts, joint purchasing agreements were accepted as compatible with Article 81 of the Treaty when the benefit of joint purchasing, which is normally a price reduction on the purchasing market, was passed on to the consumer and when members of the purchasing group were not bound by a joint purchasing obligation that forced them to acquire products of the markets concerned only via the joint purchasing group. The market shares did not play a major role.[4]

In conclusion on this point: the following criteria are of importance when the joint purchasing system of Eurovision is considered:

1. Market power on the upstream purchasing market and the downstream selling market. In this context the following have to be discussed: market definition; markets of competition between members, market shares.
2. Countervailing power effects with regard to the seller and competitors on the upstream purchasing market.
3. Benefits passed on to the consumer on the downstream market; no increase of selling power on the downstream market.

The Eurovision Joint Purchasing System of the EBU

The Eurovision joint acquisition system was first notified to the Commission in 1989. The Commission granted an exemption in 1993, which was annulled by the CFI in 1996. In 2000 the Commission granted a second exemption, which was annulled by the CFI judgment of 8 October 2002. The decision did not, however, consider the Horizontal Guidelines that were issued in 2001. The Court, of course, was not bound by the Guidelines, but if the principles set out in them are applied, they may lead to other results today.

When applying the Horizontal Guidelines, it is necessary to recall once more the system and the purpose of joint purchasing via the EBU. It has the purpose of creating a countervailing power not only to counterbalance the bargaining power of the seller but – and this is the main purpose today – to compete with the sports agencies and large media companies in Europe for the acquisition of sports rights. This is the only way to save agency costs up to 50 per cent to the rights costs (see the case of the Football World Cups 2002 and 2006) which otherwise would have to be paid by the EBU members. As a consequence, the joint purchasing system also has a solidarity effect, enabling smaller members to acquire broadcasting rights to major sports events at a price which they can afford.

Defining the Market and Assessing the Market Power

Before an assessment of the market power is made, the markets concerned need to be defined. This was, and still is, one of the major issues in the Eurovision case (see also Van de Gronden and Mortelmans, 2003, p. 13) and every legal evaluation will depend on the market definition.

The main question is: can single sports events like the Summer Olympic Games and the Football World Cup, which take place every four years, constitute a separate market? This question arises on the upstream market as well as on the downstream market, and the two markets have to be treated separately.

a) Upstream sports rights acquisition market
aa) The approach of the Commission and the Court

In the 1993 exemption the Commission did not explicitly define the market but stated: 'In particular, sports programmes can be substituted by other programmes only to a limited extent' (Para 54).

> Although international events form only a relatively small proportion of all sports broadcasting, some of them – for example, the Olympic Games or Football World Cup and European Cups – are of such widespread appeal, and of such economic importance, that their impact on the market is not adequately reflected by their expression as a mere percentage (Para. 57).

But nothing was added to corroborate this statement. In particular, the economic importance of the Olympic Games for broadcasters was not explained further.

In the 2000 exemption the Commission discussed the market definition in greater detail but still refrained from defining the relevant markets. It considered two markets as being affected by the EBU's joint purchasing system: the (upstream) sports rights acquisition market and the (downstream) broadcasting market (here differentiating between the free television and the pay-TV broadcasting market). In this context it stated:

> In conclusion, the Commission's investigation shows ... that there is a strong likelihood that there are separate markets for the acquisition of some major sporting events, most of them being international (Para 43).

The reasoning was as follows:

> Data on the viewing behaviour show that concerning these events viewing behaviour is not influenced by the coincidence of other major sporting events being broadcast simultaneously, or nearly simultaneously, that is according to the Commission, when broadcast on the same day.

For this argument, the Commission relied on a study that found that viewers of the Wimbledon Final do not watch the Football World Cup even if the Wimbledon Final is not broadcast. And viewers of the Premier League do not substitute any other major sports event broadcast on the same day (Para. 42). As examples the Commission named the Summer and Winter Olympics, the Wimbledon Finals, and the Football World Cup (Para. 42).

The Court of First Instance, in 1996, did not discuss Article 81(1) of the Treaty at all, but went straight to examine Article 81(3) without even mentioning the term 'market definition'.[5] In its 2002 decision the Court left open the market definition, following the approach of the Commission, which assumed that the Olympic Games could be a separate market, but considered that in the end it was irrelevant for the purpose of its decision (Para. 57).

The Commission's exemption did not clearly spell out it was referring to the upstream sports rights acquisition market or to the downstream broadcasting market when discussing the substitutability of major sports events like the Olympic Games and the Football World Cup.

ab) Assessment under the Horizontal Guidelines

According to the Horizontal Guidelines, the upstream market should be defined from the seller's point of view. They state:

> The definition of the relevant purchasing market follows the concept of substitutability, but with the difference to the definition of the selling markets that substitutability has to be defined from the viewpoint of supply and not from the viewpoint of demand (Para. 120).

In other words: the supplier's alternatives are decisive in identifying the competitive constraints on the purchasing market. As a consequence, the upstream purchasing market should always be defined depending on the product which the supplier sells: for the IOC the Olympic Games and for FIFA the Football World Cup. On this market, the EBU is one of several actors, like IMG, Sport five, Kirchsport (now Infront), Murdoch, Octagon, and others who are regularly bidding for major sports events like the Olympic Games and the Football World Cup.

b) *The downstream 'selling' markets: the broadcasting markets and the television advertising markets*

The 'selling market' in the case of joint acquisition by EBU is not a resale market, but the broadcasting market and, with regard to some members, the television advertising market. The EBU does not resell broadcasting rights since it is the members which acquire the rights and pay for them direct, the EBU's role being that of a coordinator and formal rights holder.

ba) The link between the broadcasting market and the television advertising market

With regard to downstream market the Commission stated that the acquisition of exclusive rights to certain major sporting events has a strong impact on the downstream television markets in which the sports events are broadcast and it defined the markets as free-to-air and pay-TV broadcasting markets (See *2000 exemption*, Para. 47).

This definition of the downstream market is in line with Commission case law in other matters. The Commission usually defines free-to-air or free access television, that includes advertising-funded private television and public television financed indirectly through the licence fee and partly through advertising as a relevant product market separate from that of pay-TV.[6]

In the following the market definition will be discussed only with regard to free television, firstly since the members of the Eurovision joint acquisition group of EBU do not provide pay-TV channels of any importance and secondly because there is a sublicensing system for pay-TV in place which was not challenged by the parties or the Court.

The Commission rightly states that in the free television market there is only a trade relationship between programme supplier and advertising industry, whereas in pay-TV the commercial relationship is established between the programme supplier and the viewer as a subscriber.[7] What are therefore the decisive parameters for assessing the market power on the free television market, the audience share or the share on the television advertising market?

The Commission tends to mention both criteria when assessing the market power of a broadcaster, not indicating clearly which should be more relevant.[8]

This approach seems debatable, at least in those countries where advertising restrictions prevail. In other words, even an audience share of a public broadcaster has only a marginal effect on the advertising revenue of its competitors when it cannot enter the television advertising market. This point was acknowledged by the Commission in *RTL/Veronica/Endemol*, where the three companies wanted to create the joint venture Holland Media Group (HMG) that according to the Commission, would have led to an audience share of 40 per cent and to an advertising market share of 60 per cent. At the same time the main competitor, the Dutch public broadcaster, would have accounted for an audience share of 37 per cent, similar to HMG, and to a television advertising market share of 31 per cent, that was half of the HMG market share.[9] By focussing on the advertising market share the Commission declared the joint venture as incompatible with the Common market because it created a dominant position for HMG on the television advertising market.

In the end, the structural remedies offered by the parties put an end to that concern.

bb) Separate broadcasting market for the broadcasting of single major sports events?

The Commission's 2000 exemption did not give a clear indication as to whether it favoured a narrow market definition with regard to major sports events on only the upstream market of sports rights acquisition (see above) or also on the downstream broadcasting market. The CFI's judgment interpreted the exemption decision in the latter way (see also the CFI judgment of 8 October 2002, Para. 54).

On close consideration, however, it does not seem convincing to have a separate downstream market for the Olympic Games or for the Football World Cup. This may be explained by means of the example of the Olympic Games by following a three-pronged test applied by the Commission in other sports antitrust cases. The Commission states that if a programme has (1) outstanding audience share, (2) branding quality, and (3) if it reaches a specific audience, it shall not be regarded as substitutable with other programming.[10]

When applying the test the following has to be considered:

Competition is a process, and services are rendered over time. Consequently, relevant time-periods must be determined. Competition between broadcasters is mostly determined by programme differentiation. The broadcaster's programmes may be specialised (dedicated channels) or they may be mixed programme services. In the end, it is the mix over time which defines the service offered, and the time-period defines the relevant market. The predominant question for any broadcaster is not how to attract as many viewers as possible for a given broadcast production but how to achieve a (sufficiently high) audience share for (at least) a complete broadcasting season. Any broadcaster, whether or not it has already established itself on the market, needs some 'special offers' on a regular basis to attract and to maintain the attention of the potential audience, but no broadcaster would deny that the ultimate challenge for its full programme package is to maintain a more or less permanent share of the audience as a whole. From the viewpoint of broadcasters (and rights marketing agencies), therefore, the differences between each sport, or each sports event, do not create as many separate markets for the corresponding broadcasting rights.

Of course, the Olympic Games are the most prestigious of all international sports events. They constitute a climax for virtually all sports; athletes – and even professional sportsmen – compete for personal and national honour, rather than – as most do the rest of the time – for financial recompense. The

Olympic ideal itself is the outstanding characteristic which makes both the Summer and the Winter Games such unique events. Practically everyone, including people not normally interested in sports programming, will at some time or other watch some Olympic programming. It is for this reason that public service broadcasters regard the Olympic Games as an absolute 'must' and as an indispensable part of their service to all sections of the public.

From a purely commercial point of view, however, the television programming value of the Olympic Games is nothing out of the ordinary. There are, of course, some outstanding events and moments in the Games, but apart from the Opening Ceremony and perhaps a few finals in major sports, even those outstanding events usually attract only average audiences. In particular, such moments of high audience appeal are embedded in literally hundreds of hours of programming with only rather modest appeal.

Applying the three-pronged test to the Olympic Games, the Commission would have to consider the following:

1. High audience shares?

The Olympic Games do not, overall, attract high audiences. The reasons are firstly that they cover a wide range of sports of different audience appeal and secondly that they spread out over a relatively long period (15 to 17 days) with sports action continuing throughout the whole day.

It is true that the audience share, i.e. the relative percentage of viewers, for Olympic programming can be comparable to premium fiction programming, but still not with Football which regularly reaches market shares of 30 per cent and more. For example, according to the Global Television Report of Sports Marketing Surveys, the 2000 Summer Olympics achieved an overall audience share of 24.6 per cent, and the 2002 Winter Olympics an audience share of 22.9 per cent. However, for the economic value of the programming two aspects have to be considered.

Firstly, the relatively high audience shares are merely the result of viewing percentages in non-prime time, which is less attractive for advertising and sponsorship. As the Global Television Report of Sports Marketing Surveys points out, the major effect of Olympic coverage in Europe is to increase the market share outside prime time by up to 10 per cent. Secondly, the audience share does not account for the *actual viewing rate*, i.e. the total number of viewers, which is decisive for fixing the costs for advertising spots.

The average viewing rate for the Olympic Games is much lower even than for premium fiction programming. The 1992 Summer Olympics, the last Summer Olympic Games to take place in the European time zone, obtained 1.3 million viewers in Spain (out of 33 million potential viewers), 1.4 million in Italy (out of 55.2 million), and 4.3 million in Germany (out of 71 million).[11]

These figures were even lower in 2000 and 2002: The 2000 Olympic Summer Games secured an average prime-time viewing rate of 1.8 million viewers in France (out of a potential audience of 53 million), and 1.3 million in non-prime time. In Spain in prime time 0.9 million (out of a potential audience of 38 million), in the UK 4.84 million in prime time (out of a potential audience of 54.5 million).[12] In Germany, the 2000 Summer Olympics obtained average audience figures of 1.74 million (out of a potential audience of 71 million), the 2002 Winter Olympics secured a viewing rate of 2.73 million which was exceptional and due to the very successful performance by German athletes. Of course, the Olympic Games include high points such as the Opening Ceremony of the Summer Olympics, in 2000 with 6.56 million viewers in Germany, but this is exceptional. Most competitions broadcast live do not obtain high viewing rates, in Germany only less than half of the competitions broadcast live obtained more than 1 million viewers (out of 71 million potential viewers).[13]

To compare: the most successful crime fiction programming of ARD, the 'Tatort', obtains in prime time an average of 7.9 million viewers, and even the repeats attract an average of 4.5 million viewers.[14]

2.   Branding character?

To be able to develop a brand image for a channel, programming needs to be broadcast throughout the year on a regular basis and must attract viewers not only for one or two competitions but for the event as a whole. Sixteen days of Olympic Games is just too short a period to guarantee high viewing levels for long periods or for the audience to become accustomed to viewing a particular channel. And Summer Olympic Games taking place every four years will not be able to let the viewer associate a channel as 'the Olympic Games channel', probably not even as 'the Olympic sports channel'. The lack of branding ability could also explain why M6 was not interested in the 2000 Olympic Games when it was offered the whole Olympic Games at exactly the same price as was France Télévision.

3.   Specific audience?

Also with regard to the type of audience, the Olympic Games are not comparable to football. Firstly, the Olympics are broadcast live all day, and are therefore unable to reach specifically the so-called most sought-after viewers (i.e. age groups 16–20 and 35–40). Secondly, the specific character of Olympic Games is to attract the general audience, and not a particular one. That is to say, all sections of the population should find something of interest when watching the Olympic Games on television, may it be ice-dancing, may it be weightlifting, hockey or curling, and so on.

To conclude with regard to the definition of the downstream market. Under the Commission's three-pronged test, the Olympic Games cannot be regarded as a separate market. In particular they are not comparable to regularly-scheduled football matches which are prime time programming and which receive as prime-time programming much higher rating figures. With the Football World Cup and the European Football Championship the result should be the same. Even with higher ratings, the broadcasting of the Football World Cup is not likely to create a branding image, since it is a four-week event once every four years. In this respect it is not comparable either with Champions League Football or with national league football that can be broadcast all year twice or three times per week.

This result of a broader market definition does not clash with Commission case law in other sports cartel cases, and particularly the recent football rights cases. Here, the Commission tends to apply a narrow market definition as, for example, in the Sport Five merger. The Commission defined the upstream sports acquisition and agency resale market narrowly as the market for the acquisition and resale of football broadcasting rights to events played annually (see Commission decision *Canal+/RTL/GJCD/JV* of 13 November 2001, Para. 21). These are not the downstream markets. The same is true for the decision *UEFA Broadcasting Rules* of 21.04.2001, where the Commission argued in favour of a narrow definition of the football rights acquisition market, directly referring to the Eurovision case (see Paras. 27–29). Here it explicitly left open the question of whether the downstream market should be defined as narrowly as the upstream market (see Para. 43).

bc) Markets of competition between members of Eurovision

Having discussed the market definitions, we can now assess which markets are covered by the joint acquisition, i.e. on which markets members of Eurovision compete with each other.

Members of the Eurovision joint purchasing group are interested only in acquiring national broadcasting licences. Consequently, they do not compete on the upstream market against each other for rights in other members' countries. In this respect the joint purchasing group is formed by *non-competing broadcasters*. The Commission considered in its *2000 exemption* that members acquire rights for other members' countries for broadcast via satellite and cable and that they are therefore in competition with members in other countries (Para. 75 of the *2000 exemption*). This is not consistent with practice. In common with commercial broadcasters, EBU members acquire national rights only and they accept the overspill of foreign programmes on to their territory by satellite and cable transmission as unintended and unavoidable. In conclusion, there is no competition between members for rights pertaining to other countries.

Only in those countries where more than one member is interested in television broadcasting rights can there be competition among broadcasters when acquiring broadcasting rights to sports events. There is more than one member in the following European countries: Denmark, Finland, France,

Germany, Norway and the United Kingdom. In all the six countries the members may compete for sports broadcasting rights on the upstream market. However, in practice there is, except for Germany, usually only one member per country participating in the joint purchasing group established for each sports rights agreement.

In the six countries mentioned above, members of Eurovision compete to a certain extent for audiences on the downstream market. However, in four of the six countries mentioned, i.e. the UK, Denmark, Finland and Norway, they do not compete against each other for advertising revenue since in each of the four countries only one of them is entitled to receive advertising and sponsorship revenue. Consequently, there is only limited competition on the downstream market.

To summarise, with just a few exceptions the joint purchasing group consists of broadcasters not competing against each other on the relevant national markets.

bd) Market shares

The market shares vary depending on whether it is television advertising shares or audience shares that are examined. The market shares in those countries with more than one Eurovision member are as follows (for 2001):

Denmark:	TV2 Denmark: 67.9 per cent on the television advertising market, 36 per cent on the broadcasting market.
	DR: 30 per cent on the broadcasting market; DR has no advertising.
Finland:	MTV3: 41 per cent on the television advertising market, 39.1 per cent on the broadcasting market.
	YLE: 43.2 per cent on the broadcasting market; YLE has no advertising.
France:	TF1: 53 per cent on the television advertising market, 32.7 per cent on the broadcasting market.
	France television: 21.8 per cent on the television advertising market, 38.2 per cent on the broadcasting market.
Germany:	ARD/ZDF: 6.3 per cent on the television advertising market, 27.6 per cent on the broadcasting market.
Norway:	TV2 Norway: 34.1 per cent on the television advertising market, 31 per cent on the broadcasting market.
	NRK: 41 per cent on the broadcasting market; NRK has no advertising.
United Kingdom:	ITV: 59.7 per cent on the television advertising market, 26.7 per cent on the broadcasting market.

> BBC: 38 per cent on the broadcasting market; the BBC has no advertising.[15]

The market shares need to be evaluated according to the degree of concentration on the respective markets. For example: the share of 6.3 per cent jointly held by ARD/ZDF on the television advertising market is very small when it is considered that the market shares of the RTL Group and of the Kirch Group are both above 40 per cent. Moreover, their combined audience share of 27.6 per cent just matches the market shares of the Kirch Group and of RTL, i.e. 25 per cent each.

As mentioned above, there is normally only *one* Eurovision member per country which participates in the joint purchasing group established for each sports rights agreement. Thus the market shares, with few exceptions, are seldom higher than 35–40 per cent, which should be acceptable in the light of the existing level of concentration on most European television markets.

The Effect of Joint Purchasing on the Upstream Sports Rights Acquisition Market with regard to the Seller and to the Competitors

It should be recalled what the Commission stated in the 2000 exemption. It considered two restrictive effects on the upstream acquisition market: firstly, the foreclosure effect with regard to non-members of the EBU (Para. 75), and secondly the restrictive effect of the joint purchasing system with regard to the competition *between* members of the EBU (Paras. 73 and 74).

From the standpoint of the Horizontal Guidelines, the assessment of the restrictive effects of the joint acquisition would lead to the following conclusions.

On the upstream market, sports rights are sold not to national broadcasters but to large sports rights agencies. The sports federations selling rights have a broad choice. For example, when the broadcasting rights for the Olympic Games are sold, there are at least five other powerful bidders (media networks and agencies) on the market: IMG, BSkyB, Kirchsport (now Infront), TEAM and Sport Five. This competitive situation was also acknowledged by the Commission in the *2000 exemption*, when it stated that the EBU's position had been *effectively* attacked by the big European media groups (Para. 55). Such an acknowledgement could be reinforced if the Commission looked at the value of the rights. In football, the EBU holds for its members only the 2004 European Football Championship and the UEFA Cup Finals. The rights to the Football World Cup and, most importantly, the Champions League are mostly held by private media groups.

From the market situation on the upstream sports rights acquisition market, it can be concluded that the seller is not negatively affected by the joint acquisition system. He is able to sell at a market price on a competitive market which does not allow for the joint purchasing system of the EBU to negotiate a price reduction. The joint purchasing system enables its members to compete with the large media groups on the upstream market with the consequence of being spared agency costs and other transaction costs.

The foreclosure effect on the upstream market of broadcasting rights to major events such as Olympic Games or the Football World Cup is not caused by the EBU, but it is in the very nature of the market that rights are sold not to competing national broadcasters but to large media networks and sports rights agencies. The existence of the EBU has two positive effects: it increases competition and it leads to lower purchasing costs since no agency profits have to be paid for.

Since the broadcasting rights would be acquired direct from the members of the Eurovision joint purchasing group, they cannot be traded on a resale market. As the CFI states in its judgment of 8 October 2002:

> ... the situation appears to be different when the transmission rights for sporting events are acquired by an agency which buys those rights in order to resell them, or when they are bought by a media group which only has operators in certain other Member States, since that group will tend to enter into negotiations with operators in other Member States to sell those rights. In that case, despite the exclusive purchase of the rights, other operators still have the opportunity to negotiate their acquisition for their respective markets (Para. 67).

It is thus true that national broadcasters are being foreclosed from the resale market. However, it may be wondered if this is really of relevance as long as there is competition on the upstream market that allows the national broadcasters to bid for the rights via the agencies and networks, and as long as the EBU joint purchasing system fulfils its pro-competitive effects.

Without the joint acquisition, EBU members were required to bid for broadcasting rights sold by sports rights agencies. Thanks to the joint acquisition system, they can acquire the rights direct saving transaction costs that they would have to pay to allow for, in particular, the agency's profit margin. Thus the effect of the joint purchasing system is to keep costs low. In the light of the Horizontal Guidelines, this should be the decisive aspect.

With regard to the restrictive effect on competition between members, it has already been noted that members do not compete for rights in other members' countries. Only where there is more than one member would competition between them be restricted. Such restrictive effects have no negative effects either on the seller or on the competitor, since on the upstream market there is a sufficient level of competition and national broadcasters would not compete on the upstream market.

Effects on the Downstream Markets

The Commission argues that the joint acquisition of sports rights by EBU members leads to foreclosure on the downstream market because national competitors are deprived of broadcasting the Olympic Games or the Football World Cup, i.e. an outstanding event that attracts large audiences (Para. 75). But what would be the economic effect of this foreclosure? From the point of view of the Horizontal Guidelines, joint purchasing can be regarded as pro-competitive when lower purchasing costs resulting from the exercise of buying power are passed on to the consumer (see Para. 128) and when there are no foreclosure effects on the downstream television markets. Below it will be argued that: (a) the competitors on the free television market are still able to broadcast attractive programming and to receive high audience figures; (b) the benefit of saving transaction costs is passed on to the consumer.

a) What is the effect of the foreclosure?
Since sports broadcasting rights are acquired on an exclusive basis, as is accepted by the Commission and the CFI, it has to be acknowledged that competing broadcasters would be excluded from the market if the Olympic Games or the Football World Cup were defined as separate markets also on the downstream broadcasting markets. However, the effects on the audience share and on the advertising share would be marginal.

On the television broadcasting market the competitor for a sports programming has many possibilities for keeping its advertising share high by showing attractive programming. If we take the yearly average audience share of television broadcasters it will be noted that the Olympic Games and the Football World Cup influence this share only marginally. For example, the audience share of ARD and ZDF in 2001 was 27.1 per cent. In 2002, the year of Winter Olympic Games in Salt Lake City and the Football World Cup in Japan and Korea, both of which events were very successful for the German national team, the audience share rose by only 1.1 per cent, to 28.2 per cent.[16] When the reasons for the increase are analysed it should be borne in mind that the year 2002 was an election year in Germany. Consequently, the impact of the sports broadcasting on the yearly audience share may have been even less since ARD and ZDF also gained higher audiences from their information programming. Consequently, the market shares on the *television advertising market* should be even less influenced by broadcasting major sports events which do not take place regularly throughout the year, such as the Olympic Games and the Football World Cup.

Furthermore, with regard to the advertising market it is impossible for EBU members to make use the benefits of joint acquisition to coordinate their behaviour, since, as mentioned earlier, with the exception of the three countries France, Germany United Kingdom, they do not compete on this market. Moreover, in Germany, since the market share on the advertising market covered by public broadcasters is extremely small, the joint acquisition by ARD and ZDF should as well not be relevant to the advertising market. This has also been acknowledged by the national cartel authority with regard to the joint acquisition of broadcasting rights to national events in the case of *SportA*, a sports rights agency jointly owned by ARD and ZDF.

Moreover, it has to be considered that only a small proportion of sports rights is acquired by EBU members *via EBU*. The total non-EBU member sports hours increased from 39 per cent in 1990 to 81 per cent in 1999. In other words, EBU members registered only 19 per cent of the total European sports hours in 1999.[17] The share of such sports rights acquired via *joint purchasing* by the EBU members is even smaller, since most of the sports events broadcast on television are purchased individually by the EBU members.

This is also due to the fact that the EBU does not hold the rights to major (international) events, such as the UEFA Champions League, Football World Cup, UEFA Cup matches, qualifying matches for the European Football Championship and to the Football World Cup, Formula 1, Ice Hockey World Championships, World Championships Sky Flying, Basketball, Handball, Wimbledon Tennis, World Rugby Cup, British and US Open Golf Tournaments, World Volleyball Championships, The ATP Tennis Tour, etc.

b) Does the consumer receive the benefit?
The marginal economic effects would be compensated for since the benefit of lower purchasing costs due to joint acquisition by the EBU would be passed on to the consumer.

With particular regard to broadcasting rights for the Olympic Games and the Football World Cup, the benefit is passed on to the consumer in two ways. Firstly, the coverage of both events is very widespread. When the CFI in its judgment of 8 October 2002 complained that RTP in Portugal did not broadcast five matches in the 1994 Football World Cup (Para. 72) it did not consider the point that these were matches scheduled simultaneously and could not therefore be transmitted live, although they were transmitted on a deferred basis. Concerning the Olympic Games, the daily programming covers, by live conference, every major competition of interest and normally every competition final.

Furthermore, the Olympic Games are an event that cannot be split up into parts. Olympic broadcasting can be characterised as a programme put together on the basis of short-term decisions by the director, who has to choose from the different multilateral signals which moments of an event to broadcast. These decisions will often be made at the last minute, depending on the performance of national athletes or teams. Since there are many competitions taking place in parallel, it is not abusive behaviour if these parallel matches or races are shown as deferred highlights only.

The second benefit is that each EBU member is spared transaction costs because it buys the broadcast rights direct via the EBU from the rights holder, on the basis on one single contract, and not from the sports rights agency. There are thus no such transaction costs to be refinanced by advertising and sponsorship. Every acquisition via a sports rights agency – the Football World Cup 2002 has demonstrated this – leads to enormous additional expense. The saving of transaction costs is of particular help to members in smaller countries, who can thus afford to acquire major sports events.

For the consumer it would be disadvantageous if broadcasters had to acquire broadcasting rights via sports rights agencies only. They would always have to pay for the agencies' profit margins, i.e. the higher rights and transaction costs would have to be recuperated by the broadcaster through advertising and sponsorship, which ultimately means by the consumer. This would be the result if the public broadcasters could not act as a joint acquisition group.

CONCLUSION

On the upstream market of acquisition of sports rights the effect of joint acquisition by EBU members can be regarded as pro-competitive since it helps the EBU to compete with the big European media groups. On the downstream market the only cases of relevance are those where there are more than two members of Eurovision participating in the joint acquisition group established for a sports rights agreement. With regard to those (rare) cases it can be noted that the anti-competitive effects for the competitor are marginal, and that the effects are compensated for because the benefits of joint purchasing are passed on to the consumer. Consequently, it is economically efficient that the EBU can continue to be a competitor on the upstream market, and by doing so, can save transaction costs that otherwise would have to be paid by its members and passed on to the consumer, if sports rights to major sports events could only be acquired by national broadcasters via a sports rights agency.

NOTES

1. The opinions expressed here are purely personal. This chapter has not been updated since the conference in Neuchâtel in 2003.
2. EGTA News.
3. See epd Medien 2001, 16/17, p. 13, and 18, p. 11.
4. See e.g., *National Sulphuric Acid Association*, OJ [1980] L 260/24, [1980] CMLR 429; *ARD/MGM* OJ [1989] L 284/36.
5. See Judgment of the Court of First Instance of 11 July 1996, joined cases T-528/93, T-542/93, T-543-/93 and T-546/93.
6. See Commission decision *MSG* of 31.12.1994, Paras. 32 and 33; Commission decision – *Bertelsmann/CLT* of 7.10.1996, Para. 16). An exception, of course, could apply for the UK market because pay-TV is also financed by advertising, see Commission decision *Pearsons* of 29.06.2000, Para. 10.
7. Commission decision *MSG* of 31.12.1994, Para. 32; Commission decision *BSkyB/KirchPayTV* of 21.03.2000, Paras. 22–23.
8. See Commission decision of *MSG* of 31.12.1994, Para. 32; Commission decision *Bertelsmann/Kirch/Premiere* of 28.5.1998 Para. 18.; Commission decision *Kirch/Mediaset* of 03.08.1999, Para. 11, Commission decision *RTL/CNN/Time Warner/n-tv* of 05.11.2002.
9. See Commission decision *RTL/Veronica/Endemol* of 20.09.1995, Para. 70.
10. See Commission Decision *UEFA Broadcasting Rules* of 19.04.2001, Paras. 24 to 41.
11. EBU.
12. Sports Marketing Surveys Ltd.
13. ARD.
14. ARD.
15. EBU, Infoadex.
16. EBU.
17. Kagan's European television Sports 2000.

REFERENCES

Emmerich, V. (2001), *Kartellrecht*, 9th ed., Munich: Beck-Verlag.

Kagan (2000), *Kagan's European Television Sports 2000*.

Van de Gronden, J. and Mortelmans K. (2003), 'Mededinging en algemene belangen: welke signale geeft de Europese rechter in de Eurovisiezaak', *Mediaforum*, 11–20.

Whish, R. (2001), *Competition Law*, 4th ed., London: Butterworths.

5. Broadcaster and Audience Demand for Premier League Football

David Forrest, Robert Simmons and Babatunde Buraimo

THE IMPORTANCE OF BROADCASTING DEMAND

Attendance demand studies constitute one of the strongest strands in the literature of sports economics. This is as it should be. Industries, and those who would regulate them, need to understand the behaviour of their customers. Accordingly, match-level attendance demand studies have explored issues such as the importance of outcome uncertainly, championship significance, star players, travel costs of visiting supporters and scheduling in accounting for variation in ticket sales. For association football, a selection of such studies is reviewed in Dobson and Goddard (2001).

In the modern era, at the highest level of professional team sports, revenue from ticket sales continues, of course, to be important but it is now less important than revenue from the sale of broadcasting rights. In season 2001–2002, the share of turnover (net of transfer fees) accounted for by broadcasting income in the English Premier League was 38 per cent. This was comfortably more than the contribution of ticket and other match day income, which was 31 per cent (information from the Premier League). In formulating policy, sports' governing bodies should therefore be as mindful of the preferences of the couch–potato audience as of those of hard-core fans who attend the games.[1]

The academic literature on television demand is, however, much thinner than that analysing patterns in live attendance. In this chapter, we aim to contribute to filling the gap. We consider both the demand characteristics of broadcasters, the immediate clients of the clubs, and those of final consumers, the television audience itself. The chapter is organised as follows. Section 2 describes the data used in our statistical analysis. Section 3 reports our modelling of broadcaster choice of which games to show. Section 4 presents regression results to account for match-to-match variation in audience ratings.

DATA

Our data relate to matches in the English Premier League in the 1990s when Sky Television, a subscription service, held exclusive rights for live television coverage. It was restricted by its contract with the Premier League to showing 60 (of a total of 380) matches per season. Audience figures for Sky are not normally in the public domain but the company was required by the Monopolies and Mergers Commission to supply match-by-match viewing figures as evidence in the inquiry into a proposed merger (subsequently ruled anti-competitive) between Sky and Manchester United. These figures are for the seasons from 1993/4 to 1997/8, so it is on the evidence for these five seasons that our empirical analysis is based.

The period in question was one of sustained growth for subscription television in general and Sky in particular. The number of subscribers to the service that carried the Premier League games increased steadily as shown in Table 5.1.

Table 5.1   Number of subscribers, 1993–1998

1993	2.281 m
1994	3.181 m
1995	4.382 m
1996	5.183 m
1997	6.074 m
1998	6.721 m

Source: Monopolies and Mergers Commission, all figures relate to first quarter of the year.

Sky's growth was, of course, in large part due to the winning of exclusive live rights for Premier League matches which was an expensive but successful part of its strategy for dominating the satellite television sector in Britain (Cave and Crandall, 2001). As its services grew in accessibility, so too did the price. The average subscription price paid to secure access to the channel showing the football increased steadily across our five seasons from £11.81 per month in 1993/4 to £19.30 per month in 1997/8.

For each season, we had a list of the 60 matches chosen for broadcast and the estimated television audience for each game. The mean audience was

0.82m in the first season, 1.40m in the last; but the range across individual matches was wide, from 0.12m to 2.86m over the whole five year period. We sought to account for such variation by estimating the role of performance variables calculated from information in various editions of the *Rothmans Football Yearbook* and we also used data on club wage bills from various editions of the Deloitte & Touche *Annual Review of Football Finance* (Touche Ross prior to 1996).

BROADCASTER SELECTION OF MATCHES FOR LIVE COVERAGE

The Premier League permitted coverage of only 60 matches per season. Modelling the choice of which games to show should reveal something about which match characteristics make a game an appealing product to the immediate purchaser, the television company. Account has, of course, to be taken of any constraints in the broadcaster's choice of games.

English Premier League games in this period (as now) were scheduled mainly for Saturday afternoons between August and May. Normally, Sky was permitted to choose two fixtures from the Saturday schedule and these games were then switched to Sunday afternoon and Monday evening for live broadcast that would not clash with other matches. In the case of matches in the first half of the season – up to the Boxing Day holiday programme (Boxing Day is the first weekday after December 25) – Sky was required to make its choice of games before the season started so that the Sunday/Monday scheduling could be incorporated into official fixture lists. After Boxing Day, Sky had the flexibility to notify its choice of future games on a week-by-week basis, presumably so that as the season progressed, it could feature matches likely to be of significance for championship, European qualification and relegation outcomes.

The contract required Sky to show each of the 20 teams in the league on at least one occasion. There was more informal pressure to restrict the frequency with which more popular teams appeared, at least for home fixtures, because the larger clubs faced pressure from season ticket holders who found Sunday and Monday games less convenient to attend than those on the traditional Saturday afternoon. Another constraint was that the league asked that 'Derby' matches between local and regional rivals should be chosen for broadcast where possible as these matches did not pose the same problems for travelling supporters who might have difficulty in covering longer distances on matches rescheduled for after work on Monday.

We estimated a probit model to test for the factors taken into account by broadcasters in their choice of games to be shown. The particular institutional arrangements described above dictate that different variables must be specified as determining selection according to whether the games were scheduled for before or after Boxing Day. For example, after Boxing Day, the television company may favour showing teams with a strong playing record in the current season and we therefore include as variables the points-per-game achieved by the teams up to (but not of course including) the subject match. But before Boxing Day, matches nominated for broadcast had been chosen even before the start of the season and so details of current form could not have influenced the decision-takers. Accordingly, for matches before Boxing Day, we substitute previous season points-per-game. Note that in the English Premier League, throughout this period, the competition awarded teams three points for a win and one for a draw. An increase in performance from one to two points per game typically raises a team from borderline relegation candidate to championship favourite.

Table 5.2   Probit estimation for selection of matches for broadcasting

	Marginal effect	(absolute) t-statistic
Season-Long Variables		
Big reputation 5	0.000043	0.27
Small reputation 5	0.000032	0.07
Relative wages	0.038	1.90
Derby	0.12	2.61
Weekend	0.09	5.22
Pre-Boxing Day Variables		
Big ppg (last)	-0.16	3.42
Small ppg (last)	0.20	3.61
Promo (premppg)	0.01	0.32
Exposure	0.05	6.23
Post-Boxing Day Variables		
Gap	-1.30	2.98
Big ppg (current)	0.24	5.99
Uncertainty	-0.70	2.68

Table 5.A.1 defines variables used here and in subsequent regression analysis. Table 5.2 reports our probit results. In the specification of the probit equation, our aim has been to test whether and to what extent factors asserted or demonstrated to matter for live attendance – club 'reputation', teams'

quality (proxied by season's wage bills), championship/qualification/ relegation significance, match outcome uncertainty, current team performance levels, expected entertainment value in terms of the rate of goal scoring – really matter to those who purchase broadcasting rights and decide which games should appear on live television.

Considering first the season-long explanatory variables, we included measures of 'reputation' for both the bigger (on this measure) and smaller team in each fixture. Reputation is indexed according to a weighted average of a club's place in the league standings over a period of years, say five, ten or 20. It has been found significant in match-level attendance demand studies, most recently by Czarnitzki and Stadtmann (2002) who found a favourable effect on attendance from achievements as long as 20 years before in the German football league. This is presumably because success attracts young, new-entrant, fans and new fans are often investing in a lifetime of support for their club. But from our results, broadcasters evidently believe that historical achievement plays no role in augmenting the appeal of a game to the couch potato audience. Bigger- and smaller-team reputation, whether measured over our reported five year span or over ten or 20 years in unreported experimentation, played no role at all in determining which games were broadcast. If individual selling of television rights were permitted, some 'big' Premier clubs in terms of attendance could not count on historical achievement to earn them abnormally high television revenue.

The other season-long variables include a measure to proxy the quality of players likely to be on show in a particular match. The measure is the sum of the relative wages of the two teams where relative wage is the ratio of a club's wage bill in a particular season to the average Premier League wage bill for that season. Thus the mean value for 'relative wages' in a match is 2.0 by construction and the range across more than 2000 matches in our sample is from 0.65 to 3.93. Our result indicates that a television company prefers to relay a match with higher quality players though the significance level is marginal.

In conformity with what one would expect from the institutional features of the arrangements between the Premier League and Sky, 'Derby'[2] matches are much more likely to be selected to be televised. And because most matches shown are from the weekend fixture list (broadcast of midweek games was rare), the 'weekend' variable is positive and highly significant.

For the pre-Boxing Day period, the striking results are the significant but opposite-signed marginal effect estimates in respect of the previous season's points-per-game for the more and less successful clubs in each fixture. The result suggests that when looking at the higher-ranked club in a fixture, Sky was less likely to pick the game the *higher* was the status of that club the previous season. When looking at the lower-ranked club in a fixture, Sky was less likely to pick a game, the *worse* was the status of that club the previous season. Our interpretation is that this is consistent with informal constraints on the number of television appearances by each team being binding. Relative success and failure are correlated across seasons. Last season's championship (relegation) contenders are likely to be this season's championship (relegation) contenders. The results suggest that, prior to Boxing Day, Sky limited its choices of games involving the best and worst teams so that it did not 'use up' its ration of teams that were likely to be involved later in the season in title- and relegation-influential games that would be very desirable to the television audience. For this pre-Boxing Day choice of matches, the variable *exposure* is also strongly significant which suggests that some teams are more 'favoured' than others for coverage in this stage of the season.

After the Christmas holiday period, Sky was able in each season to give relatively short notice of which games it intended to cover. We have been unable to find the precise period of notice that was typically given. Where relevant, we have modelled the selection decision as determined by the value of the variable (points-per-game) calculated up to the previous game to the subject match. In practice, televised games were likely to have been selected one or two weeks earlier than this but, once the season is mature, points per games are constrained by the arithmetic to be highly correlated over short time periods. Therefore we would not anticipate that specification based on more precise information could yield substantially different results.

When choice became flexible, after Boxing Day, the selection criteria adopted by Sky appear to have been those that would be suggested by the attendance demand modelling tradition of sports economics. *Gap* is our measure of the significance of a match. For most of the season, most clubs will still have something at stake. Typically, crucial issues are settled at the first (champion team), fourth (Champions League qualification), sixth (UEFA Cup qualification) and seventeenth (survivor from relegation) positions in the league. For nearly all clubs, certainly up to the penultimate month of the season, an improvement or deterioration in form could move them between the right and wrong sides of the relevant line. With this in mind, any match is more crucial if it is against a team contesting the same issue, i.e. playing in the same 'league within a league'. *Gap* is the absolute difference in points per game between the two teams in a match. Where this is low, the match matters for the settlement of an 'issue' and we would expect such matches to appeal more to the broadcaster. This is upheld by the results since the relevant marginal effect is correctly signed, large and highly significant. Such a result is consistent with the attendance demand literature's emphasis on championship significance as a positive determinant of ticket sales though that literature has not generally been updated to take account of all the pressure points in a modern European league. All such pressure points appear to have been taken into account in Sky's choice of game; but the appeal is shown to be greater for pressure points higher up the division to the extent that the result on 'bigger team points-per-game' is again large, significant and appropriately signed.

Assessment of the importance of championship significance and match-level outcome uncertainty is central in the literature on attendance demand because sports leagues have often defended anti-competitive practices by reference to a perceived need to equalise financial resources across clubs to make both the championship and individual matches more closely contested. Here, the results from a model of the broadcaster's choice of games appears to demonstrate the appeal of having more games matter for the championship. But even in an unequal league, like the Premiership, our results imply that the modern creation of effective 'leagues within leagues' permits many games to generate extra interest because they 'matter' for some issue or other.

The concepts of individual match significance and individual match uncertainty need to be separated carefully. Here, we propose a new and simple measure of uncertainty of outcome that allows for the importance of home advantage. The matches where the 'gap' in points per game between the teams is small are unquestionably significant for league standings; but they will not be the matches where uncertainty of outcome is greatest. In English soccer, home teams win nearly twice as often as away teams, so the probability of the home team winning is much greater than the probability of the away team winning where the abilities of the two teams are the same (when *gap* should be close to zero). Outcome uncertainty is greatest when a team towards the bottom of the standings plays host to a team well up in the standings (here *gap* will be rather large). Our measure of outcome uncertainty is the absolute value of the following: home advantage (measured in points per game) plus home team points per game in the current season minus away points per game in the current season. The value of 'home advantage' is taken as the difference in the previous season between points per game won by *all* home teams and points per game won by *all* away teams. Our measure of outcome uncertainty is zero where the average degree of home advantage in the league is exactly sufficient to cancel out the impact on expected outcome from a superior playing record by the visitors in a particular match. Our way of measuring *outcome uncertainty* suggests a negative sign in the probit model and we do indeed estimate a strongly significant negative sign on this variable. Television therefore appears, as one would expect, to favour screening matches where the contest is anticipated to be close.

Overall, then, Sky appears to have exhibited behaviour consistent with the assumptions or findings of sports economics. It favoured games with more (better paid) talent on show, matches of significance for some issue within the league and matches expected to be closely contested. It also appeared to take into account implicit constraints on the balance between the degree of exposure given to individual teams across the season.

AUDIENCE DEMAND

Table 5.3 displays our results from an ordinary least squares model to account for variations in the recorded size of television audience for the games shown over the five year period (the first match of the season was excluded for lack of current-season data). The functional form is log-linear. Controls this time include dummy variables for different seasons and different months in the year (the first season and August/September are the reference categories). We experimented with the inclusion of day of the week dummies but they were insignificant: Sunday and Monday audiences were not different from each other and for other days in the week there were very few observations. The results for the season dummies indicate a rising trend in audience up to, but not including, the final season in the data. This mirrors the growth in the number of subscribers and season dummy results will also incorporate the effects of any price changes as subscription rates altered from year to year. The results on the month dummies show a clear pattern with viewing highest in the midwinter months. This is in contrast to evidence on live attendance which peaks in the Spring. England enjoys a milder climate than most of Europe but there have been recent proposals for a midwinter break or even a switch to summer play. This could be costly in terms of the value of television rights. Viewership in January is estimated to be nearly one-quarter higher than in August/September and April/May and the value of television rights is likely ultimately to reflect audience size.

Many of the other variables included in our audience demand equation are similar to those employed in the probit but without the complication that decisions on games up to Boxing Day have to be taken in advance. Because there is a lot of noise in early season win-loss statistics, we experimented with modelling August/September audience size as depending on the previous season's points per game data but the results were virtually unchanged.

Reputation, based on past seasons' achievements, was statistically insignificant in the audience equation as in the selection equation. But viewers were drawn to matches where more expensive talent was on show. The coefficients on *gap* and *bigger team points per game* indicate greater interest in matches that matter, particularly those that matter in the upper end of the standings. We had no strong expectation regarding the sign of the coefficient on *Derby*. On the one hand, such matches are often contested with particular passion. On the other hand, they involve teams from a single area of the country and the rest of the national television audience may regard them as private affairs. In the event, derby matches appeared to be ranked in the television ratings no differently from other games. Their popularity with Sky was presumably just explained by the request from the Premier League that they should be given priority in the selection of games for live broadcast.

Table 5.3   Ordinary least square results for audience demand

Dependent variable: natural log of television audience		
	Coefficient	*(absolute) t-statistic*
Big reputation 5	0.00048	1.37
Small reputation 5	0.00024	0.29
Relative wages	0.22	5.27
Gap	-0.073	2.04
Big ppg (current)	0.14	4.00
Uncertainty	-0.0034	0.10
Derby	-0.0069	0.13
Exp goals	0.052	1.58
Oct	0.09	2.26
Nov	0.19	3.87
Dec	0.18	4.45
Jan	0.24	5.34
Feb	0.20	3.00
Mar	0.21	4.66
Apr/May	0.0087	0.14
Season 94/5	0.14	3.80
Season 95/6	0.36	8.50
Season 96/7	0.56	14.38
Season 97/8	0.42	6.99
Constant	12.59	113.44
R^2	0.63	
N	295	

The importance of match outcome uncertainty to football fans has been explored on several occasions in attendance demand studies. Some (since Peel and Thomas, 1988) use betting odds to derive probabilities of victory for either side but results may be sensitive to an assumption of efficiency in the betting market (Forrest and Simmons, 2002) and it is in any case difficult to separate any preference for outcome uncertainty from the preference of home supporters to see their team win. Modelling television audience demand may offer a more straightforward opportunity to assess whether outcome uncertainty matters because there is no 'home' team. What we in fact find is that outcome uncertainty appears not to matter at all. But how can this finding be reconciled with our earlier result that it matters significantly to those who choose the matches to be screened? We offer the following interpretation. For live attendance, expected closeness or otherwise of contest is important because many supporters will not want to buy a ticket and pay transport costs for a match with a high chance of being one-sided and hence tedious. For television viewers, expected closeness of contest is of low importance because, if a game does become one-sided, they can switch off or switch channel. Our data are based on set top box monitoring of audience size at one minute intervals, with audience size the average reading across the whole of a game. Thus even matches which are expected to be one-sided *and* actually become one-sided may remain interesting for long enough that measured audience size is little affected by turn-offs. For those who choose the games to be featured on television, expected closeness of contest is important even if it is not important to their subscribers. Television companies want viewers to stay switched on for the whole game because there is then a greater chance that they will view the following programme and a greater chance that they will renew their subscription next month. Notwithstanding that *uncertainty* has no impact on recorded audience figures, the provision of more evenly matched games may nevertheless raise television rights values.

'Couch potato' fans may be less purist in their appreciation of football than those who are committed enough to attend home games. Less traditional supporters are often argued to favour lots of goals and this argument lies behind various implemented or proposed rule changes such as harsher codes in sending off (to create power play situations) or even a change in the dimensions of the goal itself. We therefore included in our model a variable labelled *expected goals* which is simply the average of the mean goals per match (scored or conceded) recorded for each of the two teams in the season to date. The result was inconclusive: the coefficient was positive but just short of significant at the 5 per cent level on a one-tailed test. It is possible that the result would have been stronger for a sample where broadcast was on a free-to-view channel where the potential audience may be more genuinely 'couch potatoes'. Naturally one would guess that Sky television subscribers would include a disproportionate number of keen soccer fans who would also attend live matches.

CONCLUSIONS

The television audience for Premier League Football, as for other major sports events, dwarfs that in the stadium. This is reflected in the fact that broadcast rights revenue now exceeds that from ticket and other match day incomes and underpins the high remuneration for players in the modern era. It is not so far reflected in published studies of the determinants of television demand. Here we have attempted to model the preferences of a broadcaster selecting games to be screened and to model final audience figures. The broadcaster appears to favour the characteristics traditionally emphasised in live attendance demand studies – high quality talent on show, significance of a match for league outcomes, *ex ante* uncertainty of match outcomes – within the constraints imposed on their choices. Audience preferences are less clear-cut. That viewers appear indifferent to outcome uncertainty may be explained by the ease of switching off matches that in fact become one-sided contests. There is strong evidence that viewers do seem attracted to matches significant for League rankings and there is weaker evidence that their interest is also attracted by matches involving high scoring teams.

NOTES

1. The phrase 'couch potato' describes those who sit at home, slumped on a couch or sofa, watching television.
2. The term 'Derby' refers to matches between teams based in the same city or region where there is a tradition of strong rivalry between the two clubs and where supporters' self identity will often be bound up with which one they support.

REFERENCES

Cave, M. and R.W. Crandall (2001), 'Sports Rights and the Broadcast Industry', *Economic Journal*, 68, F4–F26.

Czarnitzki, D. and G. Stadtmann (2002), 'Uncertainty of outcome versus reputation: empirical evidence for the first German football division', *Empirical Economics*, 27, 101-112.

Deloitte & Touche (various years), *Annual Review of Football Finance*, Manchester.

Dobson, S. and J. Goddard (2001), *The Economics of Football*, Cambridge and New York, NY: Cambridge University Press.

Forrest, D. and R. Simmons (2002), 'Outcome uncertainty and attendance demand in sport: the case of English soccer', *The Statistician*, **51** (2), 229–241.

Peel, D.A. and D.A. Thomas (1988), 'Outcome uncertainty and the demand for football', *Scottish Journal of Political Economy*, 35, 242–249.

Rollin, J. (various years), *Rothmans Football Yearbook*, London: Headline.

APPENDIX

Table 5.A.1 Variable definitions

TV Audience: Audience recorded in data from the MMC on viewing figures for Sky-televised matches.

Big Reputation 5, Small Reputation 5: The larger and smaller values for a fixture of each team's reputation score where:

$$\text{Reputation} = \sum_{t=1}^{t=5} \frac{1}{x_i \sqrt{t}}$$ and x_i is the status of club i in the final standings across the four professional divisions achieved t seasons ago. Status score is highest (92) for the Champion club of the Premier League and lowest (1) for the bottom club in the bottom division.

Relative Wages: The combined relative wage of the two clubs in a fixture. Relative wage is the wage bill for a club in the particular season divided by the mean wage bill in the Premier League that season.

Big ppg (current), Small ppg (current): The larger and smaller values for a fixture of each teams' points per game in the season to date just prior to the fixture being played.

Big ppg (last), Small ppg (last): The larger and smaller values for a fixture (between two teams that were in the Premier League the previous season) of each team's points per game at the end of the previous season.

Promo (prem prg): A dummy variable (= 1 if a match involves one just promoted team) multiplied by the points per game achieved in the previous season by the team in such a fixture that had already been in the Premier League.

Gap: The absolute difference between the points per game figures to date of the two teams in a fixture.

Uncertainty: The absolute value of the following. Home advantage plus points per game to date of the home team minus points per game to date of the away team, where home advantage = mean points per game achieved by all home teams in the previous season minus points per game achieved by all away teams in the previous season.

Derby: A dummy variable set equal to one for fixtures between local or regional rivals (full list available from the authors).

Weekend: A match played as part of a weekend round of fixtures, i.e. played on Saturday, Sunday or Monday.

Exposure: For a match played pre-Boxing Day, the number of live screenings of other games involving either team in the season up to Boxing Day.

Exp goals: Average number of goals scored in matches involving either of the two teams in the season to date.

Oct, Nov, Dec, Jan, Feb, Mar, Apr/May: Dummy variables to represent the date of a fixture.

Season 94/5, season 95/6, season 96/7, season 97/8: Dummy variables to represent the season a fixture took place.

---

6. International Television Sports Rights: Risky Investments

Harry Arne Solberg

INTRODUCTION

The profitability of acquiring television sports rights depends on a wide range of factors. Some of these can fluctuate substantially, and hence cause severe financial problems for the purchasing channel. Thus it is no surprise that a number of television channels have been hit by the 'winners' curse' and suffered substantial losses from unprofitable deals. Table 6.1 presents some well-known examples from Europe.

Similar problems have also occurred regularly in the North American markets where televised sport has been a commodity since the 1960s, which is a considerably longer period of time than in Europe. It is well known that CBS (one of the major broadcasting networks) almost went bankrupt in the early 1990s after paying too much for the Major League Baseball (MLB) rights (Fort, 2003). When Fox acquired the North American Football rights (NFL) for the first time ever in 1994, they immediately sought to write off more than a third of the $1.58 billion package (Fort, 2003). In 2002, News Corporation, a media company partly owned by Rupert Murdoch, took a write-down of $909 million on unprofitable sports rights deals, while NBC (another broadcasting network) reported losses on their National Basketball Association deal (NBA) estimated at $300 million over two seasons.[1]

Due to this development, there have been indications of reversed price effects on rights fees at the start the twenty-first century. In Germany, Italy and Spain the Champions League rights were considerably reduced compared with the former value, when UEFA sold the rights for the period starting in 2003/4. Likewise, for the first time since 1992, the value of the English Premier League was also reduced when the 2004–2007 rights were sold. BSkyB paid £1.024 billion for the live rights, which was a reduction of 35 per cent per match compared to the former deal. Similarly, the BBC acquired

'Match of the Day' rights over three years at a price of £105 million while ITV paid £180 million for the former – a reduction of 43 per cent (TV Sports Markets 2003).

Table 6.1   Some unprofitable European sports rights deals²

In September 1996, **Sport 7** (a pay service channel), agreed a seven year contract with the **Dutch Eresdivisie** (the soccer elite division) for a fee of DFL 1,04 billion for nearly all the soccer matches in the Netherlands. Four months later, in December 1996, the channel collapsed, after incurring losses of DFL 100 million (BCC, 1997).

ITV-Digital was unable to fulfil its £378 million contract with the **Nationwide League** which was supposed to run from 2001 to 2004, and went bankrupt. The league brought the case to court and demanded that the owner of ITV-Digital pay the necessary amount, but lost this case. Later on, BSkyB acquired 'the remaining' part of this deal at a price of £95 million, which represented a large discount compared to the original price.

Telepiù and **Stream** lost, respectively, $300 million and $200 million from these deals during the 2001/2002 season. Thus, the renewal of the deals before the 2002/2003 **Serie A** season did not go as smoothly as before. The poorest clubs rejected the new offer from the television channels and therefore the league was delayed by two weeks. The problems were solved when the six wealthiest clubs paid the difference between the offer from television channels and what the poorest clubs demanded. As a consequence of these problems the Italian authorities recently allowed the channels to merge.

Premiere, Kirch Medias' pay-TV channel was unable to recruit enough subscribers to make the deal with the **German Bundesliga** profitable for the 2001 to 2004 period. Thus the deal was renegotiated – with the result that its value dropped by 20–25 percent.

RAI, which acquired the **Italian 2002 World Cup soccer rights**, lost a considerable amount of money due to the early exit of the Italian team. This reduced the rating figures of the remaining matches, and hence also the value of advertising slots. As a consequence there were rumours that RAI were considering legal steps against FIFA, since television pictures confirmed that it was a mistake by the referee that sent Italy home from the championship.³

TF1, which acquired the **French 2002 World Cup soccer rights**, lost €18 million due to the early exit of the national team, according to newspaper articles (Desbordes, 2003).

Canal Digital, a pay-TV channel, acquired the **Nordic 2002 World Cup soccer rights** without financial success. The channel was unable to acquire enough subscribers to make the acquisition profitable, and lost NOK 48 million.⁴

This chapter will analyse the profitability of acquiring sports rights – with special attention to international rights. The next (and theoretical) section focuses primarily on the cost structure of broadcasting in general – and secondly on sports broadcasting. This is followed by a discussion of factors that influence income, with special attention to the broadcasting of international events. It also describes how the level of competition between television channels has developed since the 1990s, and its influence on the issues in question. The empirical section presents two case studies relating to the broadcasting of matches from Euro 2000/2004 and UEFA's Champions League on Norwegian television. These studies illustrate that the popularity of sports programmes varies considerably, which has severe financial consequences for the television channels. In Norway, Euro 2004 was broadcast by TV2, a commercial public service broadcaster. It is important to bear in mind that the qualification was not finished when the rights were acquired from the European Broadcasting Union (EBU). Thus the chapter presents different scenarios about the income that the channel could have earned, depending on whether national teams qualified and their performance. This is in order to illustrate the large degree of uncertainty that a channel faces when it has to decide whether to bid for sports rights or not. Unfortunately for TV2, the Norwegian team failed to qualify.

The Champions League rights have been acquired by the Modern Times Group (MTG). The most attractive matches have been broadcast on their free-to-air channel, TV3, which has a penetration of 62 per cent of all the Norwegian TV-households.

SPORT BROADCASTING – THE SUPPLY SIDE

The Cost Structure of Broadcasting

The cost structure influences the profitability of practically all commercial activities, and sports broadcasting is no exception. The equations below provide a broad overview, with equation one distinguishing between fixed and variable costs, while equations two and three split the two categories further (Johnsen, 2001).

1. Total costs = Fixed costs + Variable costs.
2. Fixed costs = Production related costs + Sunk costs.
3. Variable costs = Variable costs of broadcasting + Variable costs of production (+ Opportunity costs).

Fixed Costs

The fixed costs are the costs that do not vary with output. Such costs cannot be altered in the short-run, whatever level of production. The first category includes *production related costs*, which are conditional on production. Contrary to the variable costs, however, they do not vary with production level. The second category is *sunk costs*, which are totally irrecoverable. The only way of disposing of them is by reselling the item which initiated them. In addition, they can be reduced if the seller agrees to renegotiate the contract.

Variable Costs

The variable costs are costs that change as output changes and can be split into three categories as seen from equation three. *The variable costs of broadcasting* vary proportionally with the quantity being broadcast, for example the total number of hours. However, these costs can vary from one programme to another. As an example, the channel has to rent a frequency to have the signals transmitted home, if the programme is a soccer match being played on another continent.

The second element is *the variable costs of production*. These can vary considerably for each individual production, for example with the number of cameras and commentators. The third element of variable costs is *the opportunity cost* which is the value of the foregone revenue from alternative actions. This cost element, however, does not represent any direct monetary outlay for the channel, which is the reason why it is placed in brackets in equation three. Nevertheless, it may still influence the construction of the optimal mixture of programmes. As an example, a channel may decide not to broadcast a sport programme even though it has the rights, if it can earn more from broadcasting another programme. Therefore the outcome from a contract which *obliges* the purchasing channel to broadcast a certain number of matches can be very different from a contract which *allows* it to broadcast the same number of matches. It is likely that the seller of the rights wants to maximise the publicity of the event – and thus also prefers the least attractive matches to be broadcast.

The production and transmission of television programmes is a typical *economies of scale* production, which usually requires considerable 'start-up' costs while the variable costs are relatively moderate. Hence, the sunk costs account for a large proportion of the total costs. As is typical for most media products, the production of television programmes is characterised by high first copy costs and low marginal distribution costs (Gaustad, 2000). This also creates substantial *economies of scale advantages* that can be utilised by distributing programmes to the largest possible audience, for example by exporting the programmes to foreign channels. Such exports also represent a cost-sharing element as it makes it possible to distribute the production costs over several channels. Furthermore, the revenues from selling to foreign channels also represents a net addition to the overall profits as long as the distribution costs are covered.

The Costs of Sport Broadcasting

If the channel has to acquire rights exclusively, then the cost structure will be influenced by the terms of the contract between the seller and the buyer. If the rights are expensive and fixed, i.e. not tied to the revenues from broadcasting the programmes, then there will be a high degree of sunk costs. Indeed, this pattern has been common for the most attractive soccer rights since the 1990s. Many European television channels have invested heavily in attractive soccer rights in order to strengthen their market position. Firstly, this development has pushed the prices to levels that were unimaginable only a few years ago. Secondly it has also enabled the sellers to dictate the contract terms. Thus, the most popular products have been sold at fixed prices, i.e. independent of the income that is generated by the broadcasting of the programmes. Hence the channels also had to carry the entire risk in case of negative shifts in demand.

As an example, TF1, the French channel, acquired the 2002 World Cup soccer rights for a fee of €60 million, while the variable costs of broadcasting (only) amounted to €8.7 million (Desbordes, 2003). Another example is TV2, a Norwegian channel which acquired the Euro 2004 rights from the European Broadcasting Union (EBU) at a price of NOK 60 million (Hauger, 2003). The production costs were estimated to be in the region of NOK 7.5 to 9 million – depending on whether Norway qualified and on their performance in the tournament. If the Norwegian team were successful, TV2 would be willing to spend more resources.[5] The EBU originally acquired the entire European rights for a price of CHF 800 million. This represented a dramatic increase from Euro 2000 which (only) cost CHF 140 million.[6] Another example is NRK's broadcasting of the 2004 Summer Olympics in Athens, where the rights fees (alone) exceed NRK's total production costs on sports programmes this year.[7]

Figure 6.1 shows the BBC's variable costs in 1998/1999 and illustrates that sport belonged to the cheaper categories, and that the variable production costs are moderate compared to other genres of programmes. Bear in mind, however, that some sports rights have become significantly more expensive since then. As an illustration, the BBC and ITV shared the 1998 World Cup soccer finals for a total fee of £5 million. This was cheap compared with the £160 million that the two channels must pay for the combined 2002 and 2006 World Cup soccer finals.[8]

Also bear in mind that as a public service broadcaster, the BBC is obliged to emphasise other concerns than those facing the commercial channels when constructing their mixture of programmes. As an example, the BBC has an objective to produce 80 per cent of programmes in-house (Solberg, 2002b). Such a policy is more expensive than buying in programmes from other channels, due to the cost-sharing element related to the latter alternative, as mentioned above. Hence, their cost structure will be somewhat different from e.g. BSkyB's, which offer their viewers a much narrower range of programmes.

Figure 6.1   Cost per hour of programme – BBC 1998/99 (£1000)

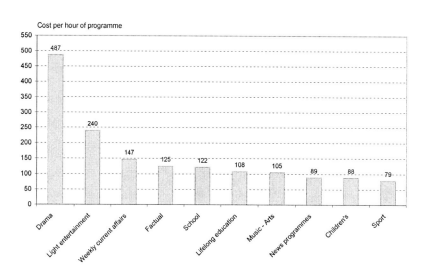

Sources: Statistical Yearbook (2000), European Audiovisual Observatory.

The Income from Sports Broadcasting

Profitability analyses of sports broadcasting also involve the income side. Commercial channels mainly earn their revenues from two sources, advertisers and viewers. The income of *advertiser channels* is broadly proportional to the size of the audience. Consequently, they always have an incentive to provide programmes which attract large audiences. However, to advertisers, not all viewers are alike. The greater the spending power of viewers and the greater their attractiveness to the advertisers, the more advertisers will pay to reach them. This creates an incentive to offer programs that households with higher income will relate to. Thus some channels have a market policy of targeting specific groups of viewers, and tie the advertising fees to the number of these viewers, instead of the gross figures.

Pay-TV channels earn their revenues from the viewers, i.e. from the consumer surplus that the viewers would have obtained if the programmes were broadcast free on air. Usually the charges are split into a two-tariff system. Firstly, there is a subscription fee, which is often split between a one-time (lump sum) fee paid when signing the subscription, and a current fee paid at regular intervals. The latter allows for adjustments if the fixed costs increase as market conditions change. The main motive behind pay-TV channels acquisition of sports rights has been to increase – or to uphold – the number of subscribers. However, there have been problems with enforcing the revenues from the viewers. Soccer fans will be looking for substitutes if the subscription fees or pay-per-view fees increase too much. In Italy, the number of viewers with pirate cards is estimated to be in the region of 2 and 4 million.[9] Another alternative is to watch the match on television in a bar or a pub.

In European broadcasting, the distinction between advertiser and pay-TV channels is quite clear. Although channels in the latter category also sell some advertising, the main revenues come from subscription and pay-per-view fees. This is different in North America, where the proportion that comes from advertising revenues is considerably higher.

In principle, a profit maximising television channel will adjust production to the level where its marginal revenue equals marginal costs. It is, however, important to bear in mind that the reception of a television signal is partly a *public good* which satisfies the non-rivalling criterion. If one person watches a programme, this does not prevent it from being received by another (Gaustad, 2000). Hence, the costs of broadcasting a programme will be unaffected by the number of viewers that watch it. To the broadcaster, the marginal cost of transmitting a programme to one additional viewer within any broadcasting market area is literally zero.

This characteristic, however, also works in reverse. Hence, a channel cannot reduce costs by broadcasting programmes to a smaller number of viewers, as is possible for private goods. If sports broadcasting yields a profit above the average rate elsewhere in the economy, this may attract new entrants to the market. The existing channels may be tempted to broadcast more sport, and new channels may also emerge. Moreover, sports programmes can also meet competition from other (entertainment) programmes.

Such impacts will cause leftward (negative) shifts in the established programmes' demand curves. This reduces the rating figures, and hence also the revenues. Furthermore, a recession in the economy can have similar effects by reducing firms' spending on advertising. In addition, a recession can also reduce the number of subscribers to pay-TV channels, assuming the products fall into the category of normal goods. Such negative impacts on income will create an incentive for all profit-maximising channels to reduce their costs. This, however, is difficult if a large proportion is sunk costs, as has been the case for some of the most attractive sports rights since the mid 1990s. As mentioned above, the only way of eliminating sunk costs is by reselling the rights or cancelling the contract.

If the buyer is a media platform that owns several channels and these have different penetration, then it will benefit from putting the most popular programmes on the channels with the highest penetration. Such a strategy will minimise the alternative costs (see equation three).

If the competition is tough, the buyers may also have to accept bundles where the popularity of the matches is mixed and uncertain. Many contracts run over several years, and the demand for the specific products can be subject to fluctuations. Some of the most attractive tournaments are even sold before the participants have qualified – or before it is decided where the tournament will take place. As an example, many European channels acquired the 2006 World Cup soccer rights – together with the 2002 tournament before Germany was elected as the host nation. Similar procedures also characterise the trade of other sporting events, e.g. the Olympic Games. The Olympics rights were sold separately until the 1998 Winter Olympics in Nagano, but have been sold in packages since then. The 2000–2008 games were sold before the hosts of the 2006 and 2008 games were selected, and the same applies to the 2010 and 2012 US rights. Such a practice represents a high degree of risk for the purchasing channels. As an example, the commercial value of the US rights will be significantly lower if the games are hosted in Asia or Europe, due to differences in time zones.

An alternative to fixed prices is tying the rights fees to the income that the programmes generate. For pay-TV channels, this can be the number of (new) subscribers, as well as pay-per-view fees. For advertising channels it can be the rating figures. Such procedures will increase the values in case buyers are risk-averse. This particularly applies to tournaments with knockout procedures, and also in cases where the rights are bundled, and/or a long time ahead of the events. Indeed, it has been arranged for some of the Olympic deals, with the fees split in fixed and variable shares (Preuss, 2000; McMillan, 1992). The fixed share has guaranteed IOC a minimum income, while the variable share has been tied to the channel's direct financial surplus from broadcasting the Olympics. However, bear in mind that revenue sharing deals create a *moral hazard* problem, since the seller will not have 100 per cent control over the actions of the buyer afterwards (McAfee and McMillan, 1987). As an example, such deals will reduce the channel's incentives to carry out extra sales efforts, since it will not keep the entire income itself. This can reverse the rights fees.

Furthermore, the television channel will have more precise information on the variables that decide the fees than the seller, such as rating figures during the core programmes and during commercials, the number of subscribers, pay-per-view fees and also lag effects which occur if viewers on sports programmes stay with the channel and continue watching other programmes.

This provides it with a motive to underreport the revenues and exaggerate the costs in order to reduce the proportion of the fee that comes from revenue sharing. See McAfee and McMillan (1987) for a more thorough analysis of these matters.

At the beginning of the twenty-first century, however, there have been signs of a reverse effect on rights fees. One reason for this is the reduction in the number of pay-TV platforms which compete for sports rights. Telepiù and Stream, the Italian channels which have shared the Serie A rights since late in the 1990s merged into Sky Italy in 2003. The same year, a similar development took place in Spain, where three pay-TV channels merged into one, Sogecable.[10] Some months earlier, the UK sports channel, ITV-Digital, was taken off the air and declared bankrupt. Some of the sellers obviously are aware that less competition can shift the market power to the buyers. Therefore the Italian Serie A clubs have taken steps toward establishing their own league channel.[11]

On the other hand, also bear in mind that many media companies involved in broadcasting have invested heavily in new digital technology at the start of the twenty-first century, and that these investments were extremely expensive. (Todreas, 1999) The only way to make them profitable is by offering viewers attractive content. As an example, more than fifty percent of BSkyB's viewers would have cancelled their subscription if the channel had lost its soccer rights, according to their own surveys. In such cases, the alternative to continuing to acquire such rights is probably going out of business – even if this requires expensive bids (Solberg, 2002a).

Collusion vs. Competition

In some markets there have been indications of collusion between channels which were competitors during the late 1990s. In the UK, the BBC and BSkyB have shared international sports rights that were originally acquired by the European Broadcasting Union (EBU). The same pattern applies to other nations where more than one channel is a member of the EBU. In Italy and Germany, informal talks between broadcasters over the rights for UEFA's Champions League have raised the spectre of possible collusion over bids, in order to avoid head-to-head competition for rights packages.[12] The two Norwegian channels, NRK and TV2, competed for sports rights during the 1990s. One example was in 1998, when TV2 submitted a very high bid for skiing rights which they knew NRK also was extremely eager to acquire. TV2's main purpose, however, was not to win the contract, but to force their rival to pay the highest possible price in order to weaken NRK's ability to submit an expensive bid on the next occasion sports rights were up for sale. As TV2 rightfully calculated, NRK outbid TV2, but to do so, they were forced to pay a price which was 400 per cent higher than the value of the former deal.[13] Since then, the situation has changed and the channels have submitted joint bids on several occasions.

Such collusion has reduced competition and hence also rights fees. However, even if some channels benefit from colluding over a certain period, this is no guarantee that the deals will be upheld forever. In order to succeed permanently, the bidders must overcome a *prisoners' dilemma* (Dixit and Skeath, 1999). The problem arises if the unsuccessful bidders value the rights for more than its selling price. This represents an incentive to bid above the agreed collusive price. It will be easier to avoid these problems in open-bid auctions than in sealed bidding, since the other channels will immediately see if any one bid is higher than originally agreed. In sealed bid auctions, the bidders learn of the deviation only after the bidding is finished. Hence any retaliation will come later.

However, if the same channels keep meeting in auctions, this will reduce their motives to break their promise. The entire flora of sports rights consists of many products, and in many markets the channels that compete for the products are more or less the same. In European soccer, there are domestic leagues and cups as well as international tournaments both for clubs and national teams. In addition, other sports also offer the channels (and viewers) a number of products. This mixture of products also characterises the markets in North America and elsewhere. Before digital technology, one single television station did not have the sufficient number of frequencies to broadcast the entire flora of sport products. This is not the case any more since digital technology, which has increased transmission capacity considerably. Hence the market has moved from a situation where frequencies were scarce to a situation where content is scarce (Todreas, 1999). Nevertheless, it is still impossible for one single channel to acquire all the sports rights, but now it is due to the extremely expensive rights fees.

If the channels are unable to collude, this can lead to behaviour which is individually rational, but collectively irrational. Let us imagine an auction where several channels are submitting bids. Each and every one of them wants to be the winner. The result of this common motive is of course that the price increases. However, the channels which lose the bidding competition also want the winning channel to pay so much that it reduces its ability to submit a high bid the next time sports rights are auctioned.

In 1996 The EBU acquired the European rights for the Olympics for the 2000–2008 period at a price of $1.4 billion, which was a massive increase compared to the former deals. The main reason for this increase was that the EBU was challenged (for the first time ever) by Rupert Murdoch's News Corporation, which in fact submitted a bid of $2 billion. The IOC, however, preferred the EBU bid for fear of Murdoch re-selling (at least some of) the games to pay service channels. This would have threatened the long-term relationship between the IOC and its sponsors, which prefer television channels with maximum penetration. Furthermore, IOC also has an objective of upholding the image of universal games, which corresponds to the objectives of non-commercial PSB channels to maintain diversity in their programme schedules. Also bear in mind that the Olympic games encompass a large number of moderately popular sports, as commercial channels tend to give priority to the most attractive sports and competitions (Preuss, 2000). Nevertheless, a fee of $1.4 billion is probably beyond the pain limit for some EBU members, particularly the licence fee based public service broadcasters. In 1998 the EBU were outbid by ISPR in the competition for the 2002 and 2006 World Cup soccer rights, maybe as a consequence of the Olympic auction two years earlier (at least partly).

TWO CASE STUDIES: UEFA CHAMPIONS LEAGUE AND EURO 2000/2004

Many sports have a number of competitions and tournaments, and the popularity of each and every product can vary substantially. Some products are unique to the viewers and thus difficult to copy or substitute without losing many viewers and hence risk a reduction in the advertising revenues, subscription fees or pay-per-view fees (Gaustad, 2000). This particularly applies to international tournaments which in general are based on knock-out procedures – at least partly. As mentioned in the former section, the rights are often sold before the teams have qualified. Hence, the acquisition of such products can be risky if the rights fees are fixed. This has been illustrated on several occasions. As mentioned above, the Italian (RAI) and French (TF1) television channels which broadcast the 2002 World Cup soccer finals suffered severe financial losses due to the unexpected early exit of their national teams. There were even rumours in the press that RAI considered suing FIFA since television pictures revealed that Italy's exit was due to a mistake by the assistant referee. To illustrate the risk related to such deals the final section of this paper presents two case studies.

UEFA's Champions League – The Scandinavian Market

The television channels which have broadcast the matches in UEFA's Champions League rights have experienced that the rating figures – and hence the advertising revenues – is influenced by the performances of local teams. When Italian clubs went through a period without success late in the

1990s, this also hit the Italian broadcasters financially. Similar effects occurred in Germany during the 2001/2002 and 2002/2003 season due to the lack of success for German teams.

The case study presented in this section is based on rating figures from the broadcasting of 116 live soccer matches from UEFA's Champions League on Norwegian television – from February 2000 to May 2003. All matches were broadcast on TV3, which is transmitted via cable and satellite and has a penetration of 62 per cent among Norwegian television households. The rating statistics were measured on several occasions during the programmes. The majority of the programmes started 45 minutes prior to the match, while some started 15 minutes before the match. The programmes in the first category contained seven commercial breaks. The first was screened just after the start of the programme. The following three breaks were screened before the start of the first half – with intervals of 8–10 minutes. Two commercial breaks were screened between the first and second half, while the last one followed immediately after the match. The programmes which started 15 minutes before the match only had the c4–c7 commercial breaks.

The rating statistics were measured by TNS Gallup Norway in a survey of about 1000 Norwegian households, equalling 2400 persons. These households have television boxes in their homes that are used to register their television viewing habits. Each television set is linked to a box that registers whether the television is on, and also to which channel. All members of the television household have their own button which registers whether they are watching or not. The members are recruited from Gallup Norway's annual Consumer and Media survey.[14] Unfortunately, we do not have accurate numbers for the targeted viewers. However, to get some idea of the financial picture we calculated the advertising revenues on the basis of the total number of viewers during the commercials. This method is common among many other television channels (see next case study).

Table 6.2   Rating figures for the broadcasting of Champions League matches on Norwegian television – during commercial breaks and matches

	C1	C2	C3	C4	1st half	C5	C6	2nd half	C7
Rating figures	48'	62'	82'	102'	245'	147'	174'	308'	135'
Duration-average (seconds)	56	241	229	252	45 min.	299	301	45 min.	308
Registrations	24	81	86	116	116	115	115	116	106

As seen from Table 6.2, the commercials drew considerably fewer viewers than the matches. In fact, the first commercial break only attracted viewers representing 18 per cent of the rating figures for the matches. The fourth break, which was screened shortly before the start of the match, attracted 37 per cent of the match audience. It was the break that was screened just before the start of the second half that achieved the highest proportion, in fact 61 per cent. On average, the rating figures during the commercials achieved 45 per cent of the rating during the matches.

The teams which qualify for the Champions League will automatically play six matches in the first group stage. Hence, the difference in income refers to the advertising revenues for an average 'Rosenborg-match' and a match involving other teams. The average length of commercials and sponsoring per match was 23 minutes and 50 seconds during the 2000–2003 period. The calculations in Table 6.3 assumed that each match has 47 commercial breaks of 30 seconds. As seen, the difference between an average 'Rosenborg-match' and a 'non-Rosenborg' match amounts to NOK 1,043,000. The difference for six matches amounts to NOK 6.258 million. Bear in mind that these figures are only based on data from the first round matches. In general the Norwegian (and Scandinavian) teams which have qualified have been eliminated in the first round.

Table 6.3   Average rating figures and advertising revenues for the broadcasting of Champions League matches on Norwegian television

	Matches including a Norwegian team (Rosenborg)	Matches including non-Norwegian teams[15]
Average rating[16]		
during matches	480,000	229,000
during commercials	216,000	98,000
Advertising revenues		
per match	NOK 1,909,000	NOK 866,000
six matches	NOK 11,455,000	NOK 5,197,000

To get a complete financial picture the cost side also has to be taken into account. Modern Times Group paid €42.3 million for the Scandinavian rights for the 2003–2006 period[17] – equivalent to NOK 346 million and an annual fee of NOK 115 million.[18] This amount, however, also includes Sweden and Denmark. Norway has 24 per cent of the total Scandinavian population, and on the basis of this proportion, the Norwegian price is calculated as NOK 27.6 million. Bear in mind that the fees during the 2000–2003 period, which is the period of the rating data, only formed 50 per cent of the value of the deal from 2004 to 2007.

These figures clearly illustrate that domestic teams can be extremely valuable. Since MTG's Scandinavian rights also include Denmark and Sweden, similar calculations can be made for these markets. The difference between a best-case scenario where teams from all the Scandinavian nations qualify – and a worst-case scenario where no teams qualify – could be in the region of NOK 25 million. This assumes that all the three teams only reach the first group stage in the best-case scenario, and that the rating figures and advertising revenues in Sweden and Denmark vary proportionally with the population. As seen from Table 6.4, the number of Scandinavian teams which have made it to the first group stage has varied considerably. Two Norwegian teams and one Swedish team qualified in the 1999/2000 season, while no teams qualified in the 2003/2004 season. For MTG, the financial difference between these two seasons can exceed NOK 20 million.

Table 6.4   Number of Scandinavian teams in Champions League (first group stage)

	Norway	Sweden	Denmark
1992/93	0	1	0
1993/94	0	0	0
1994/95	0	1	0
1995/96	1	0	1
1996/97	1	1	0
1997/98	1	1	0
1998/99	1	0	1
1999/00	2	1	0
2000/01	1	1	0
2001/02	1	0	0
2002/03	1	0	0
2003/04	0	0	0

Euro 2000/2004

The second case study relates to Euro 2000 in Belgium/Netherlands and Euro 2004 in Portugal. Table 6.5 presents the average rating figures for England and non-England matches in the UK, and for Norway and non-Norway matches in Norway for Euro 2000. The table confirms that viewers prefer their own national teams. In the UK, the non-England matches drew 43 per cent of the audience at England's matches. In Norway, the non-Norway matches drew 53 per cent of the audience at Norway's matches. England and

Norway were both eliminated in the first stage of this tournament and only played three matches. The BBC and ITV shared the matches, with two exceptions, when they both broadcast the same match simultaneously (England-Germany and the final between France and Italy). In Norway, the tournament was broadcast on NRK and TV2. NRK achieved an average rating of 1,060,000 viewers during the non-Norway matches while TV2 achieved 619,000. A similar pattern was found in the UK where matches on the BBC achieved higher ratings than those on ITV.

TV2 broadcast 14 minutes and 30 seconds of commercials per match on average during Euro 2000. This accounts for 60 per cent of what TV3 did during the Champions League matches. The difference is due to TV2's obligations as a public service broadcaster. While TV3 can devote the whole evening to sports programmes, TV2 is obliged to broadcast other programmes e.g. news programmes, which limits the number and length of commercials. However, it is worth noting that the commercials on TV2 achieved 66 per cent of the rating figures that the matches achieved, while the equivalent proportion on TV3's Champions League matches was 45 per cent.

Table 6.5   UK and Norwegian television rating figures – Euro 2000 matches[19]

| | UK | | Norway[20] | |
	England matches	*Non-England matches*	*Norway matches*	*Non-Norway matches*
Average viewers per match	15.497 mn	6.65 mn	1.530 mn	0.817 mn
Percent rating	28.3%	12.1%	41.4%	22.1%

TV2's prices for advertising vary with the season of the year, and Euro 2004 will take place in the most popular (and expensive) season. Furthermore, the price also varies with the time of the day. The prime time period is from 18.00 to 23.30, and the price of a slot during this period is 18 per cent more expensive than from 12.00–18.00.

Table 6.6 presents some scenarios of what TV2 can earn from broadcasting Euro 2004, where they will be the only Norwegian broadcaster.[21] TV2 had only one channel during Euro 2000, but this has since changed. However, in the calculations we have assumed that they will broadcast 27 matches, and that all of them will be on their main channel. This means that only one of the two last matches that are played simultaneously (in each of the four groups) in the first round will be broadcast.

The first calculation is based of TV2's own rating figures during Euro 2000, while the second is based on NRK's and TV2's joint average rating figures from the same event. Since Norway only played three matches in Euro 2000, the rating figures for these matches are based on NRK's and TV2's joint figures in both scenarios. Bear in mind that the figures only include the channel's income from selling advertising – not the sponsor revenues. At Euro 2004, there will be eight matches starting at 18.00 Norwegian time – while the others will start at 20.45.[22] Hence, all commercials will be broadcast during the *prime-time period*, except for the commercials prior to the 18.00 matches. Also bear in mind that the last two matches in each of the four groups will be played simultaneously. Based on this, the average ad-slot during the 18.00 hour matches will cost NOK 7,185 if the programme has a rating of 1 per cent.[23] Furthermore, we have not taken into account the fact that advertisers can receive quantity discounts, nor that the most attractive slots can be as much as 30 per cent more expensive than the basic price.

Therefore, the results should be read as indications rather than accurate figures. Nevertheless the figures clearly illustrate the large financial gap between a best and a worst-case scenario. The advertising revenues vary from a NOK 62.4 million low to a NOK 98 million high in the scenarios. As mentioned above, the rights cost NOK 60 million, while the production costs will amount to NOK 7.5 million (since Norway failed to qualify). Hence, TV2 will suffer a loss of NOK 5.1 million if the programmes achieve the same rating figures as in Euro 2000. On the other hand, they will make profit of NOK 14.6 million if the rating figures are identical to those jointly achieved by NRK and TV2 during Euro 2000. The alternatives are not of current interest since Norway failed to qualify, but this was not the case at the point of time when TV2 acquired the rights. TV2 could have made a profit of NOK 29 million if Norway had qualified and reached the final, assuming the rating figures were identical with NRK's and TV2's joint figures from Euro 2000. These alternative figures illustrate the large uncertainty related to investing in international sports rights.

Table 6.6   Euro 2004 – advertising revenues – some scenarios

	Norway not qualified	*Norway eliminated at group stage*	*Norway reaches the final*
Scenario 1: TV2's own rating figures at Euro 2000	62.4 mn	72.5 mn	82.7 mn
Scenario 2: TV2's and NRK's joint rating at Euro 2000	82.1 mn	90.0 mn	98.0 mn

CONCLUSION

This chapter has analysed factors that influence the profitability of acquiring sports rights. The high degree of sunk cost which characterises the broadcasting of the most attractive programmes has made several acquisitions unprofitable. This particularly applies to international tournaments where the rating figures in the respective nations are heavily influenced by the performance of national teams. Hence, acquiring such rights can be extremely risky. When national teams are eliminated, the rating figures are reduced – and hence also the value of advertising slots. The worst scenario is when national teams do not qualify.

The examples of unprofitable sports rights deals presented in the introduction contained several such examples. This extra risk does not apply to domestic leagues which do not have any elimination process. Thus, if (too) many channels suffer (too) heavy losses from the broadcasting of international competitions, this can reduce their willingness to bid for such rights. One consequence of this is that commercial channels can prioritise domestic leagues – and bid less for international competitions – as a way of reducing the risk. Certainly, this can make international tournaments cheaper.

An alternative is that the sellers agree to tie the rights fees to the income the channels receive from broadcasting the programmes. For advertising channels, this can be the rating figures, while for pay-TV channels it can be the subscription fees and/or pay-per-view fees. Such clauses will share the risk between buyers and sellers. Another advantage is that it can prevent soccer clubs from being hit by unforeseen financial problems.

There are several examples of channels being unable to pay the price they have agreed, a phenomenon that has also applied to the acquisition of domestic rights. This can cause severe problems if the clubs have entered into contracts with players and other actors, believing that income from the television deals would be stable and high. Indeed, this has been illustrated recently in Germany and England, where many clubs are in deep financial trouble due to the bankruptcies of Kirch Media and ITV-Digital.

Indirect Impacts

However, the acquisition of sports rights also generates indirect revenues, for example by increasing the number of subscribers. This will increase the overall number of viewers and hence general advertising revenues. In North America the broadcasting networks need attractive programmes to uphold their cobweb of affiliates which is important for their overall penetration rate (Solberg, 2002a). Fox's acquisition of the broadcasting rights for the National

Football League (NFL) in 1994 represents one such example. It was this acquisition that established Fox as a national broadcasting network.

Some cable operators organise referendums where the viewers vote which channels should be included in the standard package. By putting attractive programmes on less popular channels sport enthusiasts are given a motive for voting on these channels and hence ensuring that they are included in more cable packages.

If attractive sports programmes increase a channel's subscription base, this may represent an advantage the next time sports rights are auctioned. The sellers will prefer the channels with the highest penetration – other things being equal – in order to maximise the exposure of the sport and the event. This may stimulate the sports' recruitment, and in addition sponsors also want maximum exposure of themselves and their products. Hence, some channels may be willing to suffer losses in the medium term, hoping that such a strategy will pay off in the long term, e.g. in the form of lower fees than the channel otherwise would have to pay.

Moreover, it is common knowledge that a proportion of viewers tend to 'stay with the channel' and will continue watching the next programme(s). Such lag effects increase the overall rating figures and thereby the advertising revenues.

Some bundles include events that are hosted at different times in different places, for example the Olympics and World Cup soccer finals. Such events move from one continent to another. Hence the commercial values for the broadcasting channels can vary considerably due to different time zones. A television channel can be willing to take a loss on some events hoping that this will be outweighed by the other event(s). Hence, the profitability of sports rights deals cannot be judged entirely on the basis of their direct revenues and costs.

NOTES

1. http://www.gouldmedia.com/tsr.html.
2. In addition to the sources presented in the table, the remaining information is from various editions of Soccer Investor.
3. http://media.guardian.co.uk/worldcup/story/0,11974,741487,00.html.
4. http://www.telenor.com/ir/quarterly_reports/2q02/pdf_xls/2_kvartal_2002eng_godkj.pdf.
5. Bjørn Taalesen, sport director, TV2.
6. UEFA.
7. Grethe Johnsen, Sports director, Norwegian Broadcasting Corporation (NRK).
8. http://news.bbc.co.uk/sport1/hi/football/world_cup_2002/1606424.stm and http://www.wldcup.com/business/news/2001Oct/20011018_10943_html.
9. *TV Sports Markets* (2003), Vol. 7, no. 7.
10. *TV Sports Markets* (2003), Vol. 7, no. 7.
11. *TV Sports Markets* (2003), Vol. 7, no. 14.

12. *TV Sports Markets* (2003), Vol. 7, no. 7.
13. Interview with TV2's sport director, Bjørn Taalesen in Dagens Næringsliv (a Norwegian business newspaper) 31 October, 2000.
14. http://www.tns-allup.no/index.asp?tid=12003&aid=12085&active_color=#319cff&active title=&activelabel=Forbruker per cent20& per cent20Media.
15. Only including prime-time (20.45–22.45).
16. Mediacom AS. The prime time matches started 20.45 in the evening.
17. *TV Sports Markets* (2003), Vol. 7, no 1.
18. Based on exchange rate 1 August 2003: €1 = NOK8.18.
19. Barb.uk, TV Sports Market, The Norwegian Broadcasting Corporation and TV2, Norway.
20. The advertising revenue is calculated on basis of information from TV2's marketing department and Mediacom AS.
21. Based on figures in Table 6.10 and information from Birgit Eie, senior market researcher, TV2.
22. http://www.euro2004.com/Competitions/EURO/euro2004sa/Ticketing/matchlist.html.
23. http://www.tv2.no - 2003 prices.

REFERENCES

BCC – Baskerville Communications Corporation (1997), *Global TV-sports rights*, London.
Desbordes, M. (2003), 'The relationship between sport and television: the case of the French network TF1 and the World Cup 2002', Paper presented at the 5th IACE-conference, May, Neuchâtel.
Dixit, A. and S. Skeath (1999), *Games of Strategy*, New York, NY: W.W. Norton & Company.
Fort, R. (2003), *Sport economics*, Upper Saddle River, NJ: Prentice Hall.
Gaustad, T. (2000), 'The Economics of Sports Programming', *Nordicom Review*, 21, 101–113.
Hauger, K.H., Kampanje no. (Interview 2003).
Johnsen, H.W. (2001), *A Cost Perspective on Televised Sport. The Optimal Economic Utilisation of Sport's Media Rights*, Discussion Paper 02, Norwegian School of Management, Sandvika.
McMillan, J. (1992), *Games, Strategies and Managers*, New York, NY: Oxford University Press.
McAfee, R.P. and J. McMillan (1987), 'Auctions and Bidding', *Journal of Economic Literature*, **XXV**, 699–738.
Preuss, H. (2000), *Economics of the Olympic Games. Hosting the Games 1972–2000*, Sydney: Walla Wall Press in conjunction with the Centre for Olympic Studies, The University of New South Wales.
Quirk, J. and R. Fort (1999), *Hard ball. The Abuse of Power in Pro Team Sports*, Princeton, NJ: Princeton University Press.
Solberg, H.A. (2002a), 'The Economics of Television Sports Rights. Europe and the US – A Comparative Analysis', *Norsk Medietidskrift*, **9** (2), 57–80.

Solberg, H.A. (2002b), 'Cultural Prescription - The European Commission's Listed Events Regulation – Over Reaction?', *Culture, Sport, Society*, **5** (2), 1–28.

Solberg, H.A. and C. Gratton (2000), 'The Economics of TV-sports Rights – with Special Attention on European soccer', *European Journal for Sport Management*, **7** (special issue), 68–98.

Statistical Yearbook (2000), European Audiovisual Observatory.

Todreas, T.M. (1999), *Value Creation and Branding in Television's Digital Age*, Westport, CT: Quorum Books.

TV Sports Markets (2003), **7** (15).

7. The Relationship between Sport and Television: The Case of TF1 and the 2002 Football World Cup

Michel Desbordes

INTRODUCTION

The cost of showing sport on television increased sharply during the 1990s as a result of the higher costs of acquiring broadcasting rights. It currently represents between 6–10 per cent of television schedule costs (CSA 1991, 1997), although the figure is smaller when costs are looked at in terms of air time. Sport is thus an expensive part of broadcasters' strategic arsenals.

At the same time audiences have tended to fall for major events like the 2002 Champions League and Formula One events.

When the cost of acquiring broadcasting rights is added to the high production costs of televising sports events, then, in terms of management control, sport is not necessarily a financially astute choice.

This chapter is divided into two parts. First, we look at the broad direction taken by sports-related television rights in Europe. During the 1990s, there was a sharp upward trend in terms of the amounts paid for these rights (as can be seen in Tables 7.1 and 7.2 and Figure 7.1). This raises the question of whether this is a well-established trend. Is there something inevitable about the patterns observed or will things come to a halt because of the damage that televising sport can have on profitability?

The issue of just how profitable television sporting rights are for a television company forms the second part of the study. It uses a case study for the TF1 Group, which owns France's main free-to-air commercial television channel (and which is Europe's top channel in terms of turnover, audience and advertising revenue). TF1 paid 168 million euros for the French television rights to the 2002 World Cup. However, as we shall see, there were a number of areas where the French team's early exit from the competition had an unfavourable financial impact.

The case study enables us to consider how, without some form of centralised control over the way rights are sold, the high sums being paid make it difficult, or even impossible, to make a profit from the way the current European system works. It is this sort of thinking which ought to be contributing to the debate on the regulation of sport in Europe over the coming years.

TRENDS IN THE VALUE OF BROADCASTING RIGHTS

Until the 1990s, the amounts paid for television rights were comparatively low in Europe, with the balance being in favour of broadcasters (as buyers) rather than rights sellers.[1] However, during the 1990s, the way the market evolved caused the old order to change and resulted in major increases in the amounts paid (as can be seen below in Table 7.1, which shows the upward course in amounts paid for television rights and Table 7.3, which tracks changes in market structure).

Table 7.1   Growth in European television sporting rights values (in millions of US$)

	Amounts paid for television sporting rights				Increase between 1992 and 2002
	1992	*1996*	*1999*	*2002*	
Germany	319	589	931	1 377	+ 332 %
United Kingdom	350	564	873	1 262	+ 261 %
Italy	233	383	593	777	+ 233 %
France	245	379	476	615	+ 151 %
Spain	109	185	288	366	+ 236 %
Europe[2]	1 479	2 463	3 654	5 009	+ 239 %

Source: Kagan World Media, 1999.

Table 7.1 shows that over a ten-year period the price of television sporting rights more than doubled in France and increased fourfold in Germany. For Europe as a whole the average increase was 239 per cent. All the figures shown in the table were well above growth and inflation rates over the same period. Leaving aside the case of rising internet stock values on financial markets, no industrial sector recorded the sort of increases seen here. This leads to the question of whether such increases were 'normal' (in the sense of price mechanisms working in the way one would expect when a product like 'sport' is undervalued). Or was it rather a reflection of the economic circumstances of the time, where increases were fuelled by short term pre-emptive speculative behaviour in terms of acquiring these rights?

The increase in the amounts paid by television broadcasters for these rights was particularly significant for football, and it was equally applicable to the World Cup rights marketed by FIFA (Table 7.2) and the rights to show national league matches. Increases were particularly spectacular for the World Cup: from US$150m to US$350m between the 1994 and 1998 tournaments and from US$350m to US$1090m between the 1998 and 2002 tournaments.

Table 7.2   Football World Cup television rights (millions of US$ at current prices)

Year	Country	TV Rights (US$ Total)
1978	Argentina	34
1982	Spain	55
1986	Mexico	70
1990	Italy	135
1994	United States	150
1998	France	350
2002	South Korea/Japan	1,090
2006	Germany	1,330

Source: FIFA website, 2002.

Figure 7.1 highlights the fact that the increases in acquisition rights for the various national leagues were not evenly spread. In all, the biggest differences were in countries where several broadcasters had made football part of their strategic arsenals, drawing them into a bidding process that was probably more intense than anticipated (as in France and, to a lesser extent, Germany).

At the same time the major costs entailed in broadcasting these events (cameras, technical equipment, human resources etc.) have to be added to the cost of acquiring the rights to show the matches. Thus broadcasters are faced with a dilemma. While showing sporting events puts them in a positive light, it risks having negative financial effects when the package is looked at from a cost accounting perspective. In terms of costs of production per hour relative to expected audience size, variety shows, films and made-for-TV films are often much more profitable and inherently less risky than sports events (containing as they do unknown quantities in terms of the national side's results and the quality of the games).

Figure 7.1   The increase in the value of television football rights 1991–2001

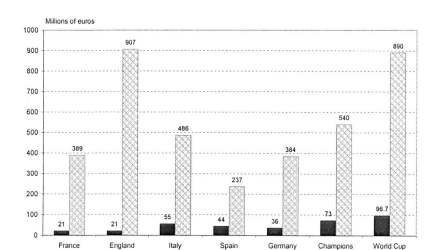

As neo-classical microeconomic theory shows, price levels are determined by market structure. Other things being equal (and in the absence of collusion or cartels) competition on the supply side will cause prices to fall. In the market for sport, the number of television channels increased during the 1990s while there was hardly any increase in the number of events available on the market. There was thus an imbalance between supply and demand during this period, causing prices to rise through the demand for sports programmes exceeding the supply available.

In 1995 FIFA went for the safe option by selling rights for the 2002 World Cup to the German media group Kirchmedia (with a cash advance of US$890 million). Kirchmedia then sold on the rights by 'parcelling them out'[3] to different countries, thus making major profits. In a two-stage process, public service broadcasters refused to pay the record amounts being asked by Kirchmedia, which were three times higher than the rights for the 1998 World Cup. For each country, Kirchmedia set prices according to the expected audience size, with prices being highest for the so-called 'Big 5' countries (the United Kingdom, Germany, France, Italy and Spain). The aim was to attract the maximum number of broadcasters so that demand would exceed supply, an approach which paid off. At some point in the process, the refusal of some public service broadcasters to accept the price that Kirchmedia was asking would have provoked fears that the World Cup matches would not be shown in a number of European countries. Subsequently, there was strong political pressure on a number of broadcasters to acquire the rights.[4] So Spain paid 198 million euros, Germany 126 million, South Korea 68 million, the UK 255 million, Italy 154 million and France 168 million.

Table 7.3   Market structure and the value of television rights

Market Structure	Event	Supplier	Bidders	TV Rights (Value)
Absolute Monopoly	2000 Winter Olympics (United States)	IOC	ABC, CBS, NBC, FOX, ESPN, Newsport, HBO, TBS, Direct TV, Showtime	$715m (NBC)
	2002 Football World Cup (World, excluding the United States)	FIFA	ABC, Cable TV, UER, Team, Kirch, IMG, UFA, CWL	$890m (Kirch)
Weak Monopoly	1997/1998 French Football Season (France)	LNF (French National Football League)	France Télévisions, TF1, Canal Plus, Canal Satellite, TPS	1300m French Francs (TF1/C+)
	1997 Formula One Grand Prix (France)	FOCA	TF1/TPS, France Télévisions, Canal Plus/Canal Satellite	250m French Francs (TF1/Canal Satellite)
Bilateral Monopoly	1992 Summer Olympics (Europe)	IOC	UER	$90m
	1983/1984 football season (France)	LNF	Cartel made up of public service broadcasters (TF1, A2 et FR3)	5m French Francs
Monopsony	1973/1974 football season (France)	League Sides	ORTF (the then French State Broadcaster)	0.5m French Francs

Source: Bourg and Gouguet, 1998, p. 228.

Paradoxically, European broadcasters did not act rationally by paying a higher price compared with the 1998 competition, since matches were going to be shown in the morning when audiences are usually at their lowest levels. It was a particularly risky bet given that it hinged on how well their national side performed.

Having looked at the figures for television rights, we can now turn to a case which illustrates the serious financial impact on a channel when the national side did badly. The case in question is that of TF1, which bought exclusive rights to cover the French team's World Cup progress. It also serves as a means for looking at the wider issues over the way the relationship between sport and television has evolved.

TF1 AND THE 2002 WORLD CUP: A CASE STUDY

TF1 – An Overview

TF1 was privatised in 1987 and is now France's main commercial free-to-view television channel, it is also Europe's largest channel. In 2002 it accounted for 95 of the top 100 viewing figures in France and has an average audience share of 33 per cent. In terms of advertising income, 2002 was a year of two contrasting halves:

- Revenue fell by 2 per cent in the first six months;
- It increased by 4.1 per cent in the second part of the year;
- The overall increase in 2002 was 0.7 per cent.

In 2003, turnover increased by 4 per cent and advertising income rose by 2 per cent.

Table 7.4 The TF1 Group

Established	1975		
Employees	2902		
Year	*2000*	*2001*	*2002*
Group turnover (millions of euros)	2220.3	2282 (+2.8%)	2624 (+ 15%)
Advertising revenue (millions of euros)	1571	1497 (-4.7%)	1507 (+0.7%)
Other interests and miscellaneous revenue (millions of euros)	649.3	785 (+20.9%)	1117 (+42.3%)

Source: www.bweeg.com.

While the fall in revenues in 2001 was the direct result of a post-September 11 crisis in advertising, and was something that was felt across the developed world, the fall in revenue in 2002 contrasted with an increase in 2003. The aim here is to see what would have happened in 2002 without the impact of the 2002 World Cup.

TF1 and the 2002 World Cup

As noted earlier, TF1 paid 168 million euros in November 2001 for the television rights to the 2002 World Cup and the 24 'top' matches of the 2006 tournament. This was the first time in France that a single channel had a monopoly over such an important event.[5] As an investment, the amount TF1 paid reflected both its monopoly and the French team's status as favourites to win the cup for the second time. But the high cost of showing the matches and the time difference between Europe and Asia did not point to hoped-for profits being high (Table 7.5).

Table 7.5   TF1's expected results from the 2002 World Cup

Cost of television Rights	60 million euros[6]
Broadcasting costs (technical equipment)	5 million euros (actual figure 8.7 million euros)
Expected financial results	Between -11 and -17 million euros (if France reached the final).
	Actual figures: between -20 and -30 million euros (according to various contradictory sources).

Sources: Les Echos, Le Figaro, Le Monde, La Lettre du Sport, Sport Finance and Marketing, L'Equipe, La Lettre du Football (compilation dans la revue de presse du CDES, années 2002 et 2003).

It may seem surprising that TF1 did not expect to make a profit from the 2002 World Cup, even if France had made it to the final. Some analysts had even floated the idea that there would have been a negative return on the investment even if France had retained the World Cup. However, this reasoning overlooks three points:

1. TF1 had also bought rights to the 2006 competition as part of the package, so profitability has to be assessed over 4 years. With no time difference, European audience levels are markedly higher, as are the advertising revenues based on audience figures
2. All merchandising products (such as DVDs)[7] have to be included.

3.   An improved image within the media and among footballing bodies from being the 'World Cup Channel'.

The Outcome of the 2002 World Cup on TF1 – or the Effect of France's 'Shock Exit'

The first matter of interest is how French audience sizes differed between the 2002 and 1998 World Cup competitions (Tables 7.6 and 7.7). When the time difference is taken into account (which meant that matches were shown in France between 8.30 in the morning and 3.15 in the afternoon) TF1 can be pleased with the audiences the matches generated. However, there is no escaping the fact that they were below those for 1998, when France was both the host nation and the winning team. Audiences were also small (in view of its daily time slot of 1845 to 2000) for the World Cup chat show *Tous Ensemble*[8] (2.9 million viewers for a daily market share of 22 per cent).

Table 7.6   1998 viewing figures for matches involving the French team

Match	Kick-Off	Average Audience	Market Share[9]	Viewing Figures
France / South Africa	9.02 pm	32.2%	68.9%	16,859,920
France / Saudi Arabia	9.00 pm	31.0%	69.1%	16,231,600
France / Denmark	4.00 pm	14.7%	77.8%	7,696,920
France / Paraguay	4.30 pm	24.1%	80.6%	12,613,610
France / Italy	4.30 pm	28.0%	87.7%	14,680,150
France / Croatia	9.00 pm	41.9%	81.7%	21,938,840
France / Brazil	9.00 pm	45.3%	86.2%	23,692,900

Source: Carat Sport, 2002.

As can be seen in Table 7.6, 16 million viewers watched France's first round matches (shown at 9pm), while the final attracted over 23 million viewers. This record was broken when the Euro 2000 France versus Italy final attracted 24.8 million viewers (in other words a market share of 90.2 per cent). For the 2002 World cup, the figures in Table 7.7 show that televised matches attracted between 4 and 16 million viewers.

From Table 7.7 it can be seen that matches involving France attracted 10 million viewers on average. While markedly lower than the levels achieved during the 1998 competition, TF1 can be pleased with the audience figures when allowance is made for time differences (with market shares ranging from 78 per cent to 90 per cent for the three first round matches). For the rest of the competition, matches attracted between 2–6 million viewers, while the final drew an audience of 12 million.

Table 7.7   Selected French viewing figures – Data for the 2002 World Cup

Match	Kick-Off	Average Audience	Market Share	Viewing Figures
France / Senegal	1.32 pm	19.7%	78.7%	10,441,000
France / Uruguay	1.31 pm	20.7%	77.5%	10,971,000
France / Denmark	8.30 am	17.9%	90.9%	9,487,000
Germany / United States	1.30 pm	10.9%	55.1%	5,777,000
England / Brazil	8.30 am	7.9%	75.9%	4,187,000
Senegal / Turkey	1.30 pm	17.6%	67.9%	9,328,000
Spain / South Korea	8.30 am	9.4%	75.5%	4,982,000
Germany / South Korea (Semi-Final)	1.30 pm	13.3%	62.1%	7,049,000
Brazil / Turkey (Semi-Final)	1.30 pm	14.4%	65.4%	7,632,000
South Korea / Turkey	12.59 pm	12.8%	55.6%	6,784,000
Germany / Brazil (Final)	1.01 pm	23.7%	77.7%	12,561,000
8.30pm Kick-Offs (Average)			*59.0%*	*2,700,000*
11.00am Kick-Offs (Average)			*48.0%*	*3,800,000*
1.30pm Kick-Offs (Average)			*53.0%*	*5,800,000*

Source: Carat Sport, 2002.

However, the *désastre français* (or France's 'nightmare performance', when the defending champions were eliminated in the first round without scoring a single goal) impacted on TF1's advertising revenue, even if its effect was not particularly significant in terms of audience figures for the first round.

Table 7.8   Cost of advertising lots for 2002 World Cup matches

Cost of 30-second advertising slot on TF1	
1st round (France playing)	60,000 euros
1st round (France not playing)	6,000 euros
1/4 Final (France not playing)	60,000 euros
1/4 Final (France not playing)	18,000 euros
Final (France not playing)	*222,000 euros*
Finale (France not playing)	*100,000 euros*

Sources: *Les Echos, Le Figaro, Le Monde, La Lettre du Sport, Sport Finance and Marketing, L'Equipe, La Lettre du Football* (compilation dans la revue de presse du CDES, années 2002 et 2003).

In the end, and given both earlier observations and the French team's poor showing, the World Cup resulted in a loss of 20 to 30 million euros.

According to TF1's President, Patrick Le Lay, the (net) cost 'only' came to 18 million euros: 60 million euros for the television rights (plus another 8 million euros for production costs) on the cost side while the advertising revenue generated by the competition came to 50 million euros (*Le Monde*, 30 September 2002).

Figure 7.2 *TF1's share price movements (euros) on the Paris stock market on 6 June(day of the goalless draw between France and Uruguay).*

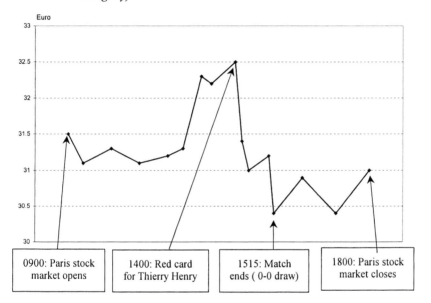

Euro

| 0900: Paris stock market opens | 1400: Red card for Thierry Henry | 1515: Match ends (0-0 draw) | 1800: Paris stock market closes |

Sources: Les Echos, Le Figaro, Le Monde, La Lettre du Sport, Sport Finance & Marketing, L'Equipe, La Lettre du Football (compilation dans la revue de presse du CDES, années 2002 et 2003).

As Figure 7.2 shows, share price movements were extremely volatile and, given the context, highly dependent on the French team's match result (for reasons mentioned earlier such as the investment represented by buying television rights at a high price, the risk of lower advertising revenues and expectations of negative year-end financial results).

The patterns observed during the France–Uruguay match were in line with TF1's share price movements during the first match, where share values fell 3 per cent when Senegal scored the opening goal against France (and went on to win the match 1-0).

If a broadcaster's share price reacts in this manner for a single match, what were the movements over the course of the entire competition? Table 7.9 sheds some light on this.

Table 7.9   TF1's share price movements (31 May–30 June)

	CAC 40[10]	TF1 β^{11}	Theoretical Movement (TF1)[12]	Actual Change	'Unexplained' Change
Change in the CAC 40 index two hours after the end of the France-Uruguay match (0-0, 6 June)	-1.30%	1.16	-1.51%	-4.40%	-2.89%
Change after the France-Senegal match (0-1, 31 May)	0	1.16	0	-2.54%	-2.54%
Change after the France-Denmark match(0-2, 10 June)	The final result did not change financial analysts' expectations, as they had already factored in France's elimination from the competition.				

Source: *La Tribune*, 28 June 2002.

From Table 7.9 we can see that TF1's share price reaction was 'exaggerated' given what would have been expected in theory from the value of its β coefficient. This demonstrates that there was a strong link between the competition and the broadcaster, with shareholders anticipating adverse financial repercussions from the team's poor showing. This might lead one to believe that an equally strong link would exist between the competition and its sponsor. However, a much more tenuous link is evident from Table 7.10 below.

Danone is France's biggest food processing group, and the French team's sponsor; it has also individually sponsored two of the members of the side (Zidane and Lizarazu) since 1998. However its share price does not seem to have been affected by the team's poor showing (Table 7.10 indicates that the share price recorded gains after the two matches in question). Similar conclusions can be drawn for other companies involved in football sponsorship such as Orange (France's No one mobile phone company and sponsor of the French league) or Carrefour (Europe's biggest supermarket group and one of the top 4 sponsors of the French team since 1998).

Table 7.10   Danone's share price movement (31 May–30 June)

	CAC 40	β	Theoretical Movement (Danone)	Actual Change	'Unexplained' Change
Change in the CAC 40 index two hours after the end of the France-Uruguay match (0-0, 6 June	-1.30%	0.4	-0.53%	0%	+0.53%
Change after the France-Senegal match (0-1, 31 May)	0	0.4	0	+0.2%	+0.2%

Source: *La Tribune*, 28 June 2002.

By way of an initial summing up, the national team's poor showing in the World Cup had three main effects on TF1 (as the company with the sole rights to show the matches). First there was the fall in audience size (only the final attracted more viewers than matches involving the French side). This caused advertising revenue to fall (down 50 per cent when the national side was not involved in a match) and led to the competition having a negative impact given that the performance over the first half of 2002 was less impressive than that for the second half. While it is hard to isolate the effect of the World Cup on figures for the first half of the year, it is likely to have played a role in the poor performance that was recorded. Finally the share price suffered, with falls on the Paris stock market reflecting a fall in confidence accompanied by expectations of a negative impact on TF1's finances. However, the investment this represented for TF1 is spread over 4 years, and covers two World Cups, so these findings must be regarded as provisional. It is worth noting that, for the 2006 competition, there will be no time difference; and it is also hard to imagine the national team's performance being any worse. Consequently, we will need to look beyond 2002 to form an overall assessment of the value of TF1's investment.

In Table 7.11 it can be seen that audiences were much higher in the countries whose teams did well. At an international level, the emergence of several new countries as forces to be reckoned with in football (like South Korea, Turkey or Senegal) also had a positive impact on televised matches. The quote from Soccer Investor below shows that most broadcasters can be satisfied with international audiences generally. But it does not necessarily follow that investment outlays showed a profit given the unprecedented high costs of acquiring the television rights. Kirchmedia gained from being the sole television rights seller for the 2002 World Cup. As the French case study showed, there was scope for debate over the way audience figures were interpreted but, at first sight, only the Brazilian channel, television Globo, made a significant profit from the competition.[13]

Table 7.11   2002 World cup television audiences

World	Average audience per match = 600 million viewers 1.5 billion for the final Cumulative audience figure for the 64 matches = 40 billion viewers
Average audience for the national side's first match	England: 23 per cent Sweden: 24.5 per cent Germany: 17.6 per cent France: 19.7 per cent Italy: 32 per cent
Italy	Audiences were higher than expected, despite the Italian team's early exit from the competition. However, like France, the cost of the television rights (80 million euros) was so high that RAI would not have broken even if 'Squadra Azzura', as the Italian national side was known, had won the cup.
Brazil	TV Globo acquired the television rights for 130 million euros. The investment this represented made an overall profit thanks to the 'historically high' audience levels achieved when the national side was playing (with a market share of between 91 and 96 per cent).
Japan	Average audience = 20 per cent. 66.8 per cent of the population watched Japan's victory over Russia, thus beating the record set during the 1964 Olympics for a volley ball match.

Source: *Soccer Investor Daily*, London, UK.

A Sports Market Surveys report on the 2002 World Cup, carried out on behalf of Kirchmedia, showed that there was a 38 per cent increase in television coverage compared with 1998, with matches being shown in 213 countries. Despite the time differences between Asia and Europe and Asia and South America, overall audience figures increased for the whole competition. Excluding China (which was covered in the study for the first time in 2002) audience figures rose by 4 per cent (an increase of 431.7 million viewers). The competition's 20 most watched matches had an average market share of 84.8 per cent. TV Globo recorded the biggest market share (94.2 per cent) when it showed the Brazil–England semi-final match (46 million viewers and an audience share of 30.2 per cent) even though the match was played at 3.30am local time. Over the course of the tournament a new record was set of 49.2 billion television hours watched and, for the first time, matches shown in public places like bars were included (2.5 billion hours).

In the third part of the chapter, we move on from looking at World Cup audiences in various countries to a more general discussion of the relationship between television channels and sport by focusing on the path followed by television rights payments in Europe.

TRENDS AND PATTERNS FOR TELEVISION RIGHTS IN EUROPE

In 2002 many sports marketing agencies and sports economists believed that the amounts paid for certain television rights had peaked. While television rights rose sharply in the 1990s (as seen in Table 7.1), the reality in demand and supply terms (falling audiences for some sporting events on the demand side and less competition because of fewer broadcasters on the supply side) pointed towards a fall in the cost of acquiring such rights. However, such a perspective fails to take account of likely changes in the way sport is structured in Europe.

General Situation Regarding Decreasing Television Rights Values in Europe

In the period covered here, several European broadcasters went into liquidation or experienced severe financial problems. As television rights are a major source of income for football clubs (see Table 7.12) this had implications for contracts signed in 2002 and 2003.

Table 7.12   Income sources for the main European football leagues

	TV Rights	*Marketing Rights*	*Ticket Sales*
France	56 %	28 %	16 %
Germany	29 %	44 %	27 %
Italy	56 %	25 %	19 %
Spain	51 %	25 %	24 %

Sources: Kirchmedia and Deloitte & Touche, 1999/2000, annual report.

Box 7.1   The case of the English football league

On 27 March 2002, British digital terrestrial pay-TV broadcaster ITV Digital experienced major financial problems and went into administration. ITV Digital spokesman Andrew Marre said that: 'Service to customers will continue and suppliers will continue to be paid'. The Football League, which was owed £178 million by ITV Digital as part of a three-year £315 million deal which began with the 2001–2002 season, saw its main source of income thrown into jeopardy.[14]

On 17 April 2002, the administrators of ITV Digital offered the Football League £62 million for the remaining two years of the television contract (instead of the original payment of £178 million). They also offered an additional £12 million in return for another year's rights, an offer that the Football League dismissed as derisory.

In July 2002, the Football League announced it has signed a new television deal for the next four seasons with satellite broadcaster BSkyB. The £95 million deal replaces the one that the Football League had with ITV Digital (which fell through after the first of the projected three years). The new deal with BSkyB is slightly cheaper per annum than the one signed for five years from 1996–2001; although £24 million is considerably short of the £89 million under the previous deal. While providing a breathing space for some clubs, it is much less than English football had expected.

Source: *Soccer Investor Daily*, 2002.

The circumstances surrounding the case involving the English football league (Box 7.1) highlight a dilemma. Should a contract for the largest amount possible be signed with a broadcaster if that contract threatens the broadcaster's financial viability and increases the risk of not being paid?

When signing a contract, other factors come into play when selecting a broadcaster, in particular the prominence that will be given to the event covered by the contract. In the 1990s, a cable channel was selected to show the Wimbledon tennis championships. However, the tournament returned to the terrestrial network (with the television rights reduced in value) because the smaller number of viewers it attracted was seen as damaging for the event's longer term prospects. Similarly, in February 2005, the French Rugby Federation opted to keep *France Télévisions* (France's public service channels) as the broadcaster for the six Nations Championship. The 5-year deal was for an amount smaller than that offered by TF1 and, as in the case of Wimbledon, was based on ensuring greater exposure for the matches.

Box 7.2 The case of the German football league

In July 2002, KirchMedia GmbH, the Kirch Group's (G.KCH) media unit that had filed for insolvency in June 2002, paid 580 million euros for the free-television, pay-TV and multimedia rights for the 2002–2003 and 2003-2004 Bundesliga seasons. It has also acquired an option to buy the 2004–2005 rights for 295 million euros plus the 2005–2006 rights for 300 million euros. The two-year deal is worth around 20 per cent less than the original 1.5 billion euros, four-year deal concluded between KirchMedia and the German League (DFL). This had to be renegotiated after just one season following KirchMedia's failure to pay the 80 million euros instalment that was due in May (ahead of its going into insolvency). KirchMedia saw off a rival bid from the Swiss rights trader AIM International, a subsidiary of the Swiss-based marketing company AIM. It is believed that AIM offered more for the rights, but that the DFL considered that AIM did not have the necessary means in place for selling on the rights to broadcasters in time for the new season (which is due to start less than six weeks after signing of the deal).

Source: *Soccer Investor Daily*, 2002.

The circumstances of the German case are fairly similar to those surrounding the English football television rights deal (see Box 7.1). KirchMedia's insolvency forced the German league into an emergency renegotiation of the deal. In such circumstances either another broadcaster can be sought (as happened in the English case) or the value of the contract can be reduced in order for it to be honoured. In both cases, the 'forced' renegotiation brought about by a broadcaster going into liquidation tips the balance (in terms of market power) in favour of those bidding for the rights, as rights suppliers need to find a solution as a matter of urgency.

Box 7.3 The case of the Italian football league

In July 2002, the new Italian League (Lega Calcio) president Adriano Galliani said that the League would refuse to agree to the demands of Italian state broadcaster RAI for smaller rights payments for the Serie A 2002–2003 season. Galliani said that RAI was offering 40–50 per cent less than the 89 million euros paid for the rights in the previous year.

Ten days later, Italian pay-TV operators Telepiù and Stream made offers to the eight Serie A clubs currently without television contracts for 2002–2003 season, but they were considerably under their asking price. The eight clubs, Atalanta, Brescia, Chievo, Como, Empoli, Modena, Perugia and Piacenza (who were collectively known under the 'Plus Media Trading Consortium') were asking for 10 million euros each for the season. Telepiù had offered 4 million euros while Stream had offered 4.5 million euros.

In August, RAI said it was no longer interested in the Coppa Italia and would not pay more than 45 million euros for the goal highlights used on the popular programme '90 Minutes' (the previous deal was for 88.8 million euros for the Cup and the Championship in 2001–2002). Finally, after intense negotiations, RAI paid 62 million euros for a three-year deal.

(to be continued)

On 20 August, Italian clubs voted to delay the start of the Serie A and Serie B season by two weeks because of the ongoing dispute over broadcasting rights. A report in the Italian newspaper *Corriere della Sera* claimed that the eight clubs, known as 'Plus Media Trading' (PMT) might set up a joint television rights company and float it on the stock market. Franco Sensi, AS Roma's President, led the negotiation for the eight clubs and finally obtained 60 million euros (7.5 million euros for each club) and the championship started on 14 September instead of 1 September.

Source: *Soccer Investor Daily*, 2002.

The Italian case highlights how the form of rights ownership (individual or collective) can influence a football league's financial balance. Television rights for the top eight clubs were negotiated individually, but the bottom eight clubs looked like having no television income for the 2002–2003 season. By acting as a cartel, their association shifted the balance within the market (without, however, getting back to the levels attained by earlier contracts).

The cases cited above indicate that in three of the 'Big 5'[15] countries the surge in the price of television rights seen in the 1990s had perhaps lost its momentum. During the course of renegotiations, broadcasters sought to bring the value of these rights down to a level more in line with market realities (in terms of potential audience and expected advertising income). But there were some exceptions – France being a case in point – where the value of television rights had not yet peaked.

France as a Special Case: Can the Value of Television Rights Still Increase?

Box 7.4 French television rights negotiations (2002–2003)

In July 2002 the French Professional League (LFP) was expected to invite bids for television rights starting from June 2004. LFP President Thiriez said that 'the LFP knew the value of its product, which includes rights for the French Ligue 1 and Ligue 2, and that television audiences for Canal Plus' football programmes were up by 16 per cent'. He dismissed ideas of any pact between the clubs and said that an exclusive offer would maintain the value of the rights. This was thought to be 450 million euros a year over a three or four year period, up by around 90 million euros on the current deal. A study by Arthur D. Little had found that were TPS and Canal Plus to merge their operations, the value of the rights could fall by as much as 250 million euros a year.

Canal Plus offered 480 million euros a year for the first three rights tranches, which included live pay-TV rights to three games, Saturday evening highlights and all live pay-per-view coverage. This was compared with around 300 million euros that it paid for the 2002-2003 season. Canal Plus was ready to pay this amount only if it could obtain exclusive rights. But the LFP Committee wanted to offer the PPV rights to TPS, which had bid 113 million euros for them (17 million euros less than Canal Plus' offer). *(to be continued)*

In December 2002, the LFP Executive Committee agreed to award exclusive rights and highlights to Ligue 1 football from 2004–2007 for 480 million euros. TPS rejected the possibility of sharing the PPV rights for a sum of 430 million euros annually. According to TPS, the LFP had abused a dominant position and that the inclusion of an exclusivity bonus in Canal Plus' offer was illegal. They made a complaint to the French competition authorities, which suspended the deal. In February 2003, the LFP Executive Committee decided to appeal against this decision.

Finally, in November 2004, Canal+ won the bidding by paying 600 million euros per year for an exclusive rights contract. This meant that rights to show the French football championship had increased in value by 55 per cent compared with the previous contract signed in 1999.

Sources: *Soccer Investor Daily,* 2002 and *Les Echos, Le Figaro, Le Monde, La Lettre du Sport, Sport Finance and Marketing, L'Equipe, La Lettre du Football* (compilation dans la revue de presse du CDES, années 2002 et 2003).

The French situation appears to be a 'special case', since the increase in the value of the French football league television rights occurred within with a somewhat inauspicious international context (in terms of reductions in the value of television right); as the examples in Boxes 1–3 show. The circumstances surrounding the French case came about as negotiations over the French television rights for the Champions League resulted in a lower price being agreed for televising the matches.

As Figure 7.3 shows, audiences for the Champions League fell by 36.4 per cent between 1997 and 2002. The two main reasons behind the fall were too many matches and the absence of French clubs during four of the championship seasons. Consequently, it was only logical for the new contract price agreed with UEFA in 2003 to be markedly lower (-45.9 per cent, as can be inferred from the figures shown in Table 7.13).

Figure 7.3   Champions League – live audiences (free-to-view channels)

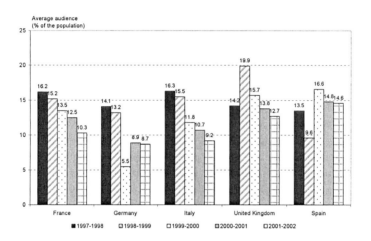

Table 7.13   French broadcasters' annual payments for Champions League television rights

	Canal Plus	*TF1*
Before 2003	55 million euros	55 million euros
2003-2006	26.5 million euros	33 million euros
Number of matches per week	15/16	1/16 (TF1 having first choice)

Source: *L'Equipe*, 8 March 2003.

UEFA stands to receive a total of 151.5 million euros less from French television broadcasters between 2003 and 2006, indicating that the amounts redistributed among the clubs will also be smaller.

The new contract that Canal+ signed in November 2004 (600 million euros per year) shows that, as far as French football is concerned, the top brand is the national league rather than a European competition (in view of the slim chances of French clubs winning a European title).

Didier Taupin from Deloitte & Touche in France argues that, compared with other countries, the new television rights contract still represents value for money for broadcasters. 'In France there are 8 million subscribers who pay to watch football on television. If you calculate the cost of football per subscriber, the new deal works out at 75 euros per person in France (compared with 44 euros for the previous deal), 75 euros in the UK and over 100 euros in Germany and Italy'.

Which therefore suggests that, in relation to other European countries, the price paid accurately reflects the true value of the television rights.

CONCLUSION: DEVELOPING A MORE RATIONAL APPROACH TO DETERMINING THE VALUE OF TELEVISION RIGHTS

In October 2002, UEFA president Lennart Johansson said at the European Broadcasting Union (EBU) Sports Group that:

> Television and football have a mutual interest in getting the balance right. We can see in certain countries the problems that can arise when this balance is not achieved, particularly when the co-ordination and fairness of collective selling is lost to the less structured approach that comes from individual selling by clubs (*Soccer Investor Daily*, 2002).

A month before, UEFA's vice-president Senes Erzik had called on European clubs to be more realistic when negotiating television rights. In his view, clubs had two alternatives:

> Either you sign a contract for a huge amount and not get paid, or you sign a reasonable, rational contract and you get fully paid. We have a situation where there have been some bankruptcies but the most attractive product in television is still football (*Soccer Investor Daily*, 2002).

These comments, coupled with the views developed earlier on the cost to TF1 of the 2002 World Cup, illustrate the pitfalls involved for broadcasters, which makes an event like the World Cup something of a double-edged sword. While sport is a means of achieving higher audience figures, and of improving the channel's image, there is equally a price to be paid in terms of the costs of acquiring the rights and in broadcasting the matches. Sometimes they are too high in relation to the hoped-for financial outcome.

These days the European system is becoming more and more professional and oriented towards making an economic profit. There is, nevertheless, a need for regulation because:

- Clubs' financial health largely depends on results on the field, so an investor has to take a major risk. Is there a way of reducing the impact of these results for the teams so as to provide a degree of security for the investment made?
- Financial differences between the clubs are growing because of cross-country inequalities in areas like tax, the law or social security contributions.[16] This means that some championship competitions, or the Champions League itself, are very often not financially advantageous (as only three or four clubs can are capable of winning the competition). Would greater harmonisation within Europe enable more potential winners to emerge within each of the competitions?

If these views were to be discussed at the European level, it could open some interesting avenues to explore. The American system, which is based on three broad regulatory principles (a fair share of television rights, a 'salary cap'[17] and a 'draft'[18] system) may serve as a model.

The three main advantages of this system are:

1. It is fair economically.
2. It creates less uncertainty and, through this, encourages investment by potential shareholders.
3. Total income is much higher thanks to negotiating collectively.[19]

For example, the value of television rights for the NFL went up from US$75 to US$ 500 million between 1975 and 1985. For the NBA (basketball) it rose from US$10 to US$400 million and for the MLB (baseball) it increased from US$20 to US$150 million.

But there are three reasons why Europeans might be scared off from adopting such a system. First, it is a closed system which is far removed from the ups and downs of league competitions; something to which most Europeans are greatly attached. Secondly, in the American system, what happens on the field is less important: a 'bad' team can remain in the league and can continue to sell lots of team-related merchandise if it has a well organised marketing strategy. Finally, the system is completely business-oriented, which some Europeans might find off-putting.

NOTES

1. In the 1970s, sports programme content sellers were seeking new media opportunities. In 1978, for example, France's national football league offered Antenne 2 (as today's public service channel France 2 was then known) the chance of showing an hour-long weekly highlights programme for 300,000 French francs (around 50,000 euros). Antenne 2 turned the offer down and it was taken up by TF1 to become 'Téléfoot'. To underline how the balance shifted in favour of sellers, the French Professional Football League sold this 'package' for 20 million euros in 2005.
2. The Kagan World Media study covers 16 European countries. Amounts shown are in US$ to facilitate comparison with the amounts paid by US television networks for broadcasting the main professional sports championships in North America.
3. This process has some similarities with speculative strategies used in the property world where large capital gains can be made by releasing a development in 'lots' rather than all at once.
4. Given football's status as the number one sport in all European countries, politicians could not countenance a situation where people were unable to watch the world's top football contest for free on television.
5. Usually in France there are at least two channels which broadcast the Olympic Games and the World Cup. In this case TF1 acquired the rights, but some of the matches and highlights were broadcast by its LCI (*La Chaîne Info*, the French equivalent of CNN) and Eurosport France subsidiaries.
6. 108 million euros have been budgeted for the 2006 World Cup.
7. In 1998, 4 million videocassettes were sold in France. Using the same figure for 2002 DVD sales gives the following result:
    - Cost of Production = 1 euro (TF1 owns the content)
    - Distribution Costs = 10 euros
    - Sale Price = 20 euros.
    In other words a possible 9 euros for each DVD sold, amounting to net income of 36 million euros for sales of 4 million copies.
8. The show's name came from the French team anthem for the 2002 competition and literally means 'all together' or 'all one'.
9. Market share is defined as the percentage of viewers watching a programme in relation to the global figure for television viewers at that time.
10. The CAC40 is the French equivalent of the Footsie and Dow Jones stock market indices in London and New York respectively. It measures the market movements of France's 40 biggest companies and serves as the reference point for the market.
11. The β coefficient measures the movement of a company's share price in relation to the overall movement of the market. A value of 1.16 indicates that for every 1 per cent rise or fall in the general market index, the company's share price rises or falls by 1.16 per cent. It can be regarded as the stock market equivalent of the elasticity measures used in consumer theory.
12. $-1.30 \times 1.16 = 1.51$ per cent.
13. We will need to wait until 2006 for definitive results.
14. ITV Digital's financial problems had a knock-on effect on the English Football League through compromising the extremely lucrative television rights contract that it had signed with the broadcaster.
15. The term 'Big 5' covers Europe's five largest football (league) markets (England, Germany, France, Italy, Spain).
16. Compared with France, the cost to an English club of a player receiving the same net monthly income is 42 per cent less.
17. The wage bill is limited at league level and is renegotiated every year with the players.
18. The teams in the lower part of the league at the end of the last season have first choice of the best players emerging from the university system.

19.   Although audiences are no longer as high as they were when Michael Jordan was the star of the 1990s, the NBA signed a contract with ABC, ESPN, and AOL Time Warner to show matches over six seasons (2001–2002 to 2007–2008). This new US$4.7bn contract was a 25 per cent increase over the previous contract.

REFERENCES

Andreff, W. and J.F. Nys (1987), *Le sport et la télévision*, Paris: Dalloz.

Andreff, W. and J.F. Nys (2001), *Economie du sport*, 4th ed., Paris: PUF.

Bourg, J.F. and J.J. Gouguet (1998), *Analyse économique du sport*, Paris: PUF.

Carat Sport (2001), *L'Image des Sports*, November, Paris.

Carat Sport (2002), *Droits et ratios TV des principales compétitions sportives en France*, June, Paris.

CSA – Conseil Supérieur de l'Audiovisuel (1997), *Sport et télévision 1991-1996: bilan de six années de régulation*, Paris.

CSA – Conseil Supérieur de l'Audiovisuel (1991), *Le sport et la télévision: analyse, avis et proposition*, July, Paris.

Desbordes, M., Ohl, F. and G. Tribou (1999), *Marketing du sport*, 1st ed., Paris: Economica.

Eurostaf (2001), *Les droits sportifs à la télévision*, July, Paris.

Halba, B. (1997), *Economie du sport*, Paris: Economica.

INA – Institut National de l'Audiovisuel (1995), Eurodience 88, June, Paris.

James, F. and H. De Camaret (1990), *Téléviser le sport*, survey Carat TV, February, Paris.

Kagan World Media (2000), *European TV Sports 2000*, June, London.

Kagan World Media (1999), *European Media Sports Rights*, April, London.

Kotler, P. and B. Dubois (2000), *Marketing Management*, Paris: Publi-Union.

Maitrot, E. and K. Nedjari (2002), *L'histoire secrète des bleus*, Paris: Flammarion.

Michel, H. (1995), *Les grandes dates de la télévision française*, Paris: PUF.

Miege, C. (2000), *Les organisations sportives et l'Europe*, Paris: Editions INSEP.

Occurence, Hickory and Koroïbos (2001), *L'Observatoire Sports et Valeurs*, March, Paris.

Pierrat, J.L. and J. Riveslange (2002), *L'argent secret du foot*, Paris: Plon.

Toussaint-Desmoulins, N. (1996), *L'économie des médias*, 4th ed., Paris: PUF.

8. Why have Premium Sports Rights Migrated to Pay-TV in Europe but not in the US?

Stefan Szymanski

INTRODUCTION

This chapter is motivated by a simple observation: why is that in Europe the majority of the most valuable sports rights have migrated to pay-TV while in the US these rights have remained available on free-to-air networks? In this context, 'most valuable' means live rights, and in Europe the most valuable rights relate to the top national league soccer championships. In the US this typically means the major leagues. In addition the Olympic Games are highly valued by consumers on both sides of the Atlantic, while some other rights attract significant interest in specific regions (PGA Golf in the US, Tour de France in much of Europe, Test Match Cricket in England).

In Italy, the UK, Germany and France the live matches of the national football tournaments are available exclusively on pay-TV, often on pay per view. Of the major football markets in Europe only Spain still has some broadcasting of live national league matches on free-to-air television. The other top club competition in European soccer, the Champions League, offers a mixture of free-to-air and pay-TV programming. Top matches involving national teams, including broadcast rights for the World Cup and the European Championship would in all probability have migrated to pay-TV had not the European Union passed legislation permitting national government to reserve sporting events of critical national significance for free-to-air broadcasters (this applies also to the Olympics). Formula One motor racing is one of the few sports to decide that, rather than sell its rights to the highest bidder, it would continue to make it rights available free-to-air. However, this merely illustrates the point: owners of sports rights in Europe can obtain more cash from pay-TV broadcasters.

In the US it is the four major national free-to-air broadcasters who continue to dominate the ownership of sports broadcast rights. CBS holds a share of NFL rights, NCAA basketball and the PGA, NBC holds the rights to the Olympics, and a share in the PGA and the NASCAR championship, ABC holds a share of NFL, NBA, NHL, the PGA and Major League Soccer as well as the Bowl Championship Series and Fox owns a share of NFL, MLB and NASCAR Rights.[1] While many of these rights are re-sold through cable packages, and Major League Baseball teams generate most of their income from selling television rights locally, frequently through cable broadcasters, it is rare for access to sporting events to be sold as premium pay-TV. The only major buyers of sports rights directly for cable distribution have been ESPN (NFL, NBA, MLB and NHL) and recently AOL Time Warner which bought a share of NBA for distribution through Turner Sports. These offerings are sold as a part of cable basic packages. For example, ESPN currently charges the highest fee for any cable sports channel, at $2 per subscriber. Thus most major sports viewed in the US are watched on free-to-air networks financed by the sale of advertising or as part of a basic cable package. The only significant premium sports events in the US have been pay-per-view boxing, and DirecTV's Sunday Ticket which enables viewers to watch out-of-market NFL games.

The chapter is set out as follows. The next section describes briefly the technology of broadcasting. Section 3 looks at the evolution of national broadcasting policy and the development of sports broadcasting in the US and in the four major European soccer markets (UK, Germany, Italy and Spain). The final section discusses some conclusions.

THE STRUCTURE OF BROADCASTING

The television industry consists of a set of vertically related markets. The nature of competition at each stage of the television industry, like any other, is determined by the nature of technology. In this respect it is developments at the final stage of the vertical chain – channel distribution – which have been the most important. Rights owners and channel providers have been greatly concerned to improve the quality of recording and editing, and these have led to huge advances in the quality of programming material. In the early days such improvements determined the evolution of the market. For example, there was little point in broadcasting baseball or cricket on television until the picture quality was good enough to allow you to see the ball. More recently, developments of cameras for filming in Formula One cars or in helmets of American Football players have enhanced the experience of watching these events. However, these developments have not radically expanded audiences or altered the economic relationships in the industry in the way that the development of broadcast platforms has done.

Figure 8.1   The vertical structure of broadcasting

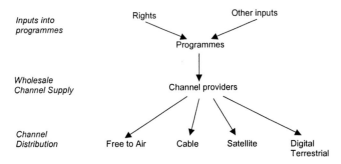

Source: OFT, 2002.

Free-to-air broadcasting relies on the transmission of signals from broadcasting antennae which, even with booster signals, typically have a maximum radius of 100 miles (Vogel, 2001, p. 176). In the US broadcasting facilities have typically been set up to serve urban areas, which have thus provided the basis for defining the country in terms of 210 broadcast markets. In 1999 there were 1616 broadcasting facilities serving these markets (Vogel, *ibid*). Because free-to-air broadcasters concentrated on cities, rural areas often found it hard to receive broadcast signals, and this was the initial impetus behind cable services, which wired households to a well located receiver. However, as technological development expanded the capacity of these wires it became attractive to connect urban households to cable services. While each cable operator tends to have a limited geographic base, cable networks, at least in theory, have the potential to connect consumers to broadcasters anywhere on the globe – just like telephony. Satellite television gives an operator a considerably wider reach or 'footprint' than any other platform. A single satellite can cover any single European country, and three or four are required to cover the US.

Significant expansion of the television market in Europe and the US ended many years ago. By 1960 90 per cent of US homes had a television, and Western Europe reached similar levels by the 1970s. Expansion in more recent years has been achieved by increasing the availability of channels. Until the recent advent of digital terrestrial television, most of this capacity expansion has occurred through the development of cable networks and satellite broadcasting. Expanding channel capacity made it possible to increase dramatically the number of broadcast hours available and thereby increase customer choice. This has also been an important factor in driving up the value of rights. When capacity was limited both consumers and suppliers had few alternatives and the controller of the distribution system could extract monopoly rents from control of the bottleneck. Relaxing capacity constraints meant not only consumer choice but also created the potential for competition between channel distributors to bid–up the rights. Thus rents have been increasingly extracted upstream by the rights holders. A not unnatural response to this development has been vertical integration. As competition in broadcasting has emerged, platform owners have increasingly tried to control content, justifying this on the grounds that financing the overheads implicit in running a broadcast system requires guaranteed access to content. However, critics have frequently been concerned that the desire to control content has been motivated by the desire to pre-empt competition in one way or another. Hence the issue of exclusivity has raised fundamental problems on both sides of the Atlantic.

THE EVOLUTION OF BROADCASTING AND NATIONAL POLICY

The following is a brief summary of the issues and policy response that have arisen in the development of broadcasting. More detailed analysis can be found elsewhere, e.g. Vogel (2001), Noam (1991), Cave and Crandall (2001), Levy *et al.* (2002).

The United States

The US free-to-air networks, CBS, NBC, ABC and now Fox, emerged between the 1930s and 1950s. These companies are essentially wholesalers of content (television channels) to television stations. Traditionally the stations affiliated to the networks, for which they received cash payments to broadcast the network's television programmes. In this way the station provided an audience for the network, enabling it to generate advertising revenue from commercial breaks. In addition, the networks own their own stations, mostly in the larger cities.

Television has been heavily regulated in the US, primarily through the Federal Communications Commission (FCC), although its decisions are frequently challenged, and overturned, in the courts. The principal restrictions on free-to-air broadcasting have been ownership rules prohibiting any company (network) controlling access to more than a fixed percentage of the population, currently set at 35 per cent of households. In addition the terms on which networks dealt with stations have been closely regulated (ensuring that the networks cannot dictate programming), networks have been obliged to create space for access of alternative programming material and have faced rules on ownership of the content (the 'fin-syn' rules), so that content providers could not control the networks. These latter were abolished in the mid 1990s, leading to mergers such as ABC and Disney (see e.g. Walker and Ferguson, 1998).

While the potential for cable broadcasting was recognised as early 1948, 'until the late 1970s the industry was restrained in order to promote the growth of traditional television broadcasting, particularly that by local independent stations' (Crandall and Furchtgott-Roth, 1996, p. 24). These regulations, aimed at protecting free-to-air systems by restricting the range of channels that cable operators could provide and ensuring access to local channel suppliers, combined first with tight municipal and then Federal rate regulation based on the premise that cable services are essentially monopolistic. Despite this cable systems have grown to the point where almost all television households are passed by cable, and two thirds of households subscribe. Moreover, the Telecommunications Act of 1996 removed most price regulation. Cable companies can typically offer many more channels than free-to-air, and critically, can charge subscription fees to generate income. This part of the broadcast industry is highly fragmented. There are over 10,000 cable systems in operation, although nearly half of these supply fewer than 500 customers, while 279 systems supply 51 per cent of cable customers (Vogel, 2001, p. 207).

Satellite broadcasting has developed at a remarkable rate in recent years, growing from 0.8m subscribers in 1990 to 18.7m in 2001, 18 per cent of television households (Levy *et al.*, 2002, p. 51). Until very recently this part of the industry was lightly regulated and indeed cable companies were obliged to grant access to programming material to satellite broadcasters, although no reciprocal obligation was imposed. Now that satellite is becoming a significant competitor, particularly in the form of DirecTV (now controlled by News Corporation) pressure for tighter regulation is growing.

Sports Programming in the US

The most successful television sport, and the model for most sports broadcasting in the US, has been the NFL. The current eight year $17bn broadcast contract dwarfs any other in sport. Television has promoted American Football from a minor sport into, arguably, the national sport. Leifer (1995) documents how the NFL was from the beginning willing to alter the game in order to fit in with the television schedules and advertising breaks. In its early years the NFL was prevented from collective selling of broadcasting rights by the courts (US v. NFL, 116 F. Supp. 310 (1953)) on the grounds that this was deliberate policy of restricting competition. However, the Sports Broadcasting Act of 1961 exempted the collective selling of 'sponsored telecasting' – usually interpreted to mean free-to-air broadcasting. From this date on NFL contracts increased rapidly in value: $4.7 million in 1962/1963 (CBS) increasing to $47 million per season by 1970, when the rights were split into three packages – Monday Night Football (ABC), NFC games (CBS) and AFC games (NBC). The fact that these matches drew huge ratings for the networks led to a continuing escalation in rights values. By 1980 they were worth $167 million and then from 1990 the contract was split into five packages, three for the networks and two for the cable channel providers ESPN and TNT, although the latter paid only 25 per cent of the total cost of $900 million per season. A similar distribution applied in 1994 when the contract was renewed (and Fox replaced CBS) for $1,137 million per season. However, the 1998 contract, worth $2,200 million per season involved only one cable channel, ESPN, who now paid more than any of the networks, although still only just over 25 per cent of the contract value. The most important development in the sale of NFL broadcast rights in recent years has been the Sunday Ticket, costing around $200 per season, which allows viewers to see all NFL matches through the satellite broadcaster DirecTV.

By contrast with the NFL, the national collective broadcast contract for MLB has never been the mainstay of broadcast income. For example, the current contract, split between Fox and ESPN is worth $559 million per year, about $17 million per team, is exceeded by the amount earned from local broadcast income ($571 million). In recent years the local broadcasting contracts have gradually shifted toward cable. In 1996 41 per cent of local broadcasts were on cable, but by 2003 the figure had risen to 69 per cent of the total. However, the prices charged for games shown on cable is relatively low. Even the New York Yankees YES channel is charged at only $1.95 per month per customer in the New York area, and this fee was only agreed after a lengthy dispute with the broadcaster Cablevision.

The UK

The fundamental difference between broadcasting in the US and Europe, including the UK, is the leading role of the state in establishing, directing and funding European broadcast systems. Thus in the UK the government established the publicly owned BBC as a vertically integrated programme maker, channel provider and broadcast distributor. The advent of commercial television in 1955 offered some competition, but these suppliers were also heavily regulated and as Noam (1991, p. 36) notes, by 1982 a typical New

York viewer with cable could watch 23 different channels, whereas a viewer in London could, at most, watch three. By 1990 the comparison was 73 channels in New York and 16 in London. Moreover, of London's 16, four were free-to-air and 12 were satellite channels – cable subscribers in the UK at this date numbered a mere 100,000 or so.

The BBC has always derived its income principally from a compulsory licence fee that is paid by all television households. Its activities are overseen by a board of governors appointed by the government and the overall remit of the Corporation is laid down in its charter which is subject to occasional revision by Parliament. For much of its existence there has been remarkably little controversy about the role and function of this organisation, its paternalistic mission being accepted by the main political parties and its impartiality unquestioned. However, in more recent years the BBC has become more controversial given the expansion of available channels and the more market oriented politics of the Thatcher era. Increasingly the BBC has sought to find a role for publicly funded broadcasting that does not simply duplicate what can be produced in the private sector. Currently this has led the Corporation to focus on the development of news and current affairs programming, and to drop out of the bidding for the more attractive, and therefore more expensive, sports rights. The BBC has also moved away from full vertical integration, contracting out a large part of its programming to independent production companies.

Commercial channels have, like the US networks, derived their main income from advertising, but in this they have been more heavily regulated (e.g. the number of minutes is limited to seven per hour). However, given the restriction on the number of channels licensed, the licensees have been extremely profitable and so have not tended to complain too vociferously about the restraints. Government has also restricted ownership to ensure that commercial broadcasters are British owned. Until 1982 the government licensed only a single channel (ITV), operated by a small number of regional franchises. A second free-to-air channel was licensed in 1982 and a third in 1997.

Cable services also developed much more slowly than in the US. Cable providers did exist for households unable to receive free-to-air signals, but these subscribers could obtain only the four licensed channels, and therefore the cable providers had no incentive to develop their systems. In the early 1980s government began licensing cable channels with the express purpose of broadening the range of entertainment available from television, but British Telecom, the most plausible entrant was banned from this market while very little cable was laid until 1991 when the government permitted cable franchises to offer telephony. This led to a massive programme of cable laying, but also required considerable industry consolidation since the government had, somewhat unrealistically for a population of 23 million households, issued nearly 100 cable licenses.

Satellite broadcasting had already started in the UK in 1989, well before cable services started to be widely available. Initially there were two competing firms carrying a narrow range of programming, but when they merged to form BSkyB (later renamed Sky) in 1990, largely controlled by News Corporation, the broadcaster developed a strategy based on selling premium movie channels and premium sports channels. To this end Sky set about acquiring a wide range of sports rights in cricket, rugby union and rugby league, tennis, motor sport, golf and so on. However, the single largest expenditure has been the acquisition of English Premier League soccer, which Sky acquired first in 1992 and has retained exclusively until 2001 and in tandem with a pay-per-view service since 2002. Satellite subscribers increased dramatically following the acquisition of Premier League rights. In 1991 subscribers numbers were just over 1 million, and by 1995 had jumped to 3 million. Toward the end of the 1990s subscriber growth appeared to slow, but then accelerated again with the introduction of digital services. By 2003 subscriber numbers had reached 6.5 million. During this period cable subscriptions also grew rapidly, approaching 4 million by the same date. However, much of the programming content for cable channels is provided by Sky on access terms overseen by a regulator.

The development of digital television in the UK also led to the creation of digital terrestrial services. The UK government has pushed heavily for broadcasters to adopt digital broadcasting and most free-to-air broadcasters supply a digital signal. However, a subscription based digital channel (ITV Digital) was also created in the late 1990s, and attracted a small number of subscribers mainly through its sale of soccer rights, some of which it bought itself and some of which it licensed from Sky. However, the company overpaid for some rights and went bankrupt in 2001.

Sports Programming in the UK

Soccer is by far the dominant television sport in the UK. Throughout the 1990s soccer rights accounted for over 50 per cent of the value of sports programming expenditure. Despite this, soccer was slow to reach UK television. Live league matches were not shown until 1982, largely due to the absence of competition for the rights. Until that time, the BBC and ITV had a no-compete pact, bizarrely endorsed by the competition authority itself in the 1970s. The broadcasters were prepared to offer very little to obtain the rights, so the members clubs of the Football League refused to make them available. As a result soccer broadcasting was restricted to major international competitions such as the World Cup and special matches such as the FA Cup

Final. This was despite the fact that broadcast coverage of other major sporting events was well established. The Football League clubs took the view that small broadcasting revenues would be insufficient to compensate for the large loss of gate they anticipated.

The clubs finally agreed to sell broadcast rights as a result of a financial crisis in the early 1980s. However, the first contract raised a mere £2.6 million to be divided among 92 clubs. Competition finally emerged in 1988, when the new satellite broadcaster bid for the rights. Although it didn't win, the BBC/ITV cartel broke down and the latter paid £11 million per season for four seasons. However, all of the matches broadcast involved the top teams of Division One, predominantly five teams, despite the fact that the income was divided among all 92 League members.

Dissatisfaction with this situation led the top teams to form the Premier League in 1992, still connected to the old Football League by the system of promotion and relegation, but selling broadcast rights and generating income only for themselves. Sky won the contract in 1992 paying £49 million per season to be divided between the 20 member clubs. The fact that rights had migrated from free-to-air to Pay-TV led to protests by fans, but this was in part dampened by the fact that Sky showed more matches (60 per season against the 18 shown previously). Sky won the contract again in 1997, paying £180 million per season, and again in 2001 paying £422 million per season for 66 matches on subscription and 40 available on pay-per-view.

While the migration to pay-TV of the Premier League was not challenged in the UK, government concerns that sporting events deemed to be of national significance might migrate to pay-TV led the introduction of 'listed events' in the 1990 Broadcasting Act. This list includes the Olympic Games, the World Cup, the FA Cup Final, the Derby, the Wimbledon Tennis Finals, the European Football Championship Finals, the Rugby World Cup Final, Cricket Test Matches played in England, Six Nations Rugby Tournament matches involving home countries, the Commonwealth Games, the Cricket World Cup, the Ryder Cup and the Open Golf Championship.

Germany, Italy and Spain

While differing in many specifics, the evolution of broadcasting and sports broadcasting in these three countries has much in common with the UK and little in common with the US. Each country has been dominated by publicly controlled and financed terrestrial broadcast monopolies until the 1970s or even 1980s. Each has permitted some competition in terrestrial television in recent years but cable television has developed only to a limited extent in each country. In each country it is satellite broadcasting that has made the greatest impact in recent years, and to which premium soccer rights have migrated.

As with the UK, one of the key catalysts for change was the 1989 European Union 'Television without frontiers' Directive which required all member states to ensure free reception of television broadcasts from other member states and prohibited the restriction of retransmission. This directive provoked member states into deregulating their own broadcast markets rather than see broadcast services run from outside their own borders. In practice this directive enabled satellite broadcasters to compete in any European state.

Unlike the UK, these countries had a longer tradition of providing extensive coverage of domestic league football, including live matches. Like the UK, soccer rights accounts for over 50 per cent of the value of all sports rights in these countries. In each case free-to-air broadcasters were soon outbid for domestic league soccer rights. In Italy pay broadcasting was introduced in 1993 and in 1999 all league matches moved to pay-per-view. In Germany, live domestic league soccer matches did not start to be shown until 1990 and from the start this was on pay-TV. Initially only one match per week was shown, but by 2000 all matches were available. In Spain most of the live broadcast rights to the national league also migrated to pay-TV by the end of the 1990s.

Each country also defined a set of listed events, but did not include domestic soccer in that definition.

WHY HAVE SPORTS RIGHTS MIGRATED TO PREMIUM PAY-TV IN EUROPE BUT NOT IN THE US?

There are (at least) four possible explanations:

1. Consumer tastes. As far as sports is concerned, Europe is a soccer monoculture. Soccer programming accounts for over 50 per cent of all broadcast rights by value in most European countries. Sporting interest is much more diverse in the US, with no one sport accounting for more than 25 per cent of all sports programming expenditure. The availability of fewer substitutes suggests that the willingness to pay of most European consumers for the programming they are most interested in will be much higher than the willingness to pay of a US consumer.

2. Economies of scale. Although the US is defined by Nielsen as 210 distinct broadcast markets, NFL matches have appeal in every segment. The domestic soccer leagues in Europe are essentially

national markets, and even the largest of these has only 34 million television households (Germany) compared to 106 million in the US. For this reason national free-to-air broadcasters in Europe cannot afford to pay nearly as much as they can in the US to acquire sports rights.

3. Contest design. In the US sports leagues have been more willing to adjust the structure of matches to meet the needs of broadcasters, particularly in relation to the timing of commercial breaks, than the governing bodies of European sports. Hence US free-to-air can generate a much larger amount of advertising income per match than their European counterparts, and so can bid more.

4. Regulation. In Europe and the US both cable and direct satellite broadcasting have historically been discouraged by regulators from competing with free-to-air broadcasters. However, the decision of the European Union in the 1980s to open television markets to increased competition ensured that pay-TV broadcasters, the only credible competitors for national free-to-air monopolies, could bid freely and acquire premium sports rights. The US has been slower to allow significant competitive entry from pay-TV providers especially for premium programming.

While each of the first three explanations has some plausibility, it is hard not to believe that regulation has played a significant role. By allowing the development of strong competing free-to-air networks the US government has ensured that these broadcasters can compete with premium pay-TV providers for the acquisition of rights in a way that the heavily regulated or publicly controlled free-to-air broadcasters of Europe could not once competition was established. However, the success of DirecTV has begun to suggest that more premium rights will migrate in the US.

One of the striking facts about sports is that the businesses which run them are so tiny given the amount of interest they generate. The Census Bureau reported in 1997 that spectator sports generate a direct income of only $14 billion domestically (0.17 per cent of GDP). One reason for this low dollar value is that teams have been unable to extract the rents they generate because mechanisms did not exist either to reach the audience or to charge that audience once it was reached. Free-to-air television reached the audience, but pay-TV offers a much greater opportunity to extract rent. Unless the US adopts a listing system, then a much greater fraction of premium rights may migrate.

Is this in the public interest? Given that fans will always want to watch the one dominant league in any sport (because they prefer to watch the best), and that entry by new leagues will always be difficult, it is not clear that allowing leagues to extract rents provides any social benefit. It might be argued that increasing revenues have funded significant improvements in broadcast quality (picture quality and so on), but it can also be argued that much of the rent has been channeled needlessly to the players. If migration continues, the players could be earning a lot more money in the near future.

NOTE

1. At the time writing in May 2003.

REFERENCES

Cave, M. and R. Crandall (2001), 'Sports rights and the broadcast industry', *The Economic Journal*, **111** (February), F4–F26.

Crandall, R. and H. Furchtgott-Roth (1996), *Cable TV: Regulation or Competition?*, Washington, DC: The Brookings Institution.

Flynn, M. and G. Richard (2001), 'An Analysis of Professional Sports Leagues as Joint Ventures', *Economic Journal*, **111**, F27–F46.

Leifer, E. (1995), *Making the Majors: The Transformation of Team Sports in America*, Massachusetts, MA: Harvard University Press.

Levy, J., Ford-Livene, M. and A. Levine (2002), *Broadcast Television: Survivor in a Sea of Competition*, Federal Communications Commission OPP Working Paper Series, 37.

Noam, E. (1991), *Television in Europe*, New York, NY: Oxford University Press.

OFT (2002), *The outcome of the OFT's competition Act investigation,* Office of Fair Trading 623, December.

Vogel, H.L. (2001), *Entertainment Industry Economics*, 5th ed., Cambridge and New York, NY: Cambridge University Press.

Walker, J.R. and D.A. Ferguson (1998), *The Broadcast Television Industry*, Boston, MA: Allyn & Bacon.

9. Economic Perspectives on Market Power in the Telecasting of US Team Sports[1]

Andrew Zimbalist

Since the 1980s the telecasting of team sporting contests in the United States has moved steadily from free television to cable. This trend, which continues today, affects both pooled/national and local television rights contracts. There are possible violations of antitrust statutes in both sets of contracts. For the consumer, this trend has meant both rapidly increasing prices and lack of access at any price in some cases. Antitrust and re-regulation policy options are available, albeit complicated by the rapidly changing technological and ownership landscape.

THE EVIDENCE ON CABLE-ISATION

A league's or team's motivation to move from broadcast to cable television is straightforward: cable produces two income streams – advertising and carriage fees; broadcast television produces only advertising. In some cases, particularly in smaller markets, a team may find it difficult to procure a contract from a broadcast station.

Table 9.1 depicts the steady trend toward cable-isation of Major League Baseball at the local level between 1987 and 2003. In 1987, the average team had 80.7 games shown locally on broadcast television and 35.1 games on cable. By 2003, these numbers had practically reversed with 41.3 games on broadcast television and 90.1 games on cable.[2] Teams that control their own cable outlet, as do the Yankees, Red Sox, Braves, Dodgers, Phillies, Twins, Blue Jays, Orioles, Astros and Royals (with more on the way), also have the ability to shelter income from MLB's increasingly costly revenue sharing system. This provides yet another impetus toward cable-isation.

Along with this migration to cable have come ever higher local media revenues for MLB teams. Together these revenues have grown from $116.9 million in 1985, to $342.1 million in 1990 to approximately $655 million in 2002 – and these represent only reported revenues (Zimbalist, 1992, p. 49; Broadcasting and Cable, 2002). Teams that own their cable or broadcast television station can shuffle revenues away from the team. Within this local media revenue total, cable has played a larger and larger role. Team revenues from local cable deals have grown from roughly $200 million in 1999, to $275 million in 2000 and to $350 million 2002 – an annual growth rate of 20.5 percent over the last three years.[3]

Table 9.1   Major league baseball migration to cable

	BROADCAST		CABLE	
	Total	Average Games	Total	Average Games
Year	*Games*	*per Team*	*Games*	*per Team*
1987	2098	80.7	914	35.1
1991	2039	78.4	1144	44.0
1996	1835	65.5	1287	50.9
1997	1668	59.6	1737	62.0
1998	1655	55.2	2058	68.6
1999	1646	54.9	2187	72.9
2000	1571	52.4	2246	75.0
2001	1507	50.2	2417	80.6
2002	1380	46.0	2478	82.6
2003	1240	41.3	2702	90.1

Sources: Broadcasting and Cable, 2002, 2003; Zimbalist, 1992, p. 157; Zimbalist, 2003, p. 147.

Similar trends have occurred in the other leagues. In the NBA, during 1997–1998 the average team televised 31 games on local free television (44.9 per cent) and 38 games on cable; during 2000–2001 the average team showed 28 games on local free television (41.1 per cent) and 40 games on cable. The shift in the NBA's national contracts has been more dramatic: in the deals expiring in 2001–2002, 48 of 142 (37.8 per cent) nationally televised regular-season games were on free television; in the deals commencing in 2002–2003, only 15 of 127 (10.6 per cent) games were on free television.

As depicted in Table 9.2, NHL national television revenues went from 30 per cent based in cable in 1993–1994 to 62.5 per cent based in cable in 2002–

2003. A similar trend has occurred in local contracts: while in 1997–1998 the average team had 63.6 per cent of locally-televised games on cable, in 2000–2001 this percentage jumped to 78.5 per cent.[4]

Table 9.2   *National hockey league migration to cable*
            US National contracts (millions of dollars per team)

Year	Broadcast TV	Cable TV
1993-94	0.7	0.3
1994-95	0.9	0.4
1995-96	1.2	0.5
1996-97	1.5	0.6
1997-98	1.7	0.6
1998-99	1.7	1.9
1999-00	1.8	2.1
2000-01	1.7	2.3
2001-02	1.7	2.7
2002-03	1.8	3.0

Source: Paul Kagan Associates, 1999a, 356-357.

The National Football League is a special case because there have been no regular-season contests locally broadcast since 1961. Nevertheless, there has been a small movement of games away from broadcast to cable television. The first NFL pooled contract for national cable was with ESPN in 1987. This contract shifted eight games that were previously on broadcast television to Sunday night cable. In 1994, the number of games on Sunday night increased to 16 and these games were now split between two cable channels, with TNT covering the first half of the season and ESPN the second half. The current contract, which began in 1998, retains 16 Sunday night cablecasts, but they are all now on ESPN.

POOLED CABLE CONTRACTS: ARE THEY LEGAL?

In 1961, under the NFL initiative, the US Congress considered granting team sports leagues an antitrust exemption to allow for leaguewide packaging of national television contracts. The resulting legislation, the Sports Broadcasting Act (SBA), allows the teams in a league to come together as a cartel for the purpose of selling an over-the-air television package to broadcast networks.

The relevant phrase in the SBA is that such packaging is allowed for '*sponsored telecasting* of the games of football, baseball, basketball or hockey'. The question then becomes what 'sponsored telecasting' means: does it refer to over-the-air broadcasting or any telecasting that contains advertising whether it be over-the-air or cable? In the early days of cable until the 1980s there was no advertising. The standard practice for ambiguously-worded legislation is to go back to a bill's legislative history.

In this case, the following clear interpretation emerges. First, the record suggests that the permission for package sales was being granted in part to ensure that all road games would be televised back to the franchises' home areas. This was necessary because the courts had previously determined that the home team has a property right in licensing the televising of games played in its park.[5] The House Judiciary Committee, therefore, decided that 'the public interest in viewing professional league sports warrants' an accommodation 'with minimal sacrifice of antitrust principles' (Roth, 1990, p. 469). This is what the SBA was meant to accomplish by promoting the viewership of games and also the more equal sharing of television revenues across teams. Since the SBA was meant to promote viewership, it would be inconsistent with the act's purpose to allow shifting of telecasting to cable.[6]

Second, the NFL was both the principal beneficiary of the SBA and the main group pushing for its passage. During congressional hearings on the bill then NFL Commissioner Pete Rozelle unequivocally asserted that the legislation was not intended to apply to cable or pay-TV. The counsel of the House Antitrust Subcommittee asked the commissioner whether he understood 'that this bill covers only the free telecasting of professional sports contests, and does not cover pay-TV'. Rozelle directly replied: 'Absolutely'. In 1982 then NFL Counsel Paul Tagliabue responded to a query from Senator Arlen Specter before the Senate Judiciary Committee as follows:

> the words "sponsored telecasting" in [the SBA] were intended to exclude pay and cable. This is clear from the legislative history and from the committee reports. So, that statute does not authorise us to pool and sell to pay and cable.[7]

This interpretation was affirmed in two subsequent court cases.[8]

Thus, the NFL, NBA and NHL national deals with cable stations and with special packages on DirecTV (e.g., *NFL Sunday Ticket*) are subject to antitrust review. In contrast, MLB's deals with ESPN and DirecTV (*Extra Innings*) as well as its own streaming of games on mlb.com may be immunised from antitrust scrutiny if its presumed exemption is valid.[9] While this distinction is significant in theory, to date it has not been particularly significant in practice. The few challenges to pooled pay-TV deals in the NFL and NBA have all been resolved with little sacrifice by the leagues. Whether the distinction becomes more meaningful in the future remains to be seen.

CHANNEL BUNDLING: IS IT LEGAL?

Cable companies bundle channels. What is known as expanded basic cable service usually offers between 40 and 70 channels of service for a single monthly fee. These channels include basic local broadcasting, national cable channels and sports channels (e.g., ESPN, ESPN2, ESPN News, ESPN Classic, Fox Sports and Regional Sports Networks or RSNs). Generally, consumers cannot choose to buy a subset of the expanded basic offering.[10]

Bundling in many circumstances can be considered a restraint of trade. Imagine walking into a department store to buy a pair of trousers and being told by the salesman that in order to buy the pair you like, you would also have to buy a particular shirt, a particular tie and two pairs of socks. Department stores do not attempt such bundling, because the consumer would not stand for it. In this case, there are many places to buy trousers. Competition curtails abuse.

Some types of bundling are allowed. Certain restaurants, for instance, offer *prix fixe* menus. They bundle an appetiser, a salad, a main course and a dessert (albeit often with choices within each category). The main reason why such bundling is legal is that consumers have a wide choice of restaurants to eat at – there is abundant competition. Secondarily, *prix fixe* menus can also offer some efficiencies to the producer which can result in either lower prices or higher quality, or both, for the consumer.

In the case of the package of sports channels offered by a cable company there is no choice. Each cable distributor selects the sports channels that will be offered on expanded basic. The consumer cannot decide, for instance, that he or she is not interested in watching replays of boxing and tennis matches from the 1970s or 1980s and, hence, does not want to subscribe to ESPN Classic. Or, until the March 31, 2003 one-year deal between Cablevision and YES, a Yankee fan could not decide that she did not want to subscribe to Fox Sports New York (FSNY) or to MSG, the two RSNs that shared coverage of the Mets.[11] Nor can a non-sports fan decide that she does not want to subscribe to any of the cable sports channels and save the corresponding $10-plus being charged monthly by the distributor.

This restriction may be more palatable to the average consumer if there were competing cable companies in local markets. With a few insignificant exceptions, however, there are not. Of the 10,157 cable systems in the United States, fewer than 100 of them have competition from another system (either another cable company or a telephone company delivering cable signals) in their area.

BUNDLING AND WELFARE

What does economic theory tell us about the effect of cable channel bundling on prices, output and efficiency? First, consider one cable company, two consumers and three cable channels. The chart below shows the hypothetical maximum value (reservation price) to each consumer of each channel per year.

Table 9.3   Hypothetical preference distribution A

	Channel A	*Channel B*	*Channel C*
Consumer 1	$70	$22	$6
Consumer 2	$36	$40	$10

If the cable company were able to engage in perfect price discrimination, charging each consumer differently for each channel, it could earn $184 in yearly revenue from these two consumers. If the cable company engaged in normal, single-part pricing, charging the inframarginal price, it could earn $128 in yearly revenue. If the cable company bundled the three channels in a package (block booking (Stigler, 1963, 152-157), it could generate $172. Since the first option is not practically available, block booking enables the cable company to increase its revenues by 37.5 per cent over normal pricing without bundles.

Chicago-type economists see no welfare loss and a possible welfare gain from this bundling. First, they would argue that from a welfare perspective it is immaterial whether surplus goes to consumers or producers. Second, they would claim that greater producer surplus may lead cable companies to expand output by adding additional cable channels that otherwise would not be profitable to produce.

We shall return to these arguments momentarily, but let us first consider a more complicated arrangement of consumer preferences. Assume there are three consumers with the following reservation prices.

In this example, perfect price discrimination would generate $224 in revenues. Regular, single-part pricing would generate $164. Bundling would generate only $120 if the cable company insisted upon selling to all consumers. If the company were revenue (and profit) maximising, however, it would bundle, price the bundle at $86, sell it only to consumers one and two, and earn $172 in revenue. The elimination of consumer three lowers output, raises deadweight loss, and lowers welfare (the sum of consumer and producer surplus).

Table 9.4   Hypothetical preference distribution B

	Channel A	Channel B	Channel C
Consumer 1	$70	$22	$6
Consumer 2	$36	$40	$10
Consumer 3	$40	$0	$0

Under perfect price discrimination, consumer surplus is 0 and producer surplus is $224 (assuming a zero marginal cost of distribution). Total surplus, therefore, is $224. Under bundling (with two consumers), consumer surplus is $12 and producer surplus is $160. Total surplus is $172. Under normal pricing and no bundling, consumer surplus is $60 and producer surplus is $164, and total surplus is $224. In this example, relative to the bundling outcome, no bundling leads to higher welfare and also avoids the wealth transfer away from consumers.

This second example accords with the findings in Adams and Yellen's 1976 article where they write that:

> bundling is inefficient by Pareto Standards: it can lead to oversupply or undersupply of particular goods ... [and] prohibition of bundling in monopolistic markets, without elimination of monopoly, can either increase or decrease the deadweight loss arising in the relevant markets (Adams and Yellen, 1976, 477, 495).

Bundling flattens the demand curve and will generally be consistent with higher profits as long as consumer tastes are both negatively correlated and not too heterogeneous (such as in the two-consumer example above.) Higher profits, in turn, generally lead to higher output. If consumption is non-rival and marginal costs are close to zero, higher output suggests greater efficiency.[12]

This observation returns us to the two-fold claim by Chicago-type economists regarding bundling. First, bundling is simply a welfare-neutral transfer from consumer to producer surplus. This is only true if it does not affect consumer behavior. If the aggregation of bundling leads to higher prices, it may reduce consumption and output.[13] If consumer behavior is unaffected, there is still a question whether the transfer is welfare-neutral. If there is a transfer from lower to higher income households, it may well reduce aggregate welfare by a utilitarian-type argument.

Second, there is a legitimate question about whether marginal costs are indeed zero or close to zero. From the perspective of the cable operator with spare capacity on the system, adding one more channel to an expanded basic package will equal the per subscriber fee charged by the channel. This fee presently ranges from negative to up to $3 per month. The negative fee arises from channels that pay the cable operator to carry their signal on the system. What is the opportunity cost to consumers for this channel to be carried instead of another channel determined by the consumer?

From the perspective of the cable operator without spare capacity, the additional channel may necessitate the use of cable boxes or even a new digital delivery system. The cost here is hardly zero.

From the perspective of the society, the marginal cost of adding another channel is the resources used to create the channel. If the cost of producing the channel is greater than the area under the society's demand curve for the channel, then efficiency is diminished by its production. A significant, dominant issue is that with channel bundling by the cable distributor the choice to allocate resources (or to sanction the allocation of resources) is not made by the consumer. This challenges basic notions of maximising welfare.

In all of these cases, the problem is aggravated by the presence of monopoly. If the consumer had choice to select among bundles or *à la carte* offerings, the welfare concerns would be alleviated. Yet, because of uneven implementation of the Telecommunications Act of 1996 and other factors, the vast majority of communities do not have effective competition among pay-TV providers. Whether this continues to be the case may well be decided by policy decisions taken by the Federal Communications Commission in the coming year.[14] We shall return to this matter below.

HIGHER PRICES

The 1996 Telecommunications Act deregulated rate setting in the industry beginning on April 1, 1999 (except for the stripped-down basic tier) on the theory that there would soon be stiff competition in all areas. The competition was expected to come from the Act's relaxation of the prohibition against telephone companies (telcos) offering cable service (and against cable companies offering telephone service) as well as from the growth of direct broadcast satellite (DirecTV and EchoStar). But, as of early 2002, competition from the telcos had materialised in only 44 of the over 10,000 markets nationwide.

According to a 2002 study by the Federal Communications Commission (FCC), in the 99 areas where there was competition between two cable distributors, average prices on expanded basic service were 6.3 per cent lower. Further, where there was competition, there were more channels offered on the expanded basic package, so that the average price per channel in areas where competition prevailed was 9.4 per cent lower (FCC 2002, pp. 4, 20, 28).[15] The US government General Accounting Office (GAO) also conducted a study in 2002 and found that the FCC survey posed several ambiguous questions, eliciting some inaccurate responses. The GAO's own survey and analysis yielded the result that when cable companies engaged in head-to-head competition in a given market, average expanded basic prices fell 17 per cent.[16]

Some competition has come from satellite services (today there are roughly 68 million US households subscribed to cable and 18 million subscribed to satellite), but satellite is not available or feasible in all areas and the product it offers can vary substantially from that of cable. Accordingly, a multiple regression analysis performed by the FCC found that the penetration of DBS in an area did not have a significant impact on the price of cable services.[17] The outcome of rate deregulation and ineffective competition in most areas, then, has been rapid price increases in cable services. Since the 1996 Telecommunications Act cable prices across the United States have gone up at three times the rate of inflation.

To a large degree, these increases have been pushed by the ever higher prices being charged by sports programmers (the national cable stations – such as ESPN, TNT or TBS – or regional sports networks). ESPN, for instance, enters into long-term contracts with cable companies with a provision that allows it to raise prices 20 per cent annually.[18] The programmers, in turn, are selling the output of games from teams that have territorial exclusivity in local media markets conferred upon them by monopoly sports leagues. In most areas there is only one regional sports network.[19] Typically, then, we have a monopoly (team) selling to a monopoly (programmer) which then sells to a monopoly (cable company), which then sells to the public. Of course, in a few areas the industry is not a monopoly but a duopoly with considerable market power and in some areas there is vertical integration among the team, programmer and distributor. Whatever the permutation in a given city, the consumer is playing against a stacked deck.

There are a few other features of this picture of concentration that also help to explain rising cable prices. Back in 1992, in an effort to protect local broadcasters against the growing power of cable companies, the US Congress passed a bill mandating retransmission consent, *inter alia*. Local broadcasters can either require the local cable company to add its station to the basic package (must carry) or it can require the cable company to obtain its consent to carry the channel. The network companies, e.g., GE/NBC, Disney/ABC, Viacom/CBS and News Corp./FOX, AOL/TimeWarner/WB, own several of their local affiliate stations covering between 35 and 45 per cent of US households.[20] Since the 1992 retransmission consent law, the rule relaxation allowing cross ownership of broadcast and cable channels, and the elimination of the FCC's Financial-Syndication rules in 1995, the national network companies have bought up and created dozens of leading cable channels. Of the 26 top-rated national cable channels 20 are owned by a national network company. Overall, the national network companies control at least 50 cable channels.[21]

Through retransmission consent the networks have derived significant economic power. It is common for the networks to require the cable companies to carry their cable channels at above market value in exchange for the right to carry the network signal. Further, according to James Gleason, Chair of the American Cable Association, the network companies include non-disclosure clauses in their retransmission consent contracts, prohibiting the cable company from revealing either the channels or their prices stipulated in the retransmission agreements. Gleason asks: 'Is it really in the public interest for all of my customers to pay for recycled soap operas?'

Thus, despite facing little competitive pressure, independent cable companies are often compelled to include certain channels in their bundle, thereby, adding to the costs of providing their packages. In a sense, through retransmission consent, the network companies indirectly are forcing the public to pay for the 'free' television they provide. While independent cable companies experience some unwanted price pressure, the cable industry as a whole continues to thrive from the lack of competition: according to Gene Kimmelman, Senior Director of Advocacy and Public Policy for the Consumers Union, the operating margin for the industry grew from $7 billion in 1997 to an estimated $18.8 billion in 2002.[22]

VERTICAL INTEGRATION

For a variety of reasons sports teams and regional sports networks have found it profitable to vertically integrate. From the perspective of a media company, ownership of a sports team can provide the programming around which to build a regional sports network. Such an option is especially alluring if it means preventing a chief rival from building an RSN in the same market. This was the avowed motivation of Rupert Murdoch in his 1997 purchase of the Los Angeles Dodgers. In December 2001 Murdoch admitted that his purchase of the Dodgers had already paid off because it enabled him to prevent Disney from creating a regional sports network in southern California (Shaikin, 2001, Sports-8).[23]

RSNs can be valuable properties, particularly in large markets. The News Corp.'s Fox Sports Net 2, which carries the Angels' and the NHL's Mighty Ducks' games, is estimated to be worth between $200 million and $300 million (Hofmeister and Newhan, 2003). New England Sports Network, which is 80 per cent owned by the Red Sox, has been valued as high as $350 million. The Yankee Entertainment and Sports (YES) network was implicitly valued at $850 million-plus, when Goldman Sachs purchased 40 per cent for $350 million in 2001.[24] Thus, by using the sports team as a fulcrum to spin off an RSN, Yankees' owner George Steinbrenner took an asset, the team, worth $600–700 million, preserved its value, and created a new asset, the RSN, worth an even larger sum.

Sports teams may derive still additional value in spawning RSNs. First, in markets where there is only one existing RSN, the team will not benefit from competitive bidding for its cable television rights. By forming an RSN or threatening to form one, the team stands a better chance of receiving market value for its rights.

Second, if the team owns the RSN, it will receive market value through its sale of advertising spots during games and the carriage fee it charges the cable distributor (of course, the RSN will be inclined to ask the cable company for a higher fee than would obtain in a competitive market and may receive it; alternatively, the RSN's asking price may be rejected – an outcome I shall discuss below). The team, however, does not have to report its revenues as team revenues. It may instead report the revenues as generated by the RSN. This latter course has three potential benefits: one, it makes the team appear less profitable which can be used in collective bargaining for leverage against the players; two, it can be used in negotiations with a city in efforts to procure public financing for a new facility; and, three, it can be used to avoid revenue sharing obligations with other teams in the league (presently, this only applies to baseball).

While vertical integration is potentially quite valuable to the sports teams, it often spells trouble for the consumer. It may also spell trouble for the integrity of competition within a given sports league.

Consider the dispute between Cablevision and YES over the carriage of New York Yankees' games on expanded basic. Cablevision is a vertically-integrated company, owning, *inter alia*, various cable distribution companies, two New York City RSNs (MSG and FSNY – Fox Sports New York) and two teams (the NBA's New York Knicks and the NHL's New York Rangers).[25] Cablevision Chairman Charles Dolan[26] was less than pleased that his company, MSG, had lost its telecasting rights to the Yankees and that his bid for the Red Sox was not accepted despite being some $90 million above that of the Henry group's bid. But more importantly, Dolan was not pleased at the prospect that his two New York City RSNs were going to face strong competition from the new upstart, YES.

Dolan's response was both clever and maddening. Dolan's Cablevision had exploited its immense market power over the years. Cablevision, the cable distributor, faced no meaningful competition in selling cable television services to 3 million of the nearly 8 million subscribers in the New York City media market. It had raised its monthly rates on its expanded basic package from $21.95 to $46.65 between 1993 and 2003.

The expanded basic package included 65 channels in early 2002. If the consumer wanted only one or two of those channels, he or she had to purchase the whole package.

Dolan's Cablevision also has enjoyed monopoly power by owning the only two RSNs in the New York City area until YES launched in early 2002 (advertisers on local cable sports programming faced a monopsony), by controlling the local broadcast rights to all professional sports teams in the greater New York City market,[27] and by owning teams in two monopoly sports leagues. Yet when asked to carry the YES network on its expanded basic package at $2 per subscriber per month, something that the three other cable distributors in New York City and dozens more in the outer market agreed to, Chuck Dolan suddenly became a populist. He argued that it was unfair to bundle the YES network into the basic package and raise the rates of all subscribers, because not all subscribers were Yankee fans. True enough. On this argument Dolan should also cease to carry ESPN, CNN, TBS, BET or a host of other cable channels on Cablevision's basic package. Also on this argument Dolan's Cablevision should not have put its own RSNs – MSG and FSNY – on the expanded basic package in roughly half of its New York markets.

The upshot of this dispute for the 2002 season was that Yankees' fans in the Cablevision area were unable to watch 130 of the team's games on cable television.[28] Monopoly power, then, led not only to higher prices and less output; in 2002 for 3 million New York households, it led to no output at all.[29]

An interesting ancillary effect of this dispute arose because Cablevision is in partnership with the News Corp. The News Corp, in turn, owned (until January 2004) the Los Angeles Dodgers, a competitor of the New York Yankees. The Dodgers not only potentially compete with the Yankees on the field, they also – along with baseball's other teams – compete with the Yankees as the team that has most aggressively pushed the player salary envelope.[30]

Similarly, the Yankees co-own the YES network via a holding company with the NBA's New Jersey Nets. The Nets were contracted to show 73 of their 82 games in 2002–2003 on the YES network. By refusing to carry YES on its expanded basic tier, Cablevision was able to derive a competitive advantage for its NBA team, the New York Knicks, over the New Jersey Nets. The NBA league office had nothing to say publicly about this apparent conflict of interest.

Whatever the motivation of Charles and James Dolan in their dispute with YES, Cablevision's resistance to the price terms of an RSN seems to have catalysed an impending price revolt among cable distributors. The days when RSNs and ESPN could announce yearly price increases of 20 per cent or more and expect the cable companies unflinchingly to pass it along to the consumer in the form of higher cable bills appear to be over. Monthly charges of $40 to $50 for expanded basic cable seem to be too much for large numbers of households to absorb during an extended period of flat incomes and high unemployment.

Paul Allen's Action Sports Cable Network (ASCN) went dark during the first week of November 2002 after AT&T Broadband, Portland Oregon's largest cable provider, refused to accept Allen's asking price – a comparatively modest 50 cents per subscriber per month. Faced with a requested price increase from $1.50 per subscriber per month to $2.20 from FSN North in Minneapolis, Time Warner chose to drop the channel. FSN North holds the cable rights to the NHL's Wild, the NBA's Timberwolves and MLB's Twins. Nearly 200,000 households lost cable access to these games until a compromise price was reached between FSN North and Time Warner cable at the end of March 2003. In Orlando, Florida, the Sunshine Network was seeking a 40 per cent rate increase to $1.26 per subscriber per month, but Time Warner found this excessive and pulled the plug on the network in January 2003. Over 700,000 households lost cable access for three months to the NBA's Magic and NHL's Lightning games until this dispute was settled in late March 2003. Meanwhile, many of ESPN's new contracts with cable distributors call for yearly price increases of 7 per cent, instead of 20 per cent.

POLICY OPTIONS

These developments are a lightning rod to consumers and politicians alike. Yankees' fans in New York unsuccessfully sought an injunction to force Cablevision to carry YES on basic cable. New Jersey Attorney General David Samson threatened to bring an antitrust suit against Cablevision. YES itself filed an antitrust action against Cablevision.

Faced with the prospect that Yankee games would be lost to New Jersey's Cablevision households for a second season in 2003, in early February 2003 the Telecommunications and Utilities Committee of the New Jersey Legislature voted four to two on a bill to compel Cablevision to carry the YES network. Then, one month later a similar bill passed the full Assembly by a 47 to 20 margin.

Various committees in the US Congress held hearings during 2003 and 2004 to consider either re-regulation or pro-competition bills for the industry. Arizona Senator John McCain opined in April 2002:

> I'm not sure an 80-year-old woman who subscribes to cable should have to pay for ESPN. I think something ought to happen. I don't know if it's competition; I don't know if it's re-regulation ... But the status quo is very unacceptable.[31]

A variety of different public policies could be employed to alleviate the bundling, carriage and pricing problems. First, the FCC could reverse its current course and promote competition among cable providers in individual markets. This could be accomplished by requiring cable distributors to provide local loop access to competitors, as was done in the telephone industry. The alternative is to wait for the maturation of DBS competition, but this might not materialise in many markets and might not benefit all consumers. DBS is limited by building or natural obstruction to certain areas or homes, and cable companies' discounted bundling of services (cable television, telephony, broadband) creates a barrier to entry. Further, when consumers live in apartment buildings or condos, the choice to add DBS service (rather than or in addition to cable) often requires a political decision.

Technological advances now offer a reasonable prospect for cable and internet services to be provided over electrical wires. Eventually, however, it appears likely that G4 wireless will become the preferred technology and competition-enhancing policy will be necessary.

Still another option, suggested by the recent Cablevision/YES agreement for the 2003 season, is to compel some level of debundling. In their settlement, Cablevision was required to carry YES in one of three ways: part of an optimum service package (at $64.95 monthly, compared to expanded basic at $46.65 monthly); part of a sports package including MSG and FSNY for $4.95 monthly; or, as a standalone channel, for $1.95 monthly (the latter two choices require subscription to the expanded basic digital package).

If Cablevision's expanded basic monthly rates are discounted under the 2003 plan to reflect the subtraction of the local RSNs, it is hard to conclude that this required debundling did not enhance consumer welfare. Non-baseball fans were not required to pay to watch the local teams. Yankees fans paid just under $2 per month on Cablevision, which was roughly what they paid on the other distributors in the New York area. Mets fans, however, had to pay either $4.95 monthly for all Mets and Yankees games or $3.90 for all Mets games (because Mets games were split between MSG and FSNY).

Pursuant to the 2003 agreement, absent a negotiated deal for subsequent seasons, YES and Cablevision agreed to submit their contract to binding arbitration. In March 2004, the three-man arbitration panel decided the terms of a carriage deal between the two entities. The decision required Cablevision to carry YES on expanded basic for six years at a price of $1.93 in 2004, with yearly increases of 4 per cent (cut from seven per cent in existing YES contracts) throughout the deal.[32]

A complementary strategy would be to extend debundling to include the national sports channels, such as ESPN and its various offshoots as well as Fox Sports.[33] ESPN has been signing long-term contracts with cable distributors that allow it to raise its carriage prices by 20 per cent per year. The package of ESPN channels can now cost over $9 a month. Prices rose again 20 per cent on August 1, 2003, though ESPN plans to offer more modest increases to distributors who pick up new ESPN channels, such as ESPN-HD and ESPN Deportes, and commit to longer term contracts. Why should all cable customers be compelled to pay $9 and upwards for national sports channel?

The theoretical claims that bundling permits more efficient pricing only hold under restrictive assumptions. As I discussed above, these arguments do not appear to be applicable to the US cable industry.

Of course, still more radical remedies are available. They include public provision of cable services with marginal cost pricing, or empowering a regulatory agency to re-establish price controls over cable monopolies. The limitation of the 1961 SBA exemption to free television could be enforced, subjecting all sports package cable and DBS deals to antitrust scrutiny. Territorial and league monopolies could also be challenged.

Rapid technological change is making new products and delivery systems economically viable with each passing year. These changes make it problematic to prescribe specific policies, but the need for competition at the delivery, programming and production levels is apparent both to promote technological innovation and to protect consumers.

NOTES

1.   An abridged and edited version of this chapter was originally published as 'Sports and Cable Television', in *The Milken Institute Review*, 2003, **5** (4), 57-66.
2.   Leading the way in 2003 was NESN and the Boston Red Sox. On September 5, 2002 the Red Sox announced that the number of games they will broadcast over-the-air in 2003 will be only 28, in contrast to 70 such games in 2002. The number of NESN telecasts in 2003 rose to 122, up from 85 in 2002.
3.   Again, actual revenue growth is likely to be considerably higher than this.
4.   These figures and those for local television contracts in the NBA come from the *Sports Business Journal* 'By the Numbers', 2002, p. 82, Paul Kagan Associates, 1999a, p. 364

and 1999b, p. 302. According to Hoehn and Lancefield (2003) in 1999 there were 127 hours of hockey on broadcast television and 1199 hours on cable.

5. *Liberty Broadcasting Systems v. National League Baseball Club of Boston, Inc.* (N.D. Ill., 1952).

6. The SBA's intention is congruent with the US Supreme Court decision in *Board of Regents of Univ. of Oklahoma v. NCAA*, 546 F. Supp. 1276, 1311 (W.D. Okla. 1982), wherein a proper standard was set for assessing broadcast rights agreements under the rule of reason. The standard was total viewership (with the number of broadcast games used as a proxy) and based on this the court held that the prevailing contract between the NCAA and the networks was illegal because it led to higher prices and lower output.

7. *Professional Sports Antitrust Immunity Hearings on S.2784 and S2821 Before the Senate Committee on the Judiciary, 97th Congress, 2d Session 41 (1982).*

8. *Chicago Pro. Sports Ltd. Partnership v. NBA*, 808 F.Supp. 646, 649-50 (N.D. Ill. 1992), and Shaw *et al.* v. NFL (ED Pa., 2000). Also see the letter from Charles Rule, Asst. Atty General, Antitrust Division, US Department of Justice, to Hon. Howard Metzenbaum, Chair, Senate Subcommittee on Antitrust, March 30, 1988.

9. MLB's contract with FOX might also be vulnerable without the exemption since the network carries some of its national games on FOX's cable affiliates. Ross, *op. cit.*, has argued that the proper reading of the Blackmun decision in *Flood v. Kuhn*, 407 US 258 (1972), would find that baseball broadcasting does not constitute a unique aspect of the baseball business and, hence, is not covered by the sport's presumed antitrust exemption. Roth also points out that the court in *Henderson Broadcasting Corporation v. Houston Sports Association*, 541 F Supp. 263 (S.D. Tex. 1982), held that:

    'The issue in the case is not baseball but a distinct and separate industry, broadcasting ... To hold that a radio station contract to broadcast baseball games should be treated differently for antitrust law purposes than a station's contract to broadcast any other performance or event would be to extend and distort the specific baseball exemption, transform it into an umbrella to cover other activities and markets outside baseball ... as a shield against the statutes validly enacted by Congress (*Ibid*, p. 271).'

10. The one-year deal signed on March 31, 2003 between Cablevision and YES for the 2003 is an exception for the moment.

11. Under the 2003 Cablevision/YES deal, a Cablevision subscriber could purchase YES alone for $1.95 monthly or a package of YES, MSG and FSNY for $4.95 monthly. The 2003 deal also provided that if the parties could not agree on a contract beyond 2003, a panel of three arbitrators would decide on what basis YES would be carried on Cablevision in the future. The panel ruled on March 23, 2004 that Cablevision must carry YES on its expanded basic package for the next six years and that YES could charge $1.93 monthly per customer in 2004 (with a 4 per cent annual increase). Since the cable delivery companies serving other parts of the NYC market have most favored nation clauses in their contracts with YES, they too will be able to benefit from the slightly lower rates promulgated by the arbitration panel.

12. By the standards applied in *Oklahoma v. NCAA*, the US Supreme Court set the output standard in terms of the number of eyeballs. Thus, the addition of a new channel does not necessarily constitute more output, especially if it is an unwanted channel. Consumers may be put off by channel clutter. In contrast, a constant number of channels, but with improved quality, may increase eyeballs (and output).

13. When airlines sell certain roundtrip tickets at a heavy discount, they are also bundling. The Saturday-night stay-over discount can affect consumer behavior in ways other than reducing consumption. It can induce passengers to spend an extra night in the visited city, to alter the dates of their trip, or to buy two separate roundtrip tickets. If nothing else, the transactions cost is increased in these instances. For a discussion of this example and other bundling issues, see: Nalebuff, 2003, Coppejans and Crawford, 1999, and Yoo, 2003.

14. FCC rulings can be challenged in court.

15.   The FCC study also performed a multiple regression analysis on the causes of price differentials controlling for other relevant factors, such as the size of the market and availability of DBS, and found that competition between cable distributors lowered prices 7–8 per cent at the 1 per cent level of significance.
16.   Testimony of William B. Shear, GAO's Acting Director of Physical Infrastructure, before the US Senate Committee on Commerce, May 6, 2003.
17.   *Ibid*, p. 28. The GAO study confirmed this result, although it did find that significant penetration by DBS into an area increased the average number of channels offered by the cable distributor.
18.   Although it is higher in some areas, as of August 1, 2003 the standard charge to the cable distributors for ESPN was $2.40 per subscriber per month. The net cost to cable companies is below this because ESPN allows the cable companies to sell a certain number of advertising spots each hour. Cox Communications says that their ad avails yield the equivalent of $0.55 per subscriber per month. Cox may also use some avails for promotional purposes. Thus, the net cost to the cable companies for ESPN is likely to be between $1.60 and $1.85 per subscriber per month. Of course, the ESPN scions have their own fees.
19.   Or, in some cases, there are two RSNs but they are both owned by the same company, as is the case in Los Angeles (Fox Sports one and two) and was the case in New York prior to the advent of YES in early 2002.
20.   In early June 2003, the FCC voted 3 to two to allow networks to increase their ownership of local affiliates. The new rules allow the networks to own a newspaper and television station in the same city, up to three television stations in the same city and to reach up to 45 per cent of US households via their owned affiliates.
21.   Testimonies of James Gleason, COO of Cable Direct and Chair of the American Cable Association, and of James Robbins, CEO of Cox Communications, before the US Senate Committee on Commerce, May 6, 2003.
22.   Gene Kimmelman, written testimony, submitted to the US Senate Committee on Commerce, Science and Transportation, hearings on the cable industry, May 6, 2003.
23.   Murdoch's News Corp. presently owns two different RSNs in the greater Los Angeles area: Fox Sports Net 1 and Fox Sports Net 2.
24.   With a minority discount, the implied value would be even higher.
25.   The RSNs (in New York and a few other cities) as well as the Knicks and Rangers are co-owned with the News Corp.
26.   The Dolan family owned 24 per cent of Cablevision's stock but controlled 75 per cent of the voting rights as of September 2002.
27.   This also refers to the period up to the formation of the YES network in October 2001. Cablevision's control over local broadcast rights for teams as well as its ownership of two local franchises enables it to limit the access to sports programming to its potential competitors in cable or satellite video distribution.
28.   Tens of thousands of fans switched to DirecTV in order to be able to watch the team. However, some areas cannot receive satellite television and other viewers were reluctant to switch because they would not be able to pick up local broadcast channels or because they purchased their internet connection and/or telephone service from Cablevision. In its suit against Cablevision, YES charged that:

> Cablevision has also improperly bundled the sale of its cable service with the sale of its online high-speed Internet access service by offering significant discounts, thereby making it impractical for a subscriber to retain the Internet access while switching to another MVPD provider, where one is available.

Complaint in *YES v. Cablevision* (S.D. N.Y., April 2002), p. 6. MVPD stands for multichannel video programming distribution.
29.   As mentioned above, this dispute was settled for the 2003 season. For 2003, Cablevision created a sports tier with MSG, FSNY and YES that sold for $4.95 a month and also allowed customers to buy YES, MSG or FSNY separately for $1.95 a month. Cablevision guaranteed YES a minimum revenue and agreed to indemnify YES for any lost

subscriber revenue on the Time Warner or Comcast systems which had most-favored-nation clauses with the YES network.
30.   The News Corp's purchase of DirecTV for $6.6 billion suggests that more manipulation and restrictive practices in the pay television market are in the offing. The purchase will give Fox more leverage vis a vis the sports leagues and teams in negotiating carriage rights. Fox has been losing leverage, as more teams have sought in recent years to create their own RSNs. One interesting question will be: how hard would DirecTV price compete with the cable companies in seeking to establish a larger market imprint? News Corp may seek higher prices for its programming from the cable operators, but it may be reluctant to enter into vigorous competition over delivery prices because it may weaken its ability to drive up programming prices. One way or the other, the acquisition will generate more market power for Murdoch's News Corp that is unlikely to be employed in the pursuit of consumer interests.
31.   *Sports Business Daily*, April 23, 2002, p. 7.
32.   Although this ruling was a clear victory for YES, YES was forced to reduce its 2003 price retroactively from $2.12 per month to $1.85 per month. The rebates cost YES around $17 million, but the new carriage deal will bring YES well over $220 million a year in subscription and advertising revenues.
33.   Because bundling is sometimes forced upon cable companies by networks via retransmission consent, such as ABC manipulating the carriage of ESPN offshoots or FOX doing the same with Fox Sports World, it would make sense for the FCC and Congress to revisit the rules surrounding retransmission consent. One obviously desirable change would be to proscribe all non-disclosure clauses.

REFERENCES

Adams, W.J. and J. Yellen (1976), 'Commodity Bundling and the Burden of Monopoly', *Quarterly Journal of Economics*, **90**, 475–498.

Broadcasting and Cable, July 29, 2002 and March 31, 2003.

Coppejans, M. and G. Crawford (1999), *Bundling in Cable Television: Incentives and Implication for Regulatory Policy,* draft manuscript, Department of Economics, Duke University.

FCC – Federal Communications Commission (2002), *Report on Cable Industry Prices*, FCC 02–107, April 4.

Hoehn, T. and D. Lancefield (2003), 'Broadcasting and Sport', *Oxford Review of Economic Policy*, **19** (4), 552–568.

Hofmeister, S. and R. Newhan (2003), 'Dodger Pitch Has a Catch', *Los Angeles Times*, January 22.

Nalebuff, B. (2003), 'Bundling, Tying and Portfolio Effects', *Department of Trade and Industry Economics paper 1*, Yale University.

Paul Kagan Associates (1999a), *The Business of Hockey*, Monterey, CA.

Paul Kagan Associates (1999b), *The Business of Basketball*, Monterey, CA.

Ross Stephen (1990), 'An antitrust analysis of sports leagues contracts with cable networks', *Emory Law Journal*, **39** (2), 463–497.

Shaikin, B. (2001), 'Fox Reaches Dodger Goals', *Los Angeles Times*, December 13.

Sports Business Journal, 'By the Numbers', 2002.

Sports Business Daily, April 23, 2002.

Stigler, G. (1963), 'United States v. Loew's Inc.: A Note on Block Booking', in P. Kurland (ed.), *The Supreme Court Review: 1963*, Chicago, IL: University of Chicago Press, 152–157.

Yoo, C. (2003), 'A New Economic Model of Television Regulation', draft manuscript, School of Law, Vanderbilt University.

Zimbalist, A. (1992), *Baseball and Billions: A Probing Look Inside the Big Business of our National Pastime*, New York, NY: Basic Books.

Zimbalist, A. and B. Costas (2003), *May the Best Team Win: Baseball Economics and Public Policy*, Washington, DC: Brookings Institution Press.

10. Baseball and the Broadcast Media

Paul D. Staudohar

INTRODUCTION

The four principal sources of revenue to major league baseball are broadcasting, gate receipts, stadium revenues, and licensing. About 40 per cent of total receipts derive from broadcasting – television (national, local and cable) and radio. By far the lion's share of broadcast revenue is from television, and its substantial payoffs have provided a bonanza to owners and players. But squabbling over the distribution of the broadcast pot has plagued the game with work stoppages. And the economic and competitive disadvantages faced by low-revenue teams, compared to their wealthy brethren, are in major part attributable to disparities in broadcast income.

This chapter explores the relationships between broadcasting and baseball, from the early days of radio through the television age. It reviews how baseball was the first sport to receive widespread exposure from broadcasting, the influence of national expansion of broadcast markets, and the role of technology. Reasons for the revenue explosion are provided. Of further interest is the economic impact of television on owners and players. Also examined are ways to make the distribution of broadcast revenues among teams more equitable, so as to promote financial health in less fortunate clubs and better competitive balance on the playing field.

RADIO

The medium of radio is important to baseball for a variety of reasons. One is historical. Radio came first, and until the 1950s it was the exclusive way in which fans received broadcast entertainment. Second, radio provided paradigms that evolved into the format for telecasts, e.g., sale of rights to broadcasters, live programming, use of paid announcers, and commercial sponsors. Third, although overshadowed by television, radio continues to provide broadcasts of virtually all games of individual teams plus national events such as the All-Star Game and World Series.

The first broadcasts of baseball occurred during the 1890s, as telegraph services paid to have reports on games sent to saloons and pool rooms (Zimbalist, 1992). Major league baseball's first radio broadcast occurred on August 5, 1921, for the game between the Pittsburgh Pirates and Philadelphia Phillies at Forbes Field in Pittsburgh (Zimbalist, 1992). The World Series in 1921 was broadcast by relay, and in 1922 and 1923 on a play-by-play basis. Helping to stimulate interest was the involvement in the Series of the New York Yankees and their popular star Babe Ruth. Nationwide broadcast of the World Series did not begin until 1926 (Battema, 2000, pp. 148, 168).

Although radio broadcasts began in the 1920s, there was no sale of rights for several years. Instead, the owners gave away the rights as a public service. They generally believed that radio coverage would reduce attendance, but acknowledged that they had to put up with some of it because of public demand. In 1929 NBC and CBS each carried the World Series on their networks, on a *pro bono* basis.

Radio broadcasts of baseball were commercialised in 1934 when Commissioner Kenesaw Mountain Landis reached a deal with the Ford Motor Company for $400,000 to sponsor the World Series for the next four years. The games were presented on all three major networks of that time, NBC, CBS, and the Mutual Broadcasting Company. In 1939 the Gillette Safety Razor Company took over sponsorship of the World Series, which it presented for the next 32 years (Rader, 1984, p. 25). Given baseball's popularity, these broadcasts captured the attention of the entire nation.

Because owners remained wary of radio's supposed affect of keeping people away from the ballpark, local broadcasting of games was not common. The main exception was William Wrigley, a chewing gum magnate who owned the Chicago Cubs. In 1925 Wrigley began giving away broadcast rights to any station that wanted to present Cubs' games, and there were multiple broadcasts of games on Chicago stations over the years. Wrigley viewed the broadcasts as free publicity that would promote the interest in his team. Ultimately he was proved to be right.

Although Cub attendance was not reduced by the broadcasts, Wrigley's example was not generally followed. In fact, in 1932 the major leagues nearly decided to ban broadcasts entirely, and in 1934 the three New York City teams (Yankees, Giants and Brooklyn Dodgers) agreed to ban radio broadcasting until 1938. The following year all major league teams broadcast on the radio for the first time, but often just games on the road.

By the 1940s and 1950s radio broadcasts of games of major league as well as minor league teams really took off. From 1945 to 1950 the number of locally operated radio stations doubled; the 'Game of the Day' on the Mutual Broadcasting Company network was broadcast on nearly 500 stations in the 1950s (Rader, 1984, p. 26). One of the oddities of local broadcasts, until the mid-1950s, was that many games were 're-created' by announcers, based on reports via telegraph from Western Union (Rader, 1984, p. 27). The most famous example of this was station WHO in Des Moines, Iowa, who used announcer Ronald 'Dutch' Reagan to re-create games of the Chicago Cubs.

Radio broadcasts were eventually overshadowed by television, but radio retains some allure today, especially for listening while motor vehicle commuting and for fans who treasure the imagery that radio broadcasts provide. A gifted radio announcer, and there are many of these, can hold listeners in thrall with creative commentary.

In 1997 all big-league teams had the option of presenting audio from their games on their own website or on the site of their flagship stations. This caused a resurgence for audiocasting, and in 2001 major league baseball decided to consolidate all of its game audio as part of a MLB.com family of sites. For access to the full season of games, listeners initially had to pay $9.95 to major league baseball, a fee that had risen to $19.95 by the 2003 season (Matthews, 2003). As a result, local radio stations that were broadcasting games online were no longer able to do so.

TELEVISION

Baseball was the first sport to be televised. On May 17, 1939, an Ivy League game between Columbia and Princeton, played at Baker Field on the Columbia campus in New York City, was televised on NBC's experimental station. The event even had a broadcaster, famous sports announcer Bill Stern. Several hundred people watched the game on a small silver screen located at the RCA Building in New York.

On August 26, 1939, the first exposure of major league baseball on television occurred, at a double-header at Ebbetts Field in Brooklyn between the Dodgers and the pennant-bound Cincinnati Reds.[1] It is estimated that fewer than 1,000 persons saw the show on nine-inch or less television sets in metropolitan New York. RCA presented the telecast, using two cameras, one behind home plate and the other at ground level near the third base dugout. Reds catcher and future Hall of Famer, Ernie Lombardi, said that he felt as though someone was 'looking over his shoulder' all day.

The Yankees in 1946 paid $75,000 to become the first team to acquire television broadcast rights. The World Series was presented live on television for the first time on NBC in 1949. A major breakthrough occurred in 1951 when a coaxial cable was completed to enable presentation of live broadcasts coast to coast (Thomson *et al.*, 1991). This prompted the 1951 playoffs between the New York Giants and the Brooklyn Dodgers to be nationally televised. Viewers were treated to Bobby Thomson's 'Shot Heard Round the World', the most dramatic home run in baseball history, winning the pennant for the Giants in the bottom of the ninth inning of the decisive game.

In 1950 only about 12 per cent of US households had television sets. While reception was sometimes of marginal quality, in black and white, the share of households with television grew rapidly, to 67 per cent in 1955 and 87 per cent in 1960 (Zimbalist, 1992, p. 149). Baseball responded to this growth in positive ways, although the lords of the game remained skeptical of the impact of television on attendance at live games, similar to their earlier reservations about radio. By the early 1950s owners had warmed to radio, perceiving that it actually stimulated demand for live attendance. Television, however, was bad for attendance in their opinion, and it was especially troublesome to the minor leagues because some viewers who could watch major league ball on television lost interest in their local minor league teams.

Prominent baseball executives Branch Rickey and Clark Griffith determined in the early 1950s that the owners should seek to collectively gain control of television broadcasting, limit its exposure, and pool income from the sale of rights (Miller, 1990, p. 6). The major leagues established rules prohibiting teams from broadcasting into other teams' territory and requiring visiting teams to get permission to broadcast. By 1953 rights to telecast a limited number of games were sold by nearly all teams.

In 1954 the major leagues submitted a plan to the US Department of Justice for a 'Game of the Week', to be negotiated by the Commissioner of Baseball. The Justice Department, however, advised the leagues that their proposal would violate federal antitrust law. Back in 1922, by US Supreme Court decision, baseball was granted immunity from the antitrust law prohibition on monopolies that restrain competition. But Congress in 1951 had conducted an investigation of this exemption, and owners were also wary of challenges to the legality of the reserve clause, binding players to clubs, which was a clear restraint of the labour market.

The owners went ahead with their plans for a game of the week on television but the arrangements were made between individual teams and the networks, rather than by the commissioner on behalf of all teams. Teams whose games appeared more often received greater revenues. Then in 1961 Congress passed the Sports Broadcasting Act. This law granted an antitrust law exemption to major team sports, enabling leagues to negotiate national broadcasting rights packages that provided for pooling of income among teams. This law cleared the way for the major leagues to establish tight control of their television rights.

With this control the symbiosis between baseball and television came into sharper focus. The owners realised that television, used judiciously, would not negatively affect attendance. They viewed it as a revenue source and a way of marketing their team to increase the size of the live gate. Television, for its part, needed sporting events to utilise airtime and attract sponsors. Especially in the early days of live video broadcasting, because of its popularity as the national pastime, baseball became a way of legitimising other television programming and was in big demand. This demand translated into hefty financial rewards to team owners. The synergism continues to the present, although the needs may not be as compelling as in the past.

An important reason why the bloom is somewhat off the rose for baseball and television is that the sports calendar has become crowded with events. In years past baseball stood alone as *the* professional team sport with national attention. NFL football began to challenge this supremacy in the 1950s and pro basketball and hockey joined the fray in the 1960s. Today, sports such as motor racing, pro wrestling, women's basketball, golf, tennis and so on flood the market with alternatives.

Also, baseball is a sport not altogether suited for television. Football and basketball games, for instance, move laterally across the television screen and utilise a larger ball that is easier to see. The baseball field, on the other hand, is spacious and features a more geometric than linear flow of play. Action away from the ball may be missed on the screen. The smaller baseball moves at high speeds, curves and can be hit high in the air. Action is less continuous, with numerous 'dead spots' that can be boring to viewers. Of course, to true fans there is nothing as intellectually stimulating as baseball, with its tradition, endless variety, subtlety and sophistication of play. But, similar to hockey, these nuances do not translate well on television. With its 162 games baseball has far more availability than pro basketball (84 games), hockey (82 games), or football (16 games), giving the sport a prolonged exposure that can dampen enthusiasm over the season, especially if playoff races are not close.

Television ratings for baseball – regular season, All-Star Game, and postseason – are all at or near historic lows. There are simply too many other things to do. Yet, baseball is hanging on, with fairly robust live attendance. Although the All-Star Game ratings are way down from earlier levels (44 per cent in 1982, 22 per cent in 1999), they are still far higher than those in other major sports' all star games (Hegedus, 2000).[2] Pro football may be the most popular American sport but baseball continues to possess the hearts of a great many fans.

BROADCAST RIGHTS

Rather than the $100,000 that it cost the Ford Motor Company to sponsor radio transmission of the World Series, its successor, Gillette, had to pony up $400,000 in the late 1930s. By the end of World War II all teams in the major leagues were selling radio rights for regular season games. Whereas teams received an average of under $1,000 each in 1933 from local broadcasts, by 1950 each franchise averaged over $200,000 annually (Rader, 1984, p. 26). The arrangements for the sale of radio rights were similar to those adopted for television. That is, rights to present national telecasts of regular season games, the All-Star Game, and the postseason are sold to networks by the leagues, with equal sharing of revenue by teams. Local rights proceeds until 1982 were exclusively retained by team owners. Some sharing has occurred since then, particularly as a result of arrangements following the 1994–1995 player strike and in the 2002 collective bargaining agreement.

NATIONAL TELEVISION

National television rights fees on a total annual basis and per team are shown in Table 10.1. The rights fees have risen steadily over the years, with especially large rises from 1980–1993. For instance, the total revenue package of $1.125 billion for the six-year period from 1984–1989 ($187.5 million per team on an annual basis) was an increase of nearly four times over the previous period.

The 1990–1993 agreement approximately doubled the revenues per team.[3] CBS, trailing the other major networks in overall ratings, sought to enhance its image by paying $1.1 billion over four years. The package included rights to the World Series, League Championship Series, All-Star Game and 12 regular season games. Shortly after the CBS deal, baseball agreed to its initial national cable contract for games with ESPN. This was a four-year deal, totaling $400 million, providing for rights to 175 games per season.

The 1990–1993 agreements were disastrous for the networks, with CBS losing about $500 million and ESPN about $150 million. CBS had rights to less than half the number of annual regular season games that had been shown under the 1984–1989 agreements with NBC and ABC, and ratings were low. Besides the low ratings, ESPN's problem was that about half of America's homes did not have access to the cable network. This marked the first time that networks had lost such large amounts on sports programming.

As a result, the 1994–1995 national television rights deal was restructured downward, cutting revenues to teams by approximately half. Baseball made an error by agreeing to a joint venture with NBC and ABC called the Baseball Network. Under this arrangement, which was originally set for six years, major league baseball received 85 per cent of the first $140 million with the networks, and got to keep 80 per cent of additional revenue. This arrangement was a mistake because it put baseball in the advertising business, responsible for selling time to sponsors on the Baseball Network, a new role that it was not well suited to perform. The ESPN agreement provided for 'up-front' money to baseball, but at $235 million over six years it was less than half the rights fees under the old agreement, and the number of weekly games was reduced from six to three.

Table 10.1   National television rights fees (millions of dollars)

Year	Amount Per Year	Annual Amount Per Year
1950	1.2	0.1
1960	3.3	0.2
1970	16.6	0.7
1976–1979	23.2	0.9
1980–1983	47.5	1.8
1984–1989	187.5	7.2
1990–1993	365.0	14.0
1994–1995	190.0	6.8
1996–2000	340.0	12.1
2001–2006*	559.0	18.6

Note: * The six-year agreement with ESPN began in 2000 and expires at the end of 2005. The bigger six-year agreement with Fox runs from 2001–2006.
Sources: Data for 1950–1979 from Zimbalist (1992, p. 49). Data from 1980–1995 from Staudohar (1996, p. 21). Data since 1995 determined by the author as presented in various published sources.

The drastic reduction in revenue was felt most acutely by the low-revenue teams that were more dependent on their equal share of the national television pot. This, in turn, led to a tough stance by the owners at the bargaining table with the players in the 1994–1995 negotiations, and was a major factor precipitating the big strike that was so debilitating to the game (Staudohar, 1997b, p. 24). Adding to the problem was that refunds had to be made to advertisers for the cancellation of the 1994 postseason games. When baseball stubbornly refused to restructure the deal, the networks angrily terminated the agreement after only two of the six years had been completed.

Termination of the television contracts turned out to be a blessing in disguise for baseball, because it was able to negotiate replacement contracts totaling $1.7 million with NBC, Fox and ESPN. This event marked the initial entry of Fox, owned by Rupert Murdoch of News Corporation, into the national baseball telecasts. Apart from the broadcast network, Murdoch's company also controls Fox Sports Net and the FX cable operation. These networks are a major force in local and regional broadcasting.

The new national network television contract is exclusively with Fox. From 2001–06 Fox has rights to the playoffs and World Series, plus 18 Saturday afternoon telecasts each year, during which it can air four different games regionally at the same time. At approximately $419 million per year, the contract provides for about a 45 per cent increase from the previous payment for the same package.

In 1999 a dispute arose between ESPN (a unit of Walt Disney Co.) and major league baseball. ESPN announced that it was switching three games from its Sunday Night Baseball program to ESPN2, the network's smaller station that reaches fewer viewers. The reason for the switch was that ESPN wanted to show three National Football League games in September because of their higher ratings (in 1998 the ratings were 8.1 for the NFL and 1.8 for baseball).[4] In a huff, baseball terminated ESPN's rights contract, effective at the end of the year. This prompted a lawsuit by ESPN to maintain its contract, and baseball filed a countersuit.

After several months of meetings, the parties agreed to a settlement. Under its terms ESPN went forward with the football telecasts but made up for the lost baseball games by showing extra games on Friday nights on ESPN and ESPN2. More importantly, the parties agreed to extend and enhance their basic rights agreement. A new six-year contract, beginning in 2000, will pay baseball an estimated $851 million. The number of telecasts will increase from 90 to 108 per season, and the deal includes certain Internet rights and rights to interactive games (Stewart, 1999). Although the television contract is for regular season games only, a separate radio arrangement was reached that includes postseason games, including the World Series, on ESPN radio. The radio rights were acquired for $46 million, or $7.7 million a year (*ibid.*).

In 2002 major league baseball presented the first game ever broadcast in video on the Internet, between the New York Yankees and the Texas Rangers. Live Internet broadcasts have potential for substantial revenue to baseball by attracting out-of-town fans who cannot get a satellite feed of a game. For the 2003 season major league baseball, in partnership with RealNetworks Inc., presented nearly 1,000 games for a fee of $79.95. For most subscribers the local team's games were blacked out and all nationally televised games were excluded. The new Internet service is expected to open up the market, because there is a significant demand by viewers for games played outside their local area, and business persons can watch games when they are traveling.

LOCAL TELEVISION

Unlike national television revenues, which are divided equally among teams, local broadcasting agreements are negotiated separately by the teams. The teams in the most lucrative markets share some of their local revenues with low-revenue teams, but they get to keep by far the biggest part. There is great disparity in local broadcasting revenue, causing a 'rich-poor' dichotomy among teams.

Until 1984 local authorities regulated the rates charged and services provided by telecommunications firms. Pursuant to the national Cable Broadcasting Act of 1984, however, cable television companies could base their charges on what the market would bear. Because some markets do not have competing firms, these companies could be monopolies. The problem that has emerged in these relatively unregulated markets is what is called 'cable-isation' or 'sports siphoning', resulting in much higher monthly fees to customers.

Suppose, for example, that games are provided to customers in a local market via 'free' public television. Teams sell rights to these games and, depending on the size of the market, may reap a tidy reward from the station. A team, however, may be able to significantly increase its revenue by selling the rights for some of its games to a cable provider which charges customers a monthly fee for its service. What is happening is that fewer games are being provided on free television and more games on pay cable. Thus games are siphoned from a situation of no charge to customers to a situation where customers have to pay extra for baseball.

The siphoning is illustrated in Table 10.2. It shows that the average number of broadcast (free television) games per team fell from 65.5 in 1996 to 55.2 in 1998. This is a decline of 16 per cent over three seasons. Meanwhile, the average number of games presented on cable television rose from 50.9 in 1996 to 68.6 in 1998, an increase of nearly 35 per cent. Only a few years ago more games were shown on free television than cable. Now the situation has reversed, as significantly more games are shown on cable. On the plus side, however, more games are being televised on the *combined* broadcast and cable outlets, as seen in Table 10.2.

Table 10.2   Baseball games shown on broadcast and cable television

	Broadcast TV		Cable TV		Combined	
Year	*Total games telecast*	*Average # of telecasts per team*	*Total games telecast*	*Average # of telecasts per team*	*Total games telecast*	*Average # of telecasts per team*
1994*	1,823	65.1	1,432	51.1	3,203	114.4
1995*	1,784	63.7	1,232	45.9	3,016	107.7
1996	1,835	65.5	1,287	50.9	3,259	116.4
1997	1,668	59.6	1,737	62.0	3,405	121.6
1998	1,656	55.2	2,059	68.6	3,715	123.8

Note: * Numbers reflect games planned prior to strike-shortened season. Actual numbers were lower.
Source: McAvoy *et al.*, 1998, p. 24.

The main reason for the shift from free or network television to cable is that cable has a dual revenue stream, from sale of advertising as well as from fees that are paid by subscribers. NBC, CBS, and other networks have only one major revenue source, which is from sale of advertising. For viewers in outlying areas, television picture quality on cable is better than with a conventional antenna. Another factor is that there are significant expenses incurred by the networks that create a cost disadvantage compared to cable. Although some cable operators, such as ESPN and Fox Sports Net, have news divisions and spend money on program development and on-air promotions, the proportionate costs to networks for these functions are higher. As a result, cable companies have a clear-cut financial edge over networks in bidding for local broadcast rights.

The impact of this trend is that fans are paying more money to see baseball on local television. Proportionately more games are shown on pay cable, as games move from the free tier to a higher-paid tier. What is more, as noted by Andrew Zimbalist, this escalation doesn't necessarily stop with basic cable. There is a higher tier of 'expanded cable service', where more games are being shown, and beyond that would come the still higher tier of pay-per-view (PPV) (Zimbalist, 1992, p. 156). PPV has been successful for major boxing events and is used for college football game viewing. It may be that PPV will appear on the baseball menu in the future.

A possible harbinger of the future is recent arrangements involving the Boston Red Sox and the New York Yankees (Badenhausen *et al.*, 2002, Zimbalist, 2003). In 2002 the Red Sox were sold to a group headed by John Henry for $700 million, far eclipsing the previous record sale price of $323 million for the Cleveland Indians in 2000. The reason the Red Sox commanded such a high price is that the sale included not only Fenway Park but an 80 per cent interest in the New England Sports Network. Although the ball club actually lost money the year before the sale, the sports network is a cash cow that recently had agreed to arrangements that more than doubled the number of viewers for Red Sox games.

Another value of this kind of cross-ownership is that teams owning sports networks have flexibility in what they report for cable fees. In effect, these teams can put revenues from baseball operations into the sports network for accounting purposes. These revenues are then exempted from the revenue sharing arrangements in baseball, discussed below. Thus, the Red Sox and other teams who either own cable networks or are owned by a media company can shelter revenues that would otherwise have to be paid to other teams.

The holding company for the Yankees is called YankeesNets, a partnership involving the Yankees, New Jersey Nets basketball team, and the New Jersey Devils hockey team. In 2001 YankeesNets settled a lawsuit with Madison Square Garden Network, a cable company owned by Cablevision Systems Inc., which had previously televised Yankee games. This enabled YankeesNets to start their own regional sports network, which is called Yankees Entertainment and Sports (YES).

The purpose of this new network is to change the way teams control their television rights. Instead of charging a flat fee to a cable provider for the rights to televise its games, YankeesNets can get more revenue by eliminating the middleman. Thus it can obtain revenue both from cable operators to carry the network and from advertisers on its programs. Eventually YES wants to have its own transmission capability, which would eliminate the need for arrangements with an outside cable operator.

YES and Cablevision continued to wage a legal and public relations battle over channel space and rights fees. Although YES was carried on 35 other regional cable companies, Cablevision did not show its telecasts because it was unwilling to pay extra fees to broadcast Yankee games. In 2003 the parties reached a one-year agreement which provides an a la carte arrangement in which consumers will get YES programming only if they pay for that service. YES is not available on basic cable. On the other hand, consumers can get YES separately or in a package with two additional regional sports channels established by Cablevision, without having to receive other cable programming.

Several other baseball, basketball and hockey franchises are forming their own regional sports channels, emulating the Red Sox and Yankees. These newly established networks would likely prefer to have their games carried by local cable companies as part of the basic programming package, because there would be more consumers under this arrangement. But if, as with the

YES-Cablevision deal, consumers have to pay extra to view games, it would not only reduce overall viewership but could redirect the business model towards the *à la carte* arrangement. It may be that the Yankees are so unique that they can have it their own way in the market. But if the Yankees are successful with their new venture, it will create incentives for other franchises and cable operators to try to follow suit. The bottom line for some cable customers would be greater value from programming, because viewers who do not like baseball would no longer have to pay for it as part of the basic cable package.

Two other points should be noted briefly. One is the compensatory payments by superstations. The Atlanta Braves and Chicago Cubs games, for example, are televised on stations that can transmit signals nationally. The Braves' games are broadcast throughout the nation on the cable television network founded by Ted Turner. This aroused the attention of other owners who felt that Turner should pay for this privilege. Therefore, in 1985, at the urging of Commissioner Peter Ueberroth, Turner agreed to pay nearly $30 million to major league baseball over five years in exchange for no restriction on the number of games he could telecast (Staudohar, 1996, p. 21). It is only fair that superstations share with baseball owners some of the money they make from advertisers on the broadcasts.

A second point concerns the recent network strategy of trying to squeeze money out of local affiliates. As noted above, the costs to the networks of broadcasting baseball have escalated over the years. Added to this are the big rights fees that networks pay to football, basketball, hockey, and other sports. Traditionally, the major television networks – NBC, CBS, and ABC – have paid their affiliated stations between $150 and $200 million annually (Flint, 2000). Cable television companies, on the other hand, are paid by their affiliates for the programming they provide (*ibid.*). Because of the spiraling costs of programming, especially for buying sports rights, the networks are seeking to phase out payments to affiliates, and hope eventually to reverse the money flow so affiliates are paying them, similar to what happens with the cable providers.

RETURNS TO OWNERS

Television technology is changing rapidly. High-definition programming is already available, with its images that rival movie theater clarity. The technology is still evolving and the equipment that most people have in their homes is limited to the extent that high-definition signals can be received. Similar to the transition from audio to video in the 1950s, the early twenty-first century holds great promise for expanded forms of entertainment with interactive qualities. Who will control the flow of programming to households, through sources such as satellite, fibre optic wire and coaxial cable remains to be seen. Competition among content providers and distributors will likely create numerous options for consumers.

One of the interesting challenges for owners in baseball and other sports is how technology will affect the electronic transmission of games to viewers and how to take advantage of the changes. Baseball ownership is gravitating increasingly toward individuals and corporations that can facilitate vertical integration of the sport, such as broadcasters and broadcast sponsors.

Although the future may foretell rapid rises in domestic revenues to baseball from broadcasting through technological change causing an increased demand by viewers, the past several years until the late 1990s were relatively flat. This is illustrated in Table 10.3. Revenues after the 1994–1995 strike slowed for a time and then picked up as fan interest revived. Both the networks and baseball are looking for new ventures to increase profitability. League expansion, PPV, and new stadiums with luxury boxes galore are important aspects of this quest. Also attractive is international marketing of the sport. In this regard, baseball has lagged behind football, basketball and hockey. However, major league baseball is seeking to increase its international exposure. The 2000 season began with a two-game series in Japan between the Cubs and Mets at the Tokyo Dome, the first ever outside North America. In subsequent seasons games were scheduled overseas. Baseball has several foreign television rights holders, including NBC Europe; Channel 5 in England; TBS, NHK, and FUJI-TV in Venezuela; Televisa in Mexico; TSN in Canada; and iTV in Korea (Johnson, 2000). With about one-fourth of the players in the major leagues born outside of the US, the potential for international marketing would seem bright.

Even though baseball's television ratings are down, rights fees have been rising at a reasonably healthy clip. This seems to defy rationality. Why would networks continue to shovel out money to baseball when ratings are low and money might be lost? The answer is that the networks view their sports contracts beyond the simple issue of direct profit or loss. For instance, Fox has paid enormous sums for sports television rights, a money loser in its own right. But ownership of major league sports programming has provided significant increases in the overall prime-time ratings on Fox, and the value of its affiliated stations has increased by far more than the cost of the sports telecasts (Geer, 1997, p. 52). Disney, which owns ABC and ESPN, has stimulated sales at its theme parks, catalog, broadcasting, film and team-sports units through sports programming.

Table 10.3   Major league baseball's media revenues (millions of dollars)

Team	1990	1993	1996	1999
NY Yankees	69.4	63.0	69.8	73.0
Chicago Cubs	24.2	36.0	29.3	71.0
Atlanta	20.0	35.0	30.3	66.0
NY Mets	38.3	46.1	30.9	54.0
Los Angeles	29.7	34.0	31.8	48.0
Baltimore	22.5	27.4	30.6	40.0
Arizona				39.0
Anaheim	24.0	26.7	18.3	38.0
Chicago White Sox	24.2	26.2	24.3	38.0
Boston	34.1	38.0	30.9	36.0
Cleveland	20.0	23.7	21.6	36.0
Colorado		5.0	22.8	34.0
Philadelphia	35.0	28.0	21.4	33.0
Detroit	22.3	30.3	24.7	32.0
San Francisco	23.3	27.5	25.5	32.0
Seattle	17.0	21.0	17.2	32.0
Toronto	28.0	31.6	28.4	32.0
Florida		5.0	23.9	30.0
Houston	24.2	26.2	22.3	30.0
St. Louis	27.4	27.0	25.7	30.0
Texas	24.6	27.5	24.3	30.0
Cincinnati	21.8	25.0	21.5	27.0
Oakland	21.2	27.4	25.2	27.0
Tampa Bay				27.0
San Diego	25.1	25.0	16.5	25.0
Milwaukee	19.0	21.5	15.1	24.0
Pittsburgh	20.0	23.5	17.7	22.0
Kansas City	19.0	21.0	16.5	21.0
Minnesota	19.6	22.3	20.4	20.0
Montreal	20.0	24.0	19.4	18.0
Average	25.9	27.7	25.2	35.5

Sources: *Financial World*, 9 July 1991, 42-43; 10 May 1994, 52; 17 June 1997, 47; and Costas, 2000, 65.

The international angle is also part of the symbiosis. At the time Rupert Murdoch of News Corp. was buying the Los Angeles Dodgers from Peter

O'Malley, one of the attractions to Murdoch was his international presence, with broadcasting and sports (soccer, rugby) holdings in Europe and elsewhere in the world. O'Malley was quoted, regarding baseball's missed opportunities internationally, as follows:

> We're behind basketball, behind football, behind hockey – we're fourth in that race. That is sad to me. And there's no doubt in my mind that Fox – and Mr. Murdoch – will bring that to the party ... He will help internationalise the game more than anyone else on the horizon (Bruck, 1997, p. 82).

Also, the concept of integration among units of a media company like Disney or News Corp. has international application. Murdoch recognised this advantage when he said at News Corp.'s 1996 annual meeting:

> We have the long-term rights in most countries to major sporting events, and we will be doing in Asia what we intend to do elsewhere in the world – that is, use sports as a battering ram and a lead offering in all our pay-television operations (*ibid.* p. 86).

When Peter O'Malley sold the Dodgers for $311 million in 1998, they were the last family-owned team whose revenues were the owner's sole support. The trend, as illustrated by News Corp. and Disney, is for media companies to enter baseball as owners. Tribune Company, which owns the *Chicago Tribune*, WGN-AM radio and WGN-TV television superstation, bought out Times-Mirror Corporation, which owns the *Los Angeles Times*, *Newsday*, and other media properties. Ted Turner sold his broadcasting and cable stations (TBS, TNT, CNN) to AOL Time Warner which owns the Atlanta Braves and Atlanta Hawks. Rogers Communications, Canada's largest cable company, bought 80 per cent of the Toronto Blue Jays from Belgian brewer Interbrew in 2000. Fox owns local broadcast rights to nearly all major league teams. These are illustrations of vertical integration in baseball, with media companies owning teams, broadcast sources, and sports-programming rights.

BENEFITS TO PLAYERS

In an attempt to undercut the newly-formed American Baseball Guild, a union of players in 1946, the owners offered a pension plan to be funded by contributions from players and owners (Voigt, 1991, p. 113). The owners decided unilaterally to fund the pension program from the sale of national television and radio rights. The players were kept in the dark about details of the program for the time being.

Upon the death in 1949 of a ten-year veteran ballplayer, Ernie Bonhaur, there was no available money in the pension fund to provide for his widow. Consequently, Commissioner Happy Chandler hurriedly obtained funds by selling the television and radio rights to the World Series and All-Star Game to Gillette for the next six years, at $1 million per year (Jennings, 1990, p. 13).

When the pension plan was revised in 1956 the players were consulted. They were given a choice of a flat $1 million annual contribution or a 60 per cent share of All-Star Game receipts and all radio and television profits from the game, plus radio and television receipts from the World Series (Jennings, 1990, p. 14). Wisely, Ralph Kiner, a player representative, thought that television's promising future justified taking the percentage rather than the flat fee. This would prove to be a boon to player pensions.

In 1972 the players went on strike over the extent and nature of pension funding, causing the cancellation of 86 games at the start of the season. As a result, funding levels were raised and a cost-of-living increase was provided for retirement benefits. This successful strike, the first in the modern sports era, was conducted with Marvin Miller at the helm of the union.

The Major League Baseball Players Association (formed in 1952) hired Miller as its first full-time executive director in 1966. A former official of the Steelworkers Union, Miller brought the players together in an adversarial relationship with the owners, erasing the paternalism of the past. By 1975, in a grievance arbitration involving pitchers Andy Messersmith and Dave McNally, baseball players won the rights to become free agents (currently after six years major league experience). Combined with the opportunity of salary arbitration for players with 2.7 to six years of major league experience, free agency has become the engine for the huge increases in player salaries over the years (Staudohar, 1997a).

If free agency and salary arbitration are the engine for player salary increases, television provides the fuel. There is a strong correlation between player salaries and television revenues, both national and local. It is no coincidence that the Yankees, the team with the richest revenues from sale of local broadcast rights, is also perennially the team with the biggest payroll. As noted in Table 10.1, revenues to baseball from national television were reduced by about half as a result of the rights sale for the 1994 and 1995 seasons. Not surprisingly, average player salaries were essentially flat during the period from 1994–1996 (not considering salary reductions as a result of the strike (*ibid.*, p. 5).) The large increase in television revenue from the 2001–2006 rights sale practically guarantees that average player salaries will rise at a rapid pace in future years.

Because of the growing gap in local television revenues between the highest and lowest revenue teams, a question arises as to whether this disparity translates into success on the playing field. There has always been a positive correlation between high salaries and winning teams. If a club is successful on the playing field, salaries increase because players are compensated on the basis of past performance. Teams like the Yankees can afford to pay players more, to replace players who are injured, and to attract free agents from other clubs. The correlation is not perfect, however, as for many years small-market teams like the Oakland Athletics, Cincinnati Reds, and Minnesota Twins won the World Series. The Yankees didn't even make the playoffs from 1983–1993.

But beginning in 1995 big-market teams have dominated the playoff positions. That year, Atlanta, with the fourth-highest payroll, won the World Series over Cleveland with the seventh highest. In 1996 the three teams with the three highest payrolls – the Yankees, Baltimore Orioles and Atlanta Braves – were joined by the team with the fifth-highest payroll, St. Louis, as the final four teams in the playoffs. In 1997 Florida (fifth highest) beat Cleveland (third highest) in the World Series. In 1998 the Yankees (second-highest) swept San Diego (tenth-highest); and in 1999 it was the highest-paying team, the Yankees, sweeping the third-highest-paying team, the Braves (Costas, 2000, p. 56). In 1999 all eight teams that made the playoffs had among the top ten payrolls in baseball. The highest-payroll Yankees ($112 million) won again in 2000. Although the high-payroll Arizona Diamondbacks won the World Series over the Yankees in 2001, the relatively low-payroll Anaheim Angels won the Championship in 2002.

Of the sources of revenue to baseball, only licensing is relatively constant. Local broadcast revenue, gate receipts, and stadium revenues can be highly variable. Some so-called small-market teams like Texas and Colorado have relatively high gate receipts and stadium revenues from recently built ballparks. Thus, while the size of the media market is a crucial factor to team revenue and success, it is not the whole story.

Bellamy and Walker have done some interesting modeling to show how cities of about the same size can have significantly different revenue streams from television and attendance, with relatively high revenues in Baltimore and St. Louis, and low revenues in Milwaukee and Pittsburgh (Bellamy *et al.*, 2000). They offer a 'pinned-in' model to explain a large part of Pittsburgh's financial difficulties, in that several major league teams surround this city geographically, such as Cleveland, Cincinnati, New York, Philadelphia, Baltimore and Toronto. In contrast, under what Bellamy and Walker call the 'hinterlands model', St. Louis has little major league competition to the immediate west and south, giving it a large potential broadcast market. Also, unlike the Pirates, the Cardinals realised early the advantages of using radio and later television to expand its broadcast market and lock in generations of fans.

Although other variables weigh heavily, the local broadcast revenue factor is crucial to financial success as well as success on the field. There was some sharing of these revenues but it was relatively minor. It had to be beefed up so that rich clubs share far more of their local broadcast revenue with geographically disadvantaged clubs. Bob Costas recommended the radical change of giving half of each team's local broadcast money to its opponents, or placing this half into a national pool that would then be divided equally among all 30 clubs (Costas, 2000, 66-67). Naturally, well placed owners, like the Yankees' George Steinbrenner, or the Dodgers' Murdoch oppose significant revenue sharing. They contend that it is a free enterprise capitalistic economy. Let competition determine survival. These owners paid proportionately more to buy their clubs, so the higher returns should be theirs to keep.

On the other side are the poorer teams who feel that they are not really competitive on the playing field, because they can't afford to pay the high salaries that attract outstanding players. It seems unfortunate that a team like Montreal was unable to retain such excellent players as Randy Johnson and Pedro Martinez. Even though Montreal has done surprisingly well in maintaining a good record on the field with a very low payroll, the club has little chance of retaining superstars or advancing to the postseason.

A compromise was reached in 2002 as a result of a new collective bargaining agreement between the owners and players. The agreement provides for a greater sharing of local revenues, up from the previous 20 per cent to 34 per cent. As a consequence, over the four-year term of the agreement, almost a billion dollars could move from high-revenue to low-revenue teams (Staudohar, 2002, p. 21).

A practical argument endorsing greater revenue sharing is that teams are organised under the umbrella of a league. Leagues are joint ventures with monopoly control (territorial rights) in the defined geographic area of team operation. Unless the large-market teams play games exclusively among themselves, the small-market teams are part of the show. It has been suggested that some of the worst off of the small-market teams, such as Minnesota and Montreal, should have their franchises cancelled by the leagues. This might improve economic competition but it would be highly unfair to local fans in those cities. Assuming the leagues remain in their present form, the only way for the economically disadvantaged teams to compete effectively is to share more of the local broadcast revenue from the high-income clubs.

NOTES

1. Information about this game was obtained by the author from the archives at the National Baseball Hall of Fame and Museum in Cooperstown, New York.
2. World Series ratings have also declined significantly. See Flint, 2002.
3. Portions of the data on the two rights contracts from 1990–1995 are based on Staudohar (1996:20-21).
4. 'ESPN Countersued Over Schedule Switch', *San Francisco Examiner*, May 23,1999, p. C5.

REFERENCES

Badenhausen, K., Fluke, C., Kump, L. and M.K. Ozanian (2002), 'Double Play', *Forbes*, April 15, 92–98.

Battema, D. (2000), 'Baseball Meets the National Pastime: Baseball and Radio', in P.M. Rutkoff (ed.), *The Cooperstown Symposium on Baseball and American Culture*, Jefferson, NC: McFarland & Company Publishers, 148–168.

Bellamy, R. and J.R. Walker (2000), 'Baseball and Television: The Case of the Cubs', paper presented at the annual NINE Spring Training Conference on Baseball History and Social Policy Issues, March 18, Tucson, AZ.

Bialik, C. (2003), 'Baseball Plans Games Webcast, Blacking Out Local Teams', *Wall Street Journal*, March 11, B1.

Bruck, C. (1997), 'The Big Hitter', *New Yorker*, December 8, 82.

Costas, B. (2000), *Fair Ball: A Fan's Case for Baseball*, New York, NY: Broadway Books.

Flint, J. (2000), 'How the Top Networks Are Turning the Tables on Their Affiliates', *Wall Street Journal*, June 15, A1.

Flint, J. (2002), 'World Series Fans with TV Viewers', *Wall Street Journal*, October 29, B1.

Geer, J.F. (1997), 'Fox's Law', *Financial World*, June 17, 52.

Hegedus, N. (2000), 'Baseball Banks on All-Star Game Rantings', *Wall Street Journal*, July 10, B12.

Jennings, K.M. (1990), *Balls and Strikes: The Money Game in Professional Baseball*, Westport, CT: Praeger Publishers.

Johnson, C. (2000), 'America's Pastime Crisscrosses the Globe', *USA Today*, March 7, 16C.

McAvoy, K. *et al.* (1998), 'Cable's Batting Average Keeps Climbing', *Broadcasting and Cable*, **128** (13).

Matthews, A.W. (2001), 'Sports Leagues Tightening Grip on Web Content', *Wall Street Journal*, June 11, 81.

Miller, J.E. (1990), *The Baseball Business: Pursuing Pennants and Profits in Baltimore*, Chapel Hill, NC: University of North Carolina Press.

Rader, B.G. (1984), *In Its Own Image: How Television Has Transformed Sports*, New York, NY: The Free Press.

Staudohar, P.D. (1996), *Playing for Dollars: Labor Relations and the Sports Business*, Ithaca, NY: Cornell University Press.

Staudohar, P.D. (1997a), 'Baseball's Changing Salary Structure', *Compensation and Working Conditions*, **2** (3), 2–9.

Staudohar, P.D. (1997b), 'The Baseball Strike of 1994–1995', *Monthly Labor Review*, **120** (3), 24.

Staudohar, P.D. (2002), 'Baseball Negotiations: A New agreement', *Monthly Labor Review*, **125** (12).

Stewart, L. (1999), 'Baseball, ESPN See Air of Ways', *Los Angeles Times*, December 7, B1.

Thomson, B., Heiman, L. and B. Gutman (1991), *The Giants Win the Pennant! The Giants Win the Pennant!*, New York, NY: Zebra Books, Kensington Publishing Corporation.

Voigt, D.Q. (1991), 'Serfs versus Magnates: A Century of Labor Strife in Major League Baseball', in Staudohar, P.D. and J.A. Mangan (eds), *The Business of Professional Sports*, Urbana, IL: University of Illinois Press.

Zimbalist, A. (2003), *May the Best Team Win: Baseball Economics and Public Policy*, Washington, DC: Brooking Institution Press.

Zimbalist, A. (1992), *Baseball and Billions: A Probing Look Inside the Big business of Our National Pastime*, New York, NY: Basic Books.

Index

advertising
  advertiser 5–7, 15–16, 111, 121,
    171, 185–6, 190
  advertising 13–20, 29–30, 37, 62,
    80–83, 89, 91, 111–12,
    120–122, 132–4, 149, 154,
    160, 163, 170, 184, 188
  advertising market 80–81, 87, 89,
    90
  advertising revenues 2, 7, 15, 73,
    86, 112, 116–23, 131–7,
    142, 151, 158
audience
  audience demand 93, 100–101
  audience preferences 103
  audience rating 94
  audience share 81–3, 86–7, 138
  couch-potato audience 97

Big Five leagues 26
broadcast rights 5, 91, 103, 148–9,
  153, 156, 158, 171, 180–81,
  184, 188, 193–4
broadcasting demand 93
  determinants 3, 19, 34, 103
  match characteristics 95
  probit model 19, 96, 99
  selection criteria 98
broadcasting markets
  broadcasting markets 8, 16, 20,
    37, 79–82, 86, 89, 112
  local media market 168
  monopoly power 21, 33, 171
  premium pay-TV 4, 149, 157–8
  premium sporting rights 2, 19
  price discrimination 13, 33, 165–6
  profitability 40, 106–8, 111, 122–
    3, 126, 132, 191

rights acquisition 79–80, 82, 85–7
vertical integration 9, 21, 35, 151,
  154, 168–70, 191–3
Bundesliga 38, 48, 107, 140
bundling 9, 21, 39, 164–6, 173–4
  bundle channels 164
  bundling strategies 13
  channel bundling 20, 164–7
  debundling 173–4
business model 3, 7, 30, 35, 190
  models of TV rights management
    39, 43
  narrowcasting 35
  new business model 35
  television airtime market 35

cable
  cable network 2, 20, 150, 172,
    184, 189
  cable television 2, 4, 156, 160,
    162, 170–71, 173, 187–8,
    190
  cable-isation 160, 187
  pooled cable contracts 20, 162
cannibalising 11
college league 9
commercialisation (of sport) 16, 27
competition policy 9, 34, 41
  anticompetitive 10, 18
  antitrust 3, 82, 159, 162–3, 174
  antitrust exemption 7–9, 18, 21,
    162, 182
  antitrust law 182
  antitrust suit 172
  barrier to entry 173
  cartel 7, 9, 33, 39–42, 45, 53, 77,
    85, 90, 129–30, 141, 156,
    162

cartel practices 41
competition-enhancing policy 173
competition laws 76
competition rules 9, 11–12, 18, 41
deregulation 17, 27, 33–4, 37, 168
downstream market 3, 6, 9–12, 18,
     74–5, 77–9, 81–2, 84–6, 89,
     91
  pooled pay-TV deals 163
  separate markets 11, 74–5, 79–80,
     82, 84, 89
  substitute 2, 11, 79–80, 96, 112,
     116, 157
  upstream market 75, 77–80, 82,
     85, 87–8, 91
  vertical integration 9, 21, 35, 151,
     154, 168–70, 191–93
competitive balance 8, 10, 17–18, 21,
     25, 32–5, 38–9, 41, 47–9, 53–
     61, 179
  competitive balance index 48–9,
     53–4
  competitive dominance 16–17,
     26–7, 32, 35
  degree of uncertainty 47, 108
  revenue concentration 19, 46, 51
  turnover Gini coefficient 50–51,
     53–4, 58
  uncertainty of outcome 8, 17, 19,
     29, 31–2, 35, 99
competitive bidding 170
  auction 27, 115–16, 123
  bid 15, 19, 27, 88, 108, 114–16,
     122, 140, 142, 151, 156–8,
     170–71
  bidder 5, 8, 87, 115, 130, 147
  bidding 10, 12, 40, 59, 73, 80,
     115, 128, 141, 154, 170,
     188
  bidding competition 115
consumer surplus 4, 34, 111, 166
cost of sport broadcasting
  economies of scale 76, 109, 157
  fixed costs 108, 112
  sharing risk 76
  variable costs 108–10

delivery mechanism 4
  digital television 2, 4, 12, 20, 37,
     155

free-to-air television 5, 12–16, 19–
     20, 30, 37, 81, 108, 126,
     148–58
  internet 11–12, 30, 35, 41, 127,
     173, 186
  mobile (devices) 11, 30, 41, 136
  radio 1, 6, 21, 30, 178–82, 184,
     186, 193–5
  satellite television 4, 7, 20, 61, 94,
     150, 176
demand for sport rights
  demand function 19
  probit model 19, 96, 99
  willingness-to-pay 13, 15

European Broadcasting Union (EBU)
     3, 18, 73–5, 78–81, 85, 87–91,
     108, 110, 114–16, 144
European Commission 3, 6–14, 18,
     41, 60
European Court of Justice 41

federation 3–8, 44, 87, 140
FIFA 11, 19, 71, 80, 107, 116, 128–
     30
French First Division 11, 47
full delayed coverage 32

highlights 21, 30, 32, 40–43, 91, 128,
     141–2

image rights 29–31
IOC 5, 80, 113, 115–6, 130
Italian Lega Calcio 47, 51, 55

joint purchasing 3, 18, 70, 74–79,
     85–91
  Eurovision 11, 18, 73–6, 78–9, 81,
     85–8, 91
  horizontal guidelines 71, 74, 76–8,
     80, 87–9
  joint acquisition group 73, 81, 91
  joint purchasing system 18, 75–9,
     87–8
  transaction costs 8–9, 18, 88–91

league (club) revenues 8, 28, 44, 46
  gate receipts (revenues) 5, 18, 21,
     27, 29–30, 59, 61, 63, 178,
     195

local media revenues 61, 161
merchandising 18, 30, 38, 51, 132
sponsor(ing) 2–3, 6, 11, 30, 46,
    60, 116, 118, 121, 123, 136,
    163, 180, 183–5, 191
sponsorship 5, 18, 29–30, 73, 83,
    86, 91, 136
sports rights 2–8, 17–20, 70–82,
    86–91, 105–15, 121–3,
    148–58, 190
ticket sale 92–3, 98, 139
Liga de Futbol 38, 51

major league 6, 20–21, 27, 106, 148–
    9, 160–61, 179–86, 190–95
market power 11–12, 18, 40, 75–81,
    114, 141, 168, 171
media revenues distribution
    big-market teams 27, 33, 35, 195
    Champions League revenues 5, 44
    French redistribution system 61
    inter-team distribution 33
    mutuality 38, 42–3, 49, 59–61
    redistribution of TV rights 38–41,
        51, 57
    revenue distribution 33, 43, 47,
        51, 54
    revenue sharing 8, 10, 17–18, 20,
        60–61, 113–14, 160, 170,
        189, 196
    small-market teams 33, 195–6
    solidarity 10, 14, 38, 42–3, 45, 47,
        49, 50–51, 54, 60, 74, 78
media rights valuation 17
multi-plant firm 7

NBA 20, 106, 145, 149, 161, 163–4,
    170–72
NBC 1, 106, 130, 149, 151, 153, 169,
    180–81, 184–6, 188, 190–91
NFL 5, 106, 123, 145, 152–3, 157,
    162–3, 186
NHL 20, 149, 161, 163, 170, 172

Premier League 4–5, 7, 10–11, 18,
    26, 28–9, 38, 51–3, 57, 66, 80,
    93–7, 101–3, 106, 156
price discrimination 13, 33, 165–6
public interest 3, 5, 12, 41, 158, 163,
    169
    ban on pay-TV 15–16

crown jewels 14
    list of events 14, 156–7
    television without frontiers 14,
        157

radio 1, 6, 21, 30, 179–86, 193–5
rights marketing agencies 82
rights ownership 61, 141
    club ownership 38, 40, 47, 51, 62
    individual clubs' rights 7
    league rights 7, 106–108, 116, 155
    ownership of sports rights 17
    property rights 17, 28–9, 32–4, 41

selling arrangement 12–12
    exclusive deals 8
    exclusive rights 7–8, 11–12, 75,
        81, 94, 131, 142
    exclusivity 3, 7–11, 32, 142, 151,
        168
    exclusivity premium 33
    individual selling 8, 10, 17–18,
        97, 144
    joint (collective) selling 3, 8–11,
        17–21, 27, 29, 32–3, 144,
        152–3
    pooled rights 41
    pooling 20–21, 38–47, 51–3,58–
        62
    rights individualisation 32–5
    rights package 8, 32, 114, 182
    single package 9, 12
    supply-side cartel 39
    transaction costs 8–9, 18, 88–91
    unused rights 18, 76
siphoning 14–15, 187
Sports Broadcasting Act 153, 162,
    182
sport events, championship
    Football World Cup 11, 14, 16,
        19, 71–91, 107, 110, 113,
        116, 123–6, 128–38, 144,
        148, 155–6
    Formula One 14, 90, 126, 130,
        148–9
    major sports events 20, 73, 78, 80,
        82, 89, 91, 103
    Olympic Games 1, 5, 11, 14, 19,
        73–4, 79–90, 113, 116, 148,
        156

Olympics 1, 4, 73, 75, 80, 83–4,
        110, 113, 115, 123, 130,
        138, 148–9
    playoffs 182–3, 186, 195
    Summer Olympics 4, 75, 83–4,
        110, 130
    Wimbledon tennis 1, 11, 80, 90,
        140, 156
    Winter Olympics 1, 4, 80, 83–4,
        113, 130
    World Series 1, 180–81, 184, 186,
        194–5
sports-media business model 30, 35
sports-media product
    joint production 28
    private good 37, 112
    public good 3, 13, 112
    valuation 17, 31
sports rights agency 18, 73, 87–8,
        90–91
sports rights acquisition
    'Big Five' countries 129, 142
    collusion 19, 114–15, 129
    local broadcasting agreements 187
    mobile rights 11
    rights value 4, 102, 127, 139, 153
    telecasting rights 170
    unprofitable deals 106
sports rights migration
    anti-siphoning 14–15
    cable-isation 20, 160, 187
    migration 15, 156, 159, 161–2
    pay-TV ban 15
    to cable 20, 160–63
    to pay-TV 15, 20, 148, 156–7
subscription
    subscription 13, 15, 31, 94, 114,
        123, 155–6, 173
    subscription fee 2, 13, 100, 111–
        12, 116, 122, 152
substitutability 11, 80

team sports
    American football 21, 106, 123,
        149, 152–3, 162–3, 183,
        186, 188, 190–91
    baseball 20–21, 106, 145, 149,
        160–63, 170–73, 179–95
    basketball 5–6, 9, 21, 90, 106,
        145, 149, 163, 183, 189–91,
        193

cricket 148–9, 155–6
football (European) 11, 16–17,
        19–20, 26–28, 35, 37–43,
        45–7, 51–5, 57, 59–63, 72–
        3, 83–5, 87, 93–4, 101–2,
        128, 130, 136–7, 139–42,
        144, 148, 155–7
hockey 5–6, 9, 35, 84, 90, 162–3,
        183, 189–91, 193
rugby 6, 90, 140, 155–6, 193
soccer 15, 99, 102, 107, 109–10,
        112–17, 122, 137, 148–9,
        155, 157, 193
Telecommunications Act 152, 167–8
television industry
    broadcast platform 150
    (channels) bundling 20, 164–7
    cable television 2, 4, 156, 160,
        162, 170–71, 173, 187–8,
        190
    channels distribution 149
    economies of scale 76, 109, 157
    local broadcasters 168
    new media 5, 9, 11–12
    paid channels 4
    pay-TV 4, 7, 12–16, 20, 30–31,
        37, 40–42, 44, 46, 48, 61–3,
        69, 81, 111–14, 122, 139–
        42, 147–49, 156–8, 163,
        167
    pay-per-view 4, 13, 15–16, 31,
        40–41, 46, 48, 59, 112–13,
        116, 122, 149, 155–56, 188
    regulation3, 5, 14, 17, 20, 27–8,
        33–4, 37, 40, 47, 58–61,
        127, 145, 152, 158, 160,
        168, 173
    US cable industry174
    video on demand 41
television timeouts 6
two-tariff system 111

UEFA 11–12, 14, 26, 35–6, 38–9, 41,
        43–5, 53, 55, 60, 85, 87, 90,
        98, 106, 108, 114, 116–17,
        143–4
value of team tournaments 31, 34–5
    determinants 3, 17, 19, 34, 52, 98,
        103
    property rights arrangements 17
    tournament revenue 33–4

uncertainty of outcome 8, 17, 19, 29, 31–2, 35, 99
vertical integration 9, 21, 35, 151, 154, 168–70, 191, 193
   integrity of competition 170

regional sports network 9, 21, 164, 168–70, 189
vertically related markets 149
viewing rate 83–4